Uncertainty in American Politics

Uncertainty is a fundamental part of politics, and research needs to reflect that fact. This book represents an exciting intellectual meeting of researchers from diverse subfields to analyze how and why uncertainty affects American politics. It seeks to bridge research traditions that have seldom spoken to one another. Although used by formal theorists, empiricists, and historians in a parallel fashion for a number of years, the notion of uncertainty often has been introduced only to explain away anomalies, provide backing for a larger argument, or justify a particular methodology. Uncertainty rarely has been considered in its own right or as a concept that might connect researchers from different subfields. The authors demonstrate some of the many substantive effects that uncertainty has on the bureaucracy, voters, and elected officials. They also reveal the origins and consequences of uncertainty to remind researchers across the discipline how central the idea should be to any serious study of U.S. politics.

Barry C. Burden is Associate Professor of Government at Harvard University. He is the author, with David C. Kimball, of *Why Americans Split Their Tickets: Campaigns, Competition, and Divided Government* (2002).

T0364280

Uncertainty in American Politics

Edited by
BARRY C. BURDEN
Harvard University

CAMBRIDGE
UNIVERSITY PRESS

CAMBRIDGE UNIVERSITY PRESS
Cambridge, New York, Melbourne, Madrid, Cape Town,
Singapore, São Paulo, Delhi, Tokyo, Mexico City

Cambridge University Press
The Edinburgh Building, Cambridge CB2 8RU, UK

Published in the United States of America by Cambridge University Press, New York

www.cambridge.org
Information on this title: www.cambridge.org/9780521012126

© Cambridge University Press 2003

First published 2003

A catalogue record for this publication is available from the British Library

Library of Congress Cataloguing in Publication Data
Uncertainty in American politics / edited by Barry C. Burden.
p. cm.
Includes bibliographical references and index.
ISBN 0-521-81273-9 – ISBN 0-521-01212-0 (pb.)
1. Uncertainty – Political aspects – United States.   2. United States – Politics and
government.   I. Burden, Barry C., 1971–
JK21 .U54 2003
320.973´01–dc21   2002035075

ISBN 978-0-521-81273-3 Hardback
ISBN 978-0-521-01212-6 Paperback

Contents

Contributors

R. Michael Alvarez
California Institute of Technology

John Brehm
University of Chicago

Barry C. Burden
Harvard University

Rui J. P. de Figueiredo, Jr.
University of California-Berkeley

Matthew J. Dickinson
Middlebury College

John G. Geer
Vanderbilt University

Prateek Goorha
Vanderbilt University

Zoltan L. Hajnal
University of California-San Diego

Bryan D. Jones
University of Washington

George A. Krause
University of South Carolina

Cherie D. Maestas
Texas Tech University

Kenneth J. Meier
Texas A&M University

Laurence O'Toole, Jr.
University of Georgia

Matthew Potoski
Iowa State University

Jeffrey Talbert
University of Kentucky

Richard G. Vanden Bergh
University of Vermont

Catherine Wilson
California Institute of Technology

Uncertainty in American Politics

INTRODUCTION

Everything but Death and Taxes

Uncertainty and American Politics

Barry C. Burden

> Our Constitution is in actual operation; everything appears to promise that it will last; but nothing in this world is certain but death and taxes.
>
> –Benjamin Franklin 1789

Proverbs like Ben Franklin's tend to remind audiences of universal truths rather than inform them about new insights. In this case, humor quickly reminds us that the political world is fundamentally uncertain. In Franklin's view, uncertainty stems from the unpredictable nature of social life. Political scientists and practitioners alike know this of course, which is why prediction into the political future is seldom done. Just a few years ago it would have been difficult to find academics willing to predict publicly that Republicans would take control of Congress any time soon, that a budget surplus would be the nation's biggest problem, that a professional wrestler would become Minnesota's governor, or that a Democratic president would push aggressively for free trade. Lack of sure knowledge about the future is a key aspect of politics. While the unpredictable nature of the future surely makes political life uncertain, this important conception of uncertainty represents only a portion of the intriguing dynamics of modern U.S. politics.

As I argue in this introduction and is demonstrated throughout the chapters in this book, uncertainty arises from many sources, can take on multiple forms, and has a variety of consequences. Although most readers have an intuitive feeling for what uncertainty is, it is more important and complex than most of us assume. This revelation is important because Franklin's instinct was correct: uncertainty is everywhere. In some ways, the authors represented in this book are doing the footwork for a proverb by reminding political scientists of this basic fact, although the long-term desire of this

I thank Richard Zeckhauser for his comments.

project is to incorporate uncertainty in new ways and in new substantive areas of the discipline.

Before preceding much further, I should acknowledge that the uncertainty concept is not being introduced for the first time in this edited volume. It has already been used successfully in a number of scholarly literatures, including many fields in political science.[1] Unfortunately, its use is sometimes overly crude, often unconnected to other conceptions of uncertainty, and typically found on the margins rather than the mainstream of American politics research. Political science is an interdisciplinary field, so we learn from others' successes. It is to our advantage to learn from those who have already handled uncertainty in their theories, models, explanations, arguments, and tests.[2] The chapters in this book and research that follows them will borrow from disciplines as disparate as sociology, economics, philosophy, and psychology plus interdisciplinary efforts such as behavioral decision theory, although they all wish to say something about U.S. politics in the end. I will not try to argue that introducing uncertainty into substantive work on politics will turn a fledgling field into a natural science, but I am asserting that much research can be improved by reexamining implicit assumptions that motives, actions, structures, and outcomes in politics are certain.

I hesitate to say more about uncertainty here because the chapters to follow will largely speak for themselves. They are examples of how uncertainty has been used, is beginning to be considered in political science, and ways in which it might be incorporated in future work. They demonstrate that uncertainty is not a concept that is limited to a particular methodology or even a substantive area. Indeed, this is a critical theme motivating this project. Although it is impossible to cover all subfields in a single volume, these authors and their subjects are diverse enough to suggest how parallel studies in other fields might look.

In the remainder of this chapter I make five assertions about uncertainty and the study of American politics. They range from quite general statements

---

[1] Indeed, academics and practitioners in economics and business and management schools already devote significant attention to uncertainty, particularly in decision theory. Among other places, one can find economic treatments in the *Journal of Risk and Uncertainty*. I lack the space to review this deep literature here. For now, I propose that political science can learn a great deal about uncertainty from this work but that our applications are often more complicated because such things as the consequences of decisions, nature of the choice set, sources of uncertainty, and even who is responsible for a course of action are seldom as clear.

[2] To remind readers that uncertainty is a concept available to all researchers, I use inclusive language. Some analysts strive for general explanations, others for parsimonious models, and yet others for complete theories. So I use the terms model, theory, test, argument, explanation, and like as a group. Also, I often refer to political decision makers as "actors." Although a dispassionate term, it prevents debates about the proper unit of analysis, because an actor could be a cabinet secretary, interest group, congressional committee, voter, or executive branch agency.

that border on the philosophical to pragmatic advice for researchers, in largely that order. Although it seems that each assertion flows almost logically from those before it, each is probably more contentious than the last. I necessarily fail to make a watertight case for each assertion. Instead, I appeal to readers' wisdom and intuition and use a few examples from the subfields with which I am most familiar to underscore the points. My hope is merely that the attention this volume pays to uncertainty in U.S. politics will awaken researchers to its role as a useful concept and will provoke them to at least consider its role in the descriptions, explanations, models, and theories they develop. Much like the new institutionalism, political economy, and political psychology have begun to do, it can lead to the redevelopment of some existing work and possibly to the creation of new lines of inquiry. Let us turn now to the five assertions.

ASSERTION 1: UNCERTAINTY PERVADES POLITICAL ACTIVITY

Uncertainty is an inherent part of everything humans do. It is especially acute in the political realm. This is because politics is largely about making decisions, and decisions are seldom certain. Because people and the institutions they create are involved, uncertainty is part of what politics is. Whether one defines politics as the "authoritative allocation of values in society" (Easton 1965) or "who gets what, when, where, how" (Lasswell 1958), politics is often about choosing.[3] It follows that the study of politics – political science – is predominantly the study of how political actors make decisions. These actors include such diverse things as interest groups, state legislatures, party leaders, voters, and bureaucracies. The consequences of their choices might seem relevant only to oneself, to a group, an institution, or even the entire nation.

Political decisions are not so different from choices made in other realms, say the workplace or one's personal life. A key difference is that political stimuli are often more ambiguous. Although choosing a mate, finding a vocation, and purchasing an automobile are all affected by uncertainty, the information associated with these decisions is more immediate and concrete than is information about political choices. One might say that political stimuli are poorly defined. Perhaps because of this, the consequences of political decisions are less clear, thus heightening uncertainty. As Dahl notes in the context of the Supreme Court, "a policy decision might be defined as an effective choice among alternatives about which there is, at least initially, some uncertainty" (1957, 279). Even outside of "policy" decisions, it is the

---

[3] A decision could be made deliberately and intentionally as I imply here, or it could result as the unintentional by-product of institutional design and collective interaction. I shall refer mostly to former type, although this portrayal understates the amount of uncertainty that results for political decision making.

uncertainty that makes politics challenging for participants and interesting to those who study it.[4]

Take the case of citizens' knowledge about politics. It is widely known that Americans do not know much factual information about their political system or even its current staff (e.g., Bennett 1995; Delli Carpini and Keeter 1996). Lack of data simply makes it difficult to reach confident decisions. The informational deficit is less severe in personal, localized choices such as which breakfast cereal to purchase at the supermarket or whether to shoot or pass to a teammate in a game of basketball.

Although raising information levels often increases certainty, especially in nonpolitical settings, I argue below that this relationship is not always so simple (Assertion 3). Even in the many cases in which information is helpful, it will almost never eliminate all uncertainty about some kinds of decisions. It is impossible to acquire all of the relevant information in most settings; in other situations uncertainty would remain even in the presence of this data. Humans worry about their decisions for one reason: they are uncertain. Decision making would be trivial if all actors were certain about all relevant causes and consequences of a choice. Here is the real kicker: the necessity of decision making makes uncertainty important, whereas the ubiquity of uncertainty in decision making makes choosing difficult.

Uncertainty "may range from a falling short of certainty to an almost complete lack of conviction or knowledge especially about an outcome or result" (Merriam-Webster dictionary; <www.m-w.com>). Even this rather general definition suggests that uncertainty lies on a continuum. Accordingly, it is more accurate to think of uncertainty as an amount or degree rather than a quality that is merely present or absent. In terms of probabilities, it runs from 0 (an impossibility) to 1.0 (a certainty). Note that impossibilities are just certainties turned upside down; one is sure that something will *not* happen.

In some settings, the probability scale could be folded at the midpoint so that it runs from completely unsure to completely sure about something. (What this "something" is comes later.) Research that assumes certainty – often by remaining silent about the ways in which uncertainty enters – unrealistically requires that political actors usually find themselves at one of the endpoints of the full probability scale when making decisions. This assumption is difficult to sustain in sophisticated analyses. Moreover, in most applications it is even inappropriate to describe actors as simply "certain" or "uncertain." This artificially dichotomizes the scale by putting the two endpoints on one side and all other values on the other. At the most basic level, then, uncertainty is a variable that takes on different values across actors,

---

[4] Without moving into a philosophical discussion, I note that the constant force of entropy in the environment and lack of mortal omnipotence (even in a limited domain) guarantee that uncertainty is always with us.

situations, and time. When we say that a decision maker is uncertain, the next question asked ought to be "How uncertain?" When this issue is buttressed, the analyst moves to determining the sources, type, and eventually the consequences of the uncertainty. The chapters in this volume deal with all of the questions.

Take Downs's definition of uncertainty as simply the "lack of sure knowledge" (1957, 77). He argues that one's level of confidence depends on three factors: the removability, intensity, and relevance of the uncertainty. In other words, an actor can be quite confident about what will happen in a situation only to the degree that uncertainty is easily vanquished, is weakly felt, and is only tangentially related. Although all researchers might not agree that these three particular dimensions are the most important components of uncertainty in every application, Downs has made a genuine contribution by acknowledging that all uncertainties are not the same. Although a simple probability is a useful way to capture certainty levels in many settings, some applications require more than this common denominator to make sense of the political phenomena at hand. In line with much of their work on institutions, March and Olsen (1979) argue convincingly that organizations are plagued by several types of what they label ambiguity, a notion not far from uncertainty.

Processes that unfold over time are subject to uncertainty at the macro level, because later events are affected by earlier events. These small early events have more weight in determining outcomes but also are more likely to be random. This sort of "path dependence" suggests that many outcomes thought to be inevitable (because of efficiency or functionality) are nearly accidental (Pierson 2000). Carmines and Stimson (1989) demonstrate these points in their study of the "evolution" of race in transforming the American party system. Some important formative but largely accidental events, such as the 1958 Senate elections, began a dynamic that eventually resulted in elite and mass polarization around issues of race. Even if one could rerun the last half century of history, it is unlikely that the same chain of events would unfold.

The point of this discussion is to remind readers, as did Benjamin Franklin at the founding of our republic, that uncertainty is everywhere. It is especially keen in political contexts in which stimuli are ambiguous. Ironically, political decisions have the potential to affect a wider group of people and institutions. The idea that uncertainty is ubiquitous is not new to political scientists. Downs warns that "uncertainty is so basic to human life that it influences the structure of almost every social institution" (1957, 88). "To our minds, politics is a dynamic process filled with uncertainty" acknowledge Wright and Goldberg (1985, 716). Fenno's (1978, 10) depiction of legislators' "home styles" portrays representatives as "fraught with *uncertainty*," most of it subjective. Finally, as Cioffi-Revilla (1998) argues in his treatment of the international relations literature, uncertainty is not only ubiquitous and ineradicable, but it is consequential. It is the consequences of uncertainty that fascinate most scholars of American politics.

ASSERTION 2: AN ACTOR MAY BE UNCERTAIN ABOUT THE ACTIONS OF OTHERS, THE CONSEQUENCES OF HER OWN ACTIONS, OR EVEN HER OWN INTENTIONS

The object of uncertainty is a crucial variable in any analysis. In conceptualizing such a variable, I make a rough distinction between internal (or local) and external (or distant) sources of uncertainty. Uncertainty plays a different role for the Supreme Court justice who is unsure about how she will vote on an upcoming case than for the interest group that can not predict the outcome of a committee meeting with much confidence. The former is uncertain about her own (future or expected) behavior, while the latter is uncertain about what situation will arise or what the state of nature will be. The justice has a local source, while the interest group faces uncertainty beyond its control. They share in common the fact that uncertainty is typically related to future events, but the nature of the events differs in important ways.

Consider again the first situation, in which an actor does not know exactly what he will do when forced to make a choice. The old saying "I'll cross that bridge when I come to it" captures the idea well. This is not a bad strategy because one usually has more information about the alternatives the closer their proximity, either in time or space. Just as a college student is not sure which major he will select until forced to choose, a member of Congress is uncertain about whether she will cosponsor a potentially controversial piece of legislation. In classic political science terms, we might say the individual is cross-pressured. For both the student and the congressman, uncertainty about their own intentions arises in part from uncertainty about the consequences of their choices. The student wonders about the relative difficulty of the two majors he is considering and how helpful, again in relative terms, each will be in finding a job after graduation. The sources of uncertainty for the member of Congress are more numerous and immediate (see Kessler and Krehbiel 1996; Schiller 1995). Will her support for the bill affect how colleagues, constituents, and interest groups perceive her? How will the decision affect her credibility? Will it help or hinder the prospects for logrolling or vote trading with other members who have a substantial stake in the outcome? Are the intended consequences of the bill going to be realized and are there unintended consequences that might be realized, too? Being uncertain about the consequences of a choice makes a person even more uncertain about even what her decision will be. Uncertainty induces further uncertainty. At a minimum, uncertainty about what one will do encourages delay and further information gathering.

In the second situation, one is uncertain about something external. In rational choice settings, an actor might associate probabilities with each possible outcome. In these cases, more information might reduce uncertainty as it did in the "internal" examples above. Consider a federal agency planning its annual budget request. Because the agency is uncertain about how much of the request will actually be funded by Congress, it determines the request strategically, often asking for substantially more than it hopes to receive. The tactic of padding the budget can backfire, however, if Congress views the request as unreasonable and chooses to punish the agency by cutting more from their budget than it would have otherwise. Knowing this, the agency would like to make the largest possible request that does not inspire such a reaction. There is tremendous uncertainty in such decisions and the consequences of the funding level are grave for an organization whose existence depends on them. The agency is uncertain about what governs the interaction between the agency's choice and Congress' reaction. This uncertainty might be reduced by looking at previous interactions, because the budget process occurs annually and the same sets of players tend to interact repeatedly year after year. But environmental changes in congressional membership or economic conditions could alter the relationship in unknown ways.

A final point should be made about the targets and sources of uncertainty. Although in theory an actor could be uncertain about its own behavior or about something external such as an event or condition, being unsure about the latter usually heightens uncertainty in the former. Not knowing what the world will be like when a decision is made, what the consequences of the decision will be, or perhaps even what alternatives will be available at the time all induces uncertainty about one's own intentions. Intentions are merely planned or expected actions that can easily be confused by things outside of one's control (Fishbein and Ajzen 1975).

ASSERTION 3: UNCERTAINTY AND INFORMATION ARE OFTEN BUT NOT ALWAYS INVERSELY RELATED

Information is most useful when uncertainty arises from a mere lack of knowledge. In this case, the simple gathering of facts makes one more confident about what will occur or what the proper decision ought to be. Our modern presidency is supplied with an amazing number of information pipelines via bureaucracies such as the National Security Agency (NSC), the Central Intelligence Agency (CIA), the Department of Justice, the Council of Economic Advisors (CEA), and cabinet agencies that serve this function. The consequences of presidential actions loom large and information is relatively cheap, so it is well worth an executive's time to pursue large amounts of data. Knowing the details about disparities in welfare benefits across the states makes an administration more confident when planning a new formula for allocating welfare funds. Knowing about the military capabilities of an international terrorist group similarly makes a presidential staff more certain about how it handles the situation. There are endless examples. In the end, all other factors held constant, when available, a fact is always more useful than speculation.[5]

Other times, gathering all of the possible data, even the most difficult to acquire, would not reduce uncertainty much and would definitely not eliminate it. The marginal benefit of pursuing uncertainty-reducing information might not justify the effort either. The reason is that facts about current or past situations or events are more trustworthy than expectations about possible events, whether they be actions or the consequences of them.

Although it is true that polling, focus groups, and other research could make a presidential campaign team more certain about its fate in the upcoming election, uncertainty always remains. And this uncertainty, however small, plays a disproportionate role in the campaign organization's behavior. As in so many other contexts, there are diminishing returns from efforts to raise one's confidence about the likelihood of future events, yet uncertainty is difficult to ignore. It seems reasonable to hypothesize that small amounts of uncertainty drive out large amounts of certainty.[6] This asymmetry in weight between certainty and uncertainty is akin to an old Swedish proverb: "Worry gives a small thing a big shadow." Even a touch of uncertainty can overwhelm large amounts of sure knowledge.

Even for those motivated to pursue information to reduce uncertainty, it is possible for newly acquired data to heighten uncertainty as I have defined it.[7] Well-informed actors could actually be less certain than poorly informed actors about what will occur. New information increases uncertainty when it is inconsistent with prior information or an actor's predispositions.[8] Even though data are usually helpful, "additional information may contradict what he knows already, so that his confidence falls as he learns more"

---

[5] One might suppose that data have uncertainty associated with them as well. A belief might be just a datum about which one is (nearly) certain. I am pretty sure what the high temperature was yesterday (to the degree that I trust thermometers and those using them), but I am much less certain about what the high temperature will be tomorrow. It is a "fact" with high uncertainty that can be decreased as more information is gathered about it. It is easy to see how this argument leads to an infinite regress because one is always uncertain about the data that determine uncertainty levels associated with other data.

[6] This is akin to what Popkin (1996) calls Gresham's Law of Information: recent and personal information drives out old and impersonal information.

[7] This view of uncertainty differs from Alvarez's portrayal in which uncertainty can be removed with adequate information (Alvarez 1998; Alvarez and Brehm 1997; Alvarez and Franklin 1994; Alvarez, Brehm, and Wilson, this volume). By treating ambivalence as a form of uncertainty (about one's own opinions or intentions), I am expanding his definition of uncertainty. The differences between the two are largely semantic, but disagreements about what uncertainty is will naturally arise when many researchers deal with the concept simultaneously.

[8] For those inclined to think this way, current data that are discrepant with one's prior could increase the variance of the posterior distribution.

(Downs 1957, 78). Beyond "brute facts," Zaller (1992) has shown that more exposure to messages of all kinds may increase the conflict among "considerations" or attitudes that an actor uses in reaching a decision (Hasecke 2000).

Consider the presidential task of choosing a nominee to replace a vacancy in some appointed position, say an ambassador, cabinet secretary, or better yet a Supreme Court justice. After going over a short list of names with advisors, the president might feel confident that a particular candidate is most qualified (and most likely to earn Senate approval). Just hours before calling a press conference to announce the decision, an aide reports newly acquired, potentially damaging information about the likely nominee to the president. The president then must reconsider his intention in light of the uncertainty the new data have added.

A simple label for the president's resulting condition is *ambivalence.*[9] Strong positive and negative information exists about the potential nominee, making the president unsure about whether to move forward, either because of personal reservations about her qualifications or because of fear that a Senate rejection will be an embarrassment to the administration. It is not the lack of information but the discrepancies among various bits of data. Ironically, the uncertainty arises despite the acquisition of more data and might even be a result of it.

In other contexts, a political actor might be uncertain because he is *indifferent.* Indifference could arise from a lack of information, stemming perhaps from apathy. It also could reflect a genuine inability to choose, because the "pros" and "cons" associated with alternatives are roughly equal in number. That is, a highly informed actor might be uncertain about a decision, because ambivalence has induced indifference.

A main reason why information gathering is not guaranteed to eliminate uncertainty is that uncertainty has multiple sources, many of them outside of an actor's control. Considering the context of voting in a typical presidential election. On top of the "local" uncertainty attributable to the voter herself, which information would probably lessen, candidate behavior might induce uncertainty about such things as the likelihood that campaign promises will become government policy if he is elected (Alvarez 1998; Downs 1957; Weisberg and Fiorina 1980). In what seems like a relatively contained decision environment involving just one voter choosing between two rather well-known candidates, uncertainty looms large and enters the process at several points. Uncertainty must play an even larger role in other political contexts.

The sources of uncertainty vary from one context to another. In his classic study of Supreme Court decisions, Dahl (1957) argues that uncertainty

---

[9] Ambivalence has typically been considered in the context of public opinion, where core values are in conflict (Alvarez and Brehm 1997; Zaller 1992).

can arise from such things as a poorly defined set of alternatives, potential consequences of a decision and their likelihoods, and the expected utility of alternatives. As Jones, Talbert, and Potoski explain in Chapter 5, in some settings an actor is uncertain about which choice is best; in many other settings, the uncertainty is about the definition of the problem itself. Each of these and other sources are potent in their own right. In the congressional realm, Bach and Smith (1988) make certainty almost synonymous with predictability. Legislators benefit from a stable, predictable environment on the House floor and therefore wish to control uncertainty with rules and procedures (see Assertion 4 below and Sinclair 2000). Paradoxically, the move to unorthodox procedures to increase leaders' certainty about the content of legislation has increased uncertainty about how the bill will be handled. Also dealing with Congress, Krehbiel (1991) derives a sophisticated informational model of congressional organization based heavily on the simple assumption that legislators are uncertain about how policies translate into outcomes.[10] This is a case of inadequate or contradictory information about the consequences of a decision that induces uncertainty in the decision makers.

ASSERTION 4: POLITICAL ACTORS ARE USUALLY MOTIVATED
TO REDUCE UNCERTAINTY

Although uncertainty can be helpful in some situations, political actors generally want to minimize their own uncertainty. One is more confident about a decision and can justify it more easily when she is certain about her intentions and the outcomes associated with the choices she makes. Decision making is simply easier when uncertainty levels are low. Humans face complex environments made of networks of people and objects and other multifaceted stimuli that make wading through information daunting. Anything that can be done to reduce the great uncertainty that arises from these natural environmental features is worthwhile, as long as the costs involved do not exceed the perceived benefits (see Assertion 3). When uncertainty cannot be sufficiently reduced, decision making remains challenging. Because politics induces greater uncertainty than do some other domains, uncertainty reduction is even more important yet more difficult there.

This is not to say that actors spend most of their time fighting uncertainty. One might argue, for instance, that some actors actually relish uncertainty. Some people enjoy the thrill of watching a scary movie, opening a surprise birthday gift, or reading a novel with an unpredictable ending. Although this is true, I might counter that some of these individuals enjoy

---

[10] As an example of political actors wanting to *increase* uncertainty for others, Arnold (1990) theorizes that legislators strive to make the connections between their actions and policy outcomes uncertain to constituents by obscuring the "traceability" of actions.

the perverse certainty that uncertainty brings. Knowing that one will be shocked or surprised makes the experience predictable. Horror movies, gifts, and mystery novels are also poor analogies to politics, even if participants genuinely pursue uncertainty in these situations. They are diversions from real life with known ending points and no real consequences other than a temporary adrenaline rush or goosebumps. The rest of social life – finding a mate, raising children, finding an occupation, and like – attaches more lasting and consequential outcomes to uncertain decisions. Politics, at least for those invested in it, has even greater (negative) consequences, including policy decisions that could lead to such unpleasant consequences as an increase in crime, millions of abortions for those who views fetuses as lives, an economic recession or even depression, or heightened racial tension. This suggests a relationship between the ramifications of uncertainty and the motivation to reduce it. All else constant, as the consequences of being uncertain increase, the drive to seek certainty does as well.

Consider some examples from the field of electoral behavior. Many citizens in the contemporary United States choose not to vote in elections. Recent presidential elections manage to mobilize only half of the electorate and other U.S. elections sometimes get just 30 or 40 percent turnout. This does not necessarily mean that citizens have avoided decision making altogether as some have argued; rather, they might have chosen an alternative (abstention) that has the least uncertainty associated with it, at least for them (Lacy and Burden 1999). Candidates and their positions are cloudy mixes of issues and images and citizens get only weak signals as to what policies might result from their election, particularly in the federal system. Deferring to others with stronger opinions and more information to choose among candidates reduces uncertainty about the outcome and thus anxiety. Of course, abstainers are not always uninformed. Information and certainty often run together, but neither is a necessary condition for the other (Assertion 3). Many are highly informed but simply indifferent (Burden 1997; Downs 1957).

Recent research demonstrates that voters generally avoid candidates about whom they are uncertain (Alvarez 1998; Bartels 1986). It is ironic that while equivocation might seem a rational strategy for candidates in theory (Downs 1957; Page 1976; Shepsle 1972), voters do not actually seem to reward it. Voters tend to avoid candidates about whom they are uncertain. In many elections, particularly low information contests for Congress and state offices, the challenger is an unknown quantity (e.g., Jacobson 1997). This probably benefits the incumbent, who has a familiar name and a public record, even if it is not entirely in agreement with voters' policy preferences. Uncertainty thus favors the *status quo* and makes retrospective voting a reasonable way to make a decision on Election Day (Downs 1957; Fiorina 1981; Key 1966).

The growth in the number, size, and sophistication of interest groups has been linked to uncertainty reduction, too. In one of the better extended treatments of uncertainty in an American politics subfield, Heinz et al. (1993) argue that the structure of contemporary interest group representation is a response to uncertainty in the policy-making process. This uncertainty stems from changes including the greater importance of federal policy today, the decentralization of Congress, the plentiful information available to policy makers, and the like. Heinz and colleagues do not find evidence that a particular side such as business has gained in power or that groups have become any less myopic despite attempts by groups to counteract growing uncertainty.

Institutions often act to reduce uncertainty, too. North (1990) has argued that the primary function of an institution is to reduce uncertainty. In his framework, institutions provide stability in humans by limiting and thus structuring behavior. The price of this greater uncertainty is often inefficiency. In contrast, Krehbiel (1991) argues that the institution of Congress is designed to maximize efficiency. Congress maintains a system of standing committees to reduce a different kind of uncertainty. Committees are composed of heterogeneous policy experts to maximize informational efficiency and reduce the uncertainty that members have about the relationship between policies and their outcomes. Kingdon (1989) found that members often gather information about how they should vote on a bill by taking cues from fellow legislators, interest groups, constituents, the administration, the media, and so on. When these cues point in the same direction, as they typically do, a member's uncertainty is low and confidence high in the final vote decision. It is the lack of information, itself a source of uncertainty, that leads to the search for cues in the first place.

Predictability of processes or outcomes also reduces uncertainty. Ben Franklin's line about death and taxes suggests that unpredictability is a frequent and relentless source of uncertainty. Many government programs – entitlements and other kinds – increase annually via an automatic process. The common procedure is to "index" program benefits to inflation in some way, which produces automatic cost of living adjustments (COLAs) for recipients. Incremental budgeting also can reduce uncertainty, although fiscal patterns that evolve too slowly might eventually require dramatic change periodically too. In addition, instability in the political agenda and treatment of items on it shapes how issues are viewed (Baumgartner and Jones 1993). Politicians might prefer certainty because it aids them in containing issues. Although introducing new issues to the public agenda sometimes advantages particular politicians (Riker 1982), constraining the agenda probably has greater benefits for most. However, a policy outcome that appears certain usually causes those on the losing side to seek another venue, which might heighten uncertainty (Schattschneider 1960).

Light's (1982) study of presidential agendas argues that the office of the presidency works vigorously to reduce uncertainty. Administrations stay in the present, solving only the most pressing problems to create a stable environment. Perhaps surprisingly, the search for predictability in the environment does not foster constant monitoring. Instead, it leads to a passive "fire fighting" rather than an active "police patrol" mode of operation.[11] These are but a few examples and I shall not stretch them to argue that political actors expend resources *primarily* to minimize uncertainty. All other factors held constant, however, there are strong theoretical reasons to believe that uncertainty is minimized whenever possible. Although there might be incentives to increase the uncertainty in *another* actor's environment, politicians of all types generally like to know what's going on in their immediate surroundings. This suggests that most political actors will take a "sure thing" (at least when it appears to advantage them) than gamble on unknown outcomes. Decision theorists would say that such choosers are "risk averse." This is yet another truth captured in a proverb: "A bird in the hand is worth two in the bush."

In contrast to this portrayal of political actors as certainty seeking, "prospect theory" posits that individuals are risk averse in gains but risk acceptant in loses (Kahneman and Tversky 1979; Tversky and Kahneman 1974). Whereas risk and certainty are distinct concepts, researchers should take this as evidence that uncertainty is not a uniform phenomenon that affects all actors and all situations identically. Although uncertainty reduction is a basic motive of most political animals, we should be open to the possibility that uncertainty is not always treated the same way by all actors or in all settings. There will be situations in which actors prefer to expend modest effort to deal pragmatically with uncertainty rather than expend great effort to reduce it completely.

ASSERTION 5: UNCERTAINTY CAN AND SHOULD BE
INCORPORATED INTO POLITICAL SCIENCE RESEARCH

Knowing that uncertainty is ubiquitous in the political world and that it deeply influences the decisions that political actors make, ignoring uncertainty in studies of American politics would be a mistake. While our substantive understanding of politics should acknowledge a role for uncertainty, we also should think more seriously about how to handle it methodologically.

Here I consider two ways in which uncertainty might be treated. For those who employ formal models of political processes, uncertainty can be incorporated into models directly as assumptions. Actors can be uncertain about their own preferences, the preferences of others who are playing the same game, the "type" of player encountered in a signaling game, and even such basic features as payoffs. Games of both *incomplete* and *imperfect* information allow for uncertainty. Also useful is the notion of a risk profile, which

---

[11] McCubbins and Schwartz (1984) offer an explanation for the dominance of "fire fighting" as the way that congressional committees monitor the bureaucracy.

is based on one's willingness to gamble when probabilities of states of the world are known. Uncertainty occurs when these probabilities are unknown or are estimated poorly. Incomplete and imperfect information frameworks allow actors to be unaware of the history of a game or the payoffs players might receive. Thus, an initial move by "nature" or "chance" introduces uncertainty and might be captured through one of these models.

Even within the rational choice framework, a central feature of uncertainty is that it is subjective. In contrast, risk is based on taking chances given objective probabilities. This subjective-objective dimension is an interesting one that might be considered explicitly in particular applications (see Maestas's research in Chapter 8). Before Fenno's (1978) study of congressional home styles appeared, researchers tended to analyze incumbents' reelection efforts in terms of risk. Incumbent risk is minimal, as nine out of ten of those who run are reelected. As a result, scholars wondered aloud why irrational legislators were so worried about their own electoral fortunes and thus spent more time than was needed worrying about things like controversial roll call votes. But Fenno revealed that incumbents' beliefs are highly subjective and unsure. As long as representatives feel uncertain, researchers should treat them as such.

In quantitative applications, creative approaches are often required. Using linear regression and maximum likelihood models, one might simply assert that any uncertainty is accounted for by the error term that gets tacked onto the end of an equation. After all, the error term is just the stochastic part that makes a deterministic model estimable by accounting for "noise" in the data. While this might suffice in situations in which the actors are highly informed decision makers or they find themselves in familiar, predictable situations, it does not really tap their *substantive* uncertainty. An error term does allow for uncertainty in estimation but not necessarily on the part of the people and institutions being analyzed. It indicates randomness in the data resulting from poor measurement, inadequate specification, too few observations, or simple stochastic behavior. Methodologies themselves make *analysts* more or less uncertain about their inferences (King, Keohane, and Verba 1994). This is distinct from the uncertainty faced by *those being analyzed*. We are far more sophisticated about methodological uncertainty than substantive uncertainty, which suggests that the latter deserves more attention.

An alternative approach is to assess uncertainty directly in data collection rather than indirectly in data analysis. For instance, Alvarez and coauthors have analyzed a new series of questions in the National Election Study that follow up traditional issue questions by asking respondents how certain they are of the answers (Alvarez and Franklin 1994; Alvarez, Brehm, and Wilson in this volume; Alvarez and Glasgow 2000).[12] It now becomes possible to

---

[12] Maestas's survey of state legislative candidates used in Chapter 8 does this by asking candidates directly for their assessments of both risk and uncertainty.

"weight" respondents' attitudes and beliefs by their certainty in them. Conclusions drawn from earlier studies might have been misleading because researchers assumed that all respondents were equally (and highly) certain about their responses.

Like some other social science concepts and methodologies, uncertainty can help reconnect Americanists to comparative politics, political philosophy, and even international relations (Cioffi-Revilla 1998). Furthermore, uncertainty is a concept that can unify related social sciences including economics, psychology, and sociology. The introduction of uncertainty, in both substantive and methodological veins, has thus far been uneven across the subfields in American politics. Such a haphazard tendency might actually increase the intellectual distance between fields. In some ways, this unevenness is justified, because uncertainty plays a larger role in some realms than in others. Still, one suspects that uncertainty pervades all of social life, especially politics (Assertion 1) and has a large enough effect on processes and outcomes that it ought to be considered in its own right.

As Cioffi-Revilla (1998) argues, uncertainty is more than a mere nuisance that impedes our understanding of politics or an unpredictable force that can not be subject to systematic study. Uncertainty can be described, theorized about, measured, and explained. In line with the borrowing tradition of political science, we ought to seek ways to transfer concepts such as uncertainty from subfields in which they have been used fruitfully to new fields in which they might be. For example, uncertainty has been applied successfully to studies of legislative politics as I have suggested, so moving to judicial or presidential settings seems like a natural extension of that work (although the internal structures and processes are obviously different).

While there are compelling methodological reasons for incorporating uncertainty in the study of politics, the main motivation of this book is substantive. If we are correct in asserting that uncertainty is an inherent but variable part of all political life, it follows that descriptions, models, and theories of politics should account for it. Perhaps some actors in limited situations are close enough to certain that an abstract model of the process can assume it away, but such scenarios are probably rare, especially in more sophisticated studies in the later stages of a subfield's evolution. Early attempts at explaining a facet of American politics might neglect uncertainty initially to focus on other salient aspects, but richer analyses that follow will almost always benefit from reintroducing it.

Downs's classic *An Economic Theory of Democracy* (1957) serves as testimony to the importance of uncertainty. It is remarkable how different his predictions are once uncertainty is introduced explicitly into the model (Hinich and Munger 1995). Although most readers recall his conclusions about party convergence and rational abstention, these results are straw men developed in a world of certainty. After relaxing the assumption that governments, parties, and voters are certain, he derives a number of even grander conclusions.

He argues that uncertainty allows for such central political phenomena as leadership, persuasion, and inequality. Uncertainty might even cause government to be smaller than it would otherwise be, doing less to redistribute wealth among constituents. In electoral politics, uncertainty leads parties to adopt different ideologies and motivates voters to vote "ideologically." All of these intriguing and potentially testable hypotheses come from a relatively simple model, relying on a rudimentary notion of uncertainty. More sophisticated models, relying on subtler depictions of uncertainty will likely carry us even further.

POTENTIAL COUNTERARGUMENTS

I have portrayed my argument and its five assertions as no more than reminders of what was already known, but that is not being completely honest. I and the authors represented in the following chapters are actually suggesting something new. In doing so, I risk finding more objectors than converts. While I believe that a healthy debate about uncertainty's place in American politics is worthwhile – as would be a debate about any concept or methodology – I wish to diffuse some of the potential criticisms by addressing potential counterarguments now.

First, it might be said that uncertainty is no more than a trendy "buzz word" that adds little to our substantive understanding of politics. A similar feeling exists is some circles about hot concepts such as "endogeneity," "social capital," and "path dependence." Although some of these ideas have been more fruitful than others, we should at least consider whether, in their original forms, they provide useful conceptions that inform our models, theories, explanations, and tests. In all cases I think they have, but their lives as meaningful contributions vary tremendously. Overextension can reduce such ideas to banality.

This warns us to be cautious about the use of "uncertainty" for fear of a dismal fate. Using it to explain nearly everything political, it loses its theoretical punch. At the same time, demoting it to a mere heuristic device or throwaway line does not make full use of the interesting idea bubbling below. If it does nothing more than cause us to reevaluate our knowledge of American politics, it has served a positive purpose. But researchers have the most to gain if they are genuinely able to integrate the idea into existing and developing studies of U.S. politics. In the end, the market of ideas will determine whether uncertainty and other lingo in the social sciences are more like the Pet Rock or the ink pen.

A second counterargument that is more easily diffused is that of methodology or approach. Although I have made no rational choice arguments in this chapter, my use of uncertainty sometimes sounds like the language of formal theory. It is true that uncertainty has been employed successfully by formal theorists already, but they do not have exclusive domain over the idea nor have they gone far enough. By speaking of "strategies," "actors," "outcomes" and the like, I might unintentionally imply that uncertainty is useful only within a political economy framework. Although it is more natural for me to consider it in that environment, I do not mean to imply that the concept is not portable. Indeed, one the benefits of uncertainty is that it can be used all kinds of research. For example, in behavioral studies it might be variable or parameter to be estimated, in qualitative and historical studies it could be used to explain causal connections and avoid deterministic arguments, and in formal theories as an assumption or dimension. Because uncertainty is a ubiquitous part of the "real world" of politics, incorporating it improves the verisimilitude of our explanations – a goal favored by more traditional scholars – without adding unnecessary complexity to our models – a goal favored by formal theorists. The idea of uncertainty's inherent place in political affairs might actually bring researchers from disparate traditions closer together rather than push them further apart. This is a hope not an expectation, but it rests on the deep belief that uncertainty should not be limited to any one style of scholarship.

A final criticism that is not quickly dismissed sees my recommendations are unrealistic. Perhaps political actors really are uncertain, one might argue, but their uncertainty is minimal enough and the cost of including uncertainty in existing theories is high enough that it is better ignored. Although I do not doubt that there are cases in which uncertainty plays a small role or in which its use as a theoretical concept is limited, in most cases uncertainty helps improve our work. As with other concepts, it has the potential to strengthen existing models, theories, and explanations while also encouraging exploration on new frontiers. Because it is not possible to make a complete case for its use, I let the chapters in this volume and the larger set of works with which they connect speak for its utility. The proof is in the pudding.

One other point should be made for readers whose substantive interests are not represented in the chapters collected here. Not only are these essays models for what can be done in other subfields within American politics, they also might be used fruitfully by researchers studying politics in other nations or relationships among them. The international relations literatures on security, deterrence, trade, and the like already have made great use of uncertainty as an analytical tool (Cioffi-Revilla 1998). We contain our inferences to a limited number of works in American politics here for practical reasons but welcome others to pursue creatively other applications.

THE REMAINDER OF THE BOOK

The points made in this introduction are driven home by the contributors whose chapters follow. They cover a variety of topics – from bureaucracy to elections – and approaches – formal, empirical, and theoretical – to be as exhaustive as possible without losing sight of the book's motivation. The

remaining chapters are divided into two broad sections that roughly mirror
interests in the discipline. The first section focuses on "Elite and Institutional
Politics," the second on "Citizen and Electoral Politics."

On the institutional side, three chapters tackle bureaucracies. Contributors
tors VandenBergh and de Figueiredo posit that bureaucratic insulation is in
part a response to uncertainty about the future. To prevent a bureaucracy
from drifting from the current status quo as new actors gain control of the
policy process, today's policy makers attempt to institutionalize policy goals
in government agencies. O'Toole and Meier argue that bureaucracies by their
very nature face at least three different kinds of uncertainty. The chapter
demonstrates that uncertainty has many sources and that each type needs
to be understood on its own terms. Bureaucracies are better at managing
some of these varieties than others, but an agency must act in an uncertain world and that fundamentally affects its operation. Krause adds to this
list of sources of uncertainty by examining congressional-bureaucratic relationships. The "signal" that an agency gets from a congressional committee
about legislators' policy preferences can be more or less meaningful depending on the homogeneity of the committee. Bureaucracies are less accountable
to Congress when the signal-to-noise ratio decreases and their uncertainty
about the committee's preferences is greater.

Dickinson examines how uncertainty has shaped presidential interactions
with Congress. As other actors such as the Congress have increased the
number and quality of informational resources at their disposal, presidents
have been losing ground in bargaining situations. The rise of bargaining
uncertainty leads presidents to bolster their staffs, to fight fire with fire. Thus,
in contrast to the conventional wisdom that mere workload or complexity
lead to a growth of White House staff, Dickinson shows that uncertainty is an
important cause of staffing changes as well. Jones, Talbert, and Potoski speak
more directly about the legislative process by suggesting how uncertainty
induces policy winnowing. Legislators are uncertain about policy choices in
a multidimensional space, so the legislative reduces the dimensionality of
bills through markup and revision so that simpler, and thus more certain,
policy choices result in the end.

The second half of the book considers the place of uncertainty in mass
politics. Alvarez, Brehm, and Wilson show that uncertainty is an inherent
part of public opinion. Citizens hold a number of core political values, each of
which is important but potentially conflicting with the others. Value conflict
often leads citizens to hold uncertain policy preferences in many cases, but
leads to ambivalence and equivocation in others. Uncertainties in public
opinion might consequently be more often thought of as a principled lack of
resoluteness on policy issues rather than a disinterested lack of information
about in politics. Moving to a specific realm of electoral politics, Hajnal
explores white voters' uncertainty about black mayoral candidates. Whites
have little experience with black elected officials and fear the direction a

black incumbent might take a city government. This uncertainty reduces the likelihood that risk-averse white voters will vote for a black. This apparently changes once a black has one as uncertainty among whites drops significantly and reelection is much easier.

Maestas takes the discussion of incumbency and uncertainty further. Based on a survey of state legislative candidates, she argues that incumbent insecurity must be decomposed into risk and uncertainty. Thinking of insecurity in this two-dimensional context helps one better understand why incumbents behave as they do. Finally, Geer and Goorha explain how the advent of scientific polling techniques has reduced politicians' uncertainty about public opinion. Knowing rather than guessing about public sentiment allows elected officials to better follow opinion. But this also induces parties to minimize their differences and is likely to prevent a major political realignment in the future.

References

Alvarez, R. Michael. 1998. *Information and Elections*. Revised ed. Ann Arbor: The University of Michigan Press.

Alvarez, R. Michael, and John Brehm. 1997. "Are Americans Ambivalent toward Racial Policies?" *American Journal of Political Science* 41:345–74.

Alvarez, R. Michael, and Charles H. Franklin. 1994. "Uncertainty and Political Perceptions." *Journal of Politics* 56:671–89.

Alvarez, R. Michael, and Garrett Glasgow. 2000. "Uncertainty and Candidate Personality Traits." *American Politics Quarterly* 28:26–49.

Arnold, R. Douglas. 1990. *The Logic of Congressional Action*. New Haven, CT: Yale University Press.

Bach, Stanley, and Steven S. Smith. 1988. *Managing Uncertainty in the House of Representatives*. Washington, DC: Brookings Institution.

Bartels, Larry M. 1986. "Issue Voting under Uncertainty: An Empirical Test." *American Journal of Political Science* 30:709–28.

Baumgartner, Frank R., and Bryan D. Jones. 1993. *Agendas and Instability in American Politics*. Chicago: The University of Chicago Press.

Bennett, Stephen Earl. 1995. "Comparing Americans' Political Information in 1988 and 1992." *Journal of Politics* 57:521–32.

Burden, Barry C. 1997. "Deterministic and Probabilistic Voting Models." *American Journal of Political Science* 41:1150–69.

Carmines, Edward G., and James A. Stimson. 1989. *Issue Evolution: Race and the Transformation of American Politics*. Princeton, NJ: Princeton University Press.

Cioffi-Revilla, Claudio. 1998. *Politics and Uncertainty: Theory, Models, and Applications*. New York: Cambridge University Press.

Dahl, Robert A. 1957. "Decision-Making in a Democracy: The Supreme Court as a National Policy Maker." *Journal of Public Law* 6:279–95.

Delli Carpini, Michael X., and Scott Keeter. 1996. *What Americans Know about Politics and Why It Matters*. New Haven, CT: Yale University Press.

Downs, Anthony. 1957. *An Economic Theory of Democracy*. New York: Harper and Row.

Easton, David. 1965. *A Systems Analysis of Political Life*. New York: John Wiley and Sons.

Fenno, Richard F. 1978. *Home Style: House Members in Their Districts*. Boston, MA: Little, Brown.

Fiorina, Morris P. 1981. *Retrospective Voting in American National Elections*. New Haven, CT: Yale University Press.

Fishbein, Martin, and Icek Ajzen. 1975. *Belief, Attitude, Intention, and Behavior*. Reading, MA: Addison-Wesley.

Hasecke, Edward B. 2000. "A General Model of Uncertainty: Combining the Theories of Rational Choice and Political Psychology." Unpublished manuscript. The Ohio State University.

Heinz, John P., Edward O. Laumann, Robert L. Nelson, and Robert H. Salisbury. 1993. *The Hollow Core: Private Interests in National Policy Making*. Cambridge, MA: Harvard University Press.

Hinich, Melvin, and Michael C. Munger. 1995. *Ideology and the Theory of Political Choice*. Ann Arbor: The University of Michigan Press.

Jacobson, Gary C. 1997. *The Politics of Congressional Elections*. 4th ed. New York: Longman.

Kahneman, Daniel, and Amos Tversky. 1979. "Prospect Theory: An Analysis of Decisions under Risk." *Econometrica* 47:313–27.

Kessler, Daniel, and Keith Krehbiel. 1996. "Dynamics of Cosponsorship." *American Political Science Review* 90:555–66.

Key, V. O. 1966. *The Responsible Electorate*. New York: Vintage Books.

King, Gary, Robert O. Keohane, and Sidney Verba. 1994. *Designing Social Inquiry*. Princeton, NJ: Princeton University Press.

Kingdon, John W. 1989. *Congressmen's Voting Decisions*. 3rd ed. Ann Arbor: The University of Michigan Press.

Krehbiel, Keith. 1991. *Information and Legislative Organization*. Ann Arbor: The University of Michigan Press.

Lacy, Dean, and Barry C. Burden. 1999. "The Vote-Stealing and Turnout Effects of Ross Perot in the 1992 U.S. Presidential Election." *American Journal of Political Science* 43:233–55.

Lasswell, Harold D. 1958. *Politics: How Gets What, When, How*. New York: Meridian Press.

Light, Paul C. 1982. *The President's Agenda: Domestic Policy Choice from Kennedy to Reagan*. Baltimore, MD: The Johns Hopkins University Press.

March, James G., and Johan P. Olsen. 1979. *Ambiguity and Choice in Organizations*. Oslo: Universitetsforlaget.

McCubbins, Mathew D., and Thomas Schwartz. 1984. "Congressional Oversight Overlooked: Police Patrols versus Fire Alarms." *American Journal of Political Science* 28:165–79.

North, Douglass C. 1990. *Institutions, Institutional Change, and Economic Performance*. New York: Cambridge University Press.

Page, Benjamin I. 1976. "The Theory of Political Ambiguity" *American Political Science Review* 70:742–52.

Pierson, Paul. 2000. "Increasing Returns, Path Dependence, and the Study of Politics." *American Political Science Review* 94:251–68.

Popkin, Samuel L. 1996. *The Reasoning Voter.* 2nd ed. Chicago: The University of Chicago Press.

Riker, William H. 1982. *Liberalism Against Populism: A Confrontation between the Theory of Democracy and the Theory of Social Choice.* Prospect Heights, IL: Waveland Press.

Schattschneider, E. E. 1960. *The Semi-Sovereign People.* New York: Holt, Rinehart, and Winston.

Schiller, Wendy J. 1995. "Senators as Political Entrepreneuers: Using Bill Sponsorship to Shape Legislative Agendas." *American Journal of Political Science* 39:186–203.

Shepsle, Kenneth A. 1972. "The Strategy of Ambiguity: Uncertainty and Electoral Competition." *American Political Science Review* 66:555–69.

Sinclair, Barbara. 2000. *Unorthodox Lawmaking: New Legislative Processes in the U.S. Congress.* 2nd ed. Washington, DC: Congressional Quarterly.

Tversky, Amos and Daniel Kahneman. 1974. "Judgment under Uncertainty: Heuristics and Biases." *Science* 185:1124–31.

Weisberg, Herbert F., and Morris P. Fiorina. 1980. "Candidate Preference under Uncertainty: An Expanded View of Rational Voting." In *The Electorate Reconsidered,* ed. John C. Pierce and John L. Sullivan. Beverly Hills, CA: Sage Publications.

Wright, John R., and Arthur S. Goldberg. 1985. "Risk and Uncertainty as Factors in the Durability of Political Coalitions." *American Political Science Review* 79: 704–18.

Zaller, John R. 1992. *The Nature and Origins of Mass Opinion.* New York: Cambridge University Press.

PART 1

ELITE AND INSTITUTIONAL POLITICS

I

Bargaining, Uncertainty, and the Growth of the White House Staff, 1940–2000

Matthew J. Dickinson

A president's power, scholars agree, depends in part on the actions and advice of the scores of advisers who constitute the "presidential branch": the large, functionally specialized and hierarchically arranged White House-centered staff system that has become increasingly influential since World War II.[1] Many scholars argue that the growth in staff size and influence is linked to an expansion in presidential responsibilities during the post-1940 "modern" era (Cronin 1975; Hess 1988; Ragsdale and Theis 1997). In Clinton Rossiter's (1949) famous description, presidents since Franklin Delano Roosevelt (FDR) have acquired many more "hats," ranging from chief legislative agenda-setter to manager of economic prosperity to "leader of the free world." In response, they have recruited aides with the requisite expertise to deal with these new responsibilities, and placed them under White House direction (Moe 1985). Stephen Hess (1988, 225) succinctly summarizes this administrative logic:

Generally, [presidential staff growth] has reflected a greater participation in World affairs since World War II, a widened concept of what services government should perform, and has filled a vacuum left by the failure of state and local governments to respond to legitimate needs and the transfer of services to the federal level. The growth has also reflected popular support for an increasingly activist concept of the presidency, more complicated interrelationships between government programs, and new offices imposed on the White House by Congress. Then, too, because existing federal agencies have sometimes failed to do an adequate job, presidents have tried to fill the void by creating new White House offices.

As a general explanation for the post–World War II expansion of the presidential staff, these functionalist accounts predicated on a growth in the federal government's programmatic responsibilities are likely correct. But

---

[1] The phrase was coined by Polsby (1983) and popularized by Hart (1995b). See also Burke (1995), Gilmour (1975), and Seligman (1956).

they do not fully explain why so much of that growth has been centered within the White House Office (WHO), as opposed to the other staff agencies within the Executive Office of the Presidency (EOP). Since its formal inception in 1939, the WHO has developed into the keystone of the modern presidential staff system (Hart 1995b; Patterson 2000; Walcott and Hult 1995). As yet, however, there is little in the way of theory explaining why the White House staff has achieved such prominence (cf., Kernell 1989; Moe 1985; Ragsdale and Theis 1997).

Consider Hess's claim that much of the presidential staff's growth reflects new government programs and stronger public support for an "activist" government. In fact, the presidents who have been entrusted with the most significant program responsibilities since 1939 have *not* responded by expanding their White House staff. Roosevelt is a prime example; as president he oversaw the complete mobilization of the nation's economy for war production, and led a multination coalition to victory in World War II. Although he significantly expanded the presidential staff system by formally establishing the EOP, and placed a number of staff agencies within it where they grew larger and more influential, his White House staff scarcely grew at all during this period (Dickinson 1996). Similarly, Lyndon Johnson's "Great Society" legislative initiatives from 1964 to 1967 produced a measurable increase in his EOP, but did not have much impact on the size of his core White House staff.[2] Conversely, the White House Office grew by leaps and bounds in the late 1960s into the 1970s, and again in the 1990s, although presidents during these periods took on no new policy programs on a scale to rival Roosevelt's war mobilization or Johnson's War on Poverty.

Functionalist explanations that predicate White House staff growth on the acquisition of new presidential responsibilities, then, cannot be the whole story. Instead, I suggest another explanation: an increase in presidential uncertainty linked to the political implications of presidential bargaining. By uncertainty, I simply mean the inability of the president to predict reliably the likely outcome of his (someday her) bargaining exchanges with other political actors. In Richard Neustadt's (1990) classic analysis of presidential power, bargaining is the primary means by which presidents exercise influence on governmental and political outcomes. By negotiating transactions that appeal to the interests of other political actors, presidents build the coalitions necessary to achieve their political and policy objectives (Neustadt 1990). And by anticipating the likely impact of those bargaining outcomes on their sources of bargaining influence, presidents preserve their sources of bargaining power down the road.

---

[2] The Office of Economic Opportunity (OEO), established in 1964 and placed in the EOP to help implement Johnson's antipoverty programs, was not part of the White House Office, and in any case is more properly defined as an operating, as opposed to staff, agency (Hess 1988).

To properly assess the institutional implications of Neustadt's bargaining paradigm, one should distinguish between political capital and bargaining information. Capital refers to the raw material that presidents exchange – votes, services or others goods, and promises that political actors find useful in carrying out their own tasks. Information, in contrast, refers to the president's knowledge regarding the preferences of those with whom he bargains, and his understanding regarding the likely impact of bargaining choices on his preferred outcome and sources of bargaining influence. The distinction between bargaining capital and information parallels that made by economists regarding the difference between production and transaction costs. It is increases in presidents' information costs since 1940, I argue, that are the key to understanding the growth of the White House staff.

To bargain effectively, then, presidents require information regarding the likely outcome of their bargaining choices. Broadly speaking, that information is of two types: policy and political. Policy information refers to the technical aspects of the transaction – if consummated, will it achieve the desired objective? Political information, by contrast, concerns the preferences and strategies of those with whom the president is bargaining. Who is likely to support the deal, and who will oppose it? Effective bargaining requires information on both counts.

When Neustadt first articulated his bargaining thesis in 1960, a president's political information was acquired through interaction with relatively durable "protocoalitions" of party officials, Congressional leaders, executive branch officials, and a limited number of interested groups and media figures (Kernell 1997). In the ensuing four decades, however, these protocoalitions have fragmented because of a variety of developments, including changes to the presidential selection system, a telecommunications revolution, a proliferation of issue-oriented interest groups and, most recently, the transformation of the two parties' constituency base. The cumulative impact has produced a less insular, less stable and less politically predictable bargaining process. As a result, presidential uncertainty regarding the likely outcome of presidential bargaining choices on preferred policy outcomes and on their sources of bargaining influence has increased. In response to this growth in political "transaction" costs, successive presidents built up the White House "firm"; they recruited specialized advisers possessing the requisite information regarding other actors' preferences and likely bargaining strategies, and placed them in the White House where they would be most responsive to the president's bargaining needs.

In short, I argue that the growth of the *White House* staff since Roosevelt's presidency is due largely – although not exclusively – to successive presidents responding to a series of developments that have made presidential bargaining a more politically uncertain process. To test this claim, I first define the salient aspects of White House staff growth, focusing primarily on an increase in staff size and functional specialization since 1940. I then regress that measure against a variety of indicators designed to gauge presidential bargaining uncertainty with key political actors. The results, as reported below, lend support for the claim that bargaining uncertainty as defined here is a significant cause for the institutionalization of the White House staff since 1940. In the final section, I place this research in the larger context of the post-Watergate efforts to reduce the influence of the White House staff. What do these findings say about the likelihood – and desirability – of reform? Before addressing these questions, however, we need first to specify what we mean by the phrase White House staff. The next section addresses that task.

THE EVOLUTION OF THE WHITE HOUSE STAFF, 1940–2000

To what or whom does the phrase "White House staff" actually refer?[3] In recent years, the failure to define this term has generated more than a little controversy. In 1993, it was at the center of reporters' skepticism toward President Clinton's claim to have reduced his "White House" staff by 25 percent during his first year in office (Hart 1995a). It turns out that much of his "success" in reducing staff size was achieved by eliminating the National Office of Drug Control, which technically is not a part of the White House Office. Indeed, it is often the case that White House staff is used as a catchall phrase in the media and elsewhere to describe other staff components within the EOP, such as the Office of Management and Budget, the National Security Council, the Domestic Council or the National Economic Council, all of which are formally outside the White House Office (Patterson 2000).

As John Hart (1995b) points out, however, even when people agree regarding what the White House Office is, they still dispute its size. Estimates vary depending on whether one counts only full-time budgeted employees formally housed within the White House Office or also includes those detailed to work in the White House while on another agency's payroll. There is also the question of whether to include outside consultants, such as Dick Morris, who served as Clinton's primary adviser leading up to the 1996 election but who was never formally part of his presidential staff.

Moreover, staff size is not necessarily the best measure of White House staff influence in any case. Many critics focus more on the acquisition of new functions by the White House Office. But here, too, assessments can differ depending on whether the focus is only on senior-level staff who deal directly with the president, or includes lower-level assistants (and their assistants) who rarely if ever see the president but nonetheless may issue directives in his name. Similarly, a study of staff functions might be limited to substantive

---

[3] On efforts to define White House staff, see Seligman (1956), Gilmour (1975), Burke (1995), Hart (1995b), Wyszomirski (1991), and Light (1995).

policy or political activities, or expanded to include administrative tasks performed by lower-level "clerical" staff.

Assessments regarding the size of the White House staff, then, are inevitably colored by how one defines the population of study. Because my theory focuses on the growth in those aides who are "presidential" – that is, whose workplace incentives are influenced primarily by the president – I define "White House staff" to include any aide working in the White House Office and, beginning in 1970, in the Domestic Council staff and its various successor staffs, whose title includes the phrase "to the president."

These officials are distinguished from other presidential aides within the EOP for at least four reasons. First, they are political aides who are appointed by and serve only at the pleasure of the president; they do not require Senate confirmation nor do they have civil service status. Indeed, because they are advisers to the president, they typically do not testify before Congress. Second, their primary function is to advise the president; they have no statutory duties or "line" responsibilities. Third, these aides typically perform advising related to policy or political matters; they are not primarily responsible for "operating" or clerical tasks. Finally, the designation "to the president" signifies a higher level of responsibility not shared by other presidential aides within the White House staff.[4]

To identify these aides, I utilized the White House Office and Domestic Council staff listings printed in the *U.S. Government Manual*, which has been published annually (and sometimes more frequently) since FDR's first presidential term. To confirm that the *Manual* lists all presidential advisers whose title includes the phrase "to the president," I also utilized more detailed sources of White House aides at different periods and compared the lists. For example, an internal Eisenhower memorandum, dated March 1957, lists thirty political aides (and their assistants) serving in the White House back to June 1953.[5] Each aide whose title includes the phrase "to the president" is also listed in the *U.S. Government Manual* for those years. Nineteen years later, a 1976 internal White House study conducted by the Ford Administration lists 473 fulltime White House aides, of which 381 had career status. Among the remaining ninety-two "unclassified" or "political" aides, fifty-seven are listed in the 1976–77 *U.S. Government Manual* under White House Office. Again, these include every aide with the title of Assistant to the President, Deputy Assistant to the President or Special Assistant to the President. The thirty-five Ford White House aides not listed in the *Manual* at this time were at the bottom of the salary scale, and had titles

---

[4] There are exceptions. Andrew Goodpaster, officially Eisenhower's "Staff Secretary," performed a much more substantive role than his title would suggest. But the exceptions appear few in number.

[5] White House Office Files, Subject – Office of Staff Secretary. File: White House Grade Setup. "Office – Sherman Adams" (March 5, 1957). Dwight David Eisenhower Presidential Library.

such as Associate Director or Staff Assistant that did not include the phrase "to the president," signifying that they were performing primarily clerical duties.[6] Twenty-one years after the Ford study, the Spring 1997 edition of *The Capitol Source* – an authoritative "who's who" of government officials put out twice a year by the National Journal based on White House submissions – lists 276 aides working in the Clinton White House Office, Domestic Policy Council and National Economic Council, including ninety-nine aides whose titles include "to the president."[7] Of the latter group, ninety-eight are listed in the 1996–97 *U.S. Government Manual.*

It appears, then, that the *U.S. Government Manual* provides a comprehensive list of all presidential aides whose title includes the phrase "to the president," signifying primary responsiveness to the president's bargaining interests.[8] In practice, these are upper-level White House Office staff appointees, and their assistants, with significant policy or political functions; the listings do not for the most part include those with career status, and those who perform primarily clerical or "operating" tasks.

With certain modifications, then, this subset of assistants is the dependent variable in the analysis that follows.[9] These listings reveal that the staff has become progressively more "institutionalized" in at least three ways since 1940. First, there has been a substantial increase in staff personnel. Under Roosevelt, seven individuals are listed as working in the White House in 1940. Six decades later, under Clinton, that number has jumped to 120. There is a second, related trend: a growth in staff specialization, as indicated by the proliferation of staff titles. In his classic article describing the evolution of the U.S. House of Representatives, Nelson Polsby (1968) cites an "internal division of labor" as a key feature of an "institutionalized organization." On this dimension, based on the listing of staff titles, the WHO is

---

[6] Staff Secretary Subject File (Connor). File: White House Staff Reductions – Lists and Charts. "Summary – Unclassified Personnel" (July 29, 1976). Gerald R. Ford Presidential Library.

[7] *The Capitol Source (Spring, 1997).* (Washington, DC: National Journal, Inc.), 6–11.

[8] Other scholars have found the *Manual* a useful data source for analyzing substantive White House staffing trends. See Ragsdale and Theis (1997) and Dickinson and Tenpas (2002).

[9] Note that physicians, personal photographers, any aides serving the Vice President or First Lady, and any aide who heads another staff agency within the EOP (such as the Council of Economic Advisers or the Office of Science and Technology Policy) that exercises statutory or "line" functions are not included in my analysis. I also exclude national security advisers, including the Assistant to the President for National Security Affairs, as well as any lower-level national security aides and others who deal primarily in foreign affairs. Although the national security staff fit the criteria of White House advisers, my model does not include measures for bargaining in the international arena. The exclusion of the NSC staff significantly impacts some presidential listings. For example, the *U.S. Government Manual* 1995 listing for Clinton's White House staff includes 153 names, far more than any other president. On closer inspection, it turned out that most of these were junior members of the National Security staff who were not included in prior WHO listings. Moreover, most of these names were left off the 1996 staff list, suggesting that the 1995 list was an aberration.

clearly institutionalized. On the eve of World War II, FDR's WHO consisted primarily of two types of staff positions: his political "secretaries" and the administrative assistants. Contrast this rather sparse functional differentiation to the much more specialized Clinton White House. When Clinton left office in 2001, his staff collectively bore more than eighty titles, ranging from the Chief of Staff to the President to the Special Counsel to the President for Nominations. Of course, not every individual title signifies a unique staff function. Indeed, under some presidents, identical titles mask different staff functions. For example, each of FDR's political "secretaries" handled separate administration tasks related to his daily activities: appointments, correspondence, and press relations. Nevertheless, there has been a clear increase in the number of staff functions during this period.

A third measure of institutionalization is the degree of internal hierarchy. As the White House staff has grown larger and more functionally differentiated, it also has become internally layered. All of FDR's key advisers interacted directly with him daily, usually on a one-on-one basis. Although Truman instituted a daily staff meeting, his senior advisers still dealt directly with him. Eisenhower was the first to institute a measure of staff hierarchy by appointing Sherman Adams as his chief of staff, responsible for managing the White House on Ike's behalf. Two assistants, making Eisenhower's staff in effect a three-level hierarchy, assisted Adams in this task. By Reagan's presidency, the chief of staff had become an accepted part of the White House organization. By the end of Clinton's presidency, the addition of deputy and special assistants to the president had created a five-level White House staff hierarchy, including four layers of White House staff who almost never interacted with the president.

In the aggregate, then, the White House staff has grown larger, more functionally specialized, and more hierarchical during the last sixty years. Among these developments, perhaps the most important in terms of its impact on presidential influence is the growth in staff functional specialization. To begin, functional growth contributes to the overall increase in staff size. Moreover, several studies have shown that different functional arrangements alter the flow of information and the decision-making processes within bureaucracies (Hammond 1986; Hammond and Miller 1985; Miller 1992). The increase in staff size and expertise, as reflected in new positions, has undoubtedly helped presidents cope with the burgeoning demands on their office. As critics point out, however, it also complicates the president's managerial job. The chances for mischief are multiplied with more staff members running around acting in the president's name.

In addition, functional specialization also may fragment staff work among different perspectives. Critics of White House staff specialization complain that these titles confer "hunting licenses" to staff members, giving aides a sense of jurisdictional entitlement and contributing to staff parochialism. This might make it more difficult to act collectively on the president's broader behalf (Dickinson 1996). Finally, the increase in titles has produced a need for hierarchy to coordinate the actions of different types of aides on the president's behalf. But this layering of political appointees may diffuse staff accountability to the president (Light 1995).

By measuring annual changes in the number of aides with titles including the phrase "to the president," I develop a crude approximation of changes in staff functional specialization. Note that this approach differs from previous research that counts the total number of budgeted White House aides, including clerical aides, to assess the growth of the White House staff.[10] By restricting my analysis to the subset of higher-echelon White House staff, and excluding clerical aides and others performing primarily administrative functions, I focus more nearly on the object of much of the post-Watergate criticism of the White House staff. It is the proliferation of aides with substantive policy and political duties, but who often do not interact directly with the president, that concerns many critics (Dickinson 1996; Rourke 1991). At the same time, however, the White House staff listings, as defined here, do provide an approximate gauge of the combined impact of a change in White House staff size *and* functional specialization.

Figure 1.1 shows the degree to which staff size and functions have increased since 1940, based on the foregoing definition.

Two patterns are worth noting. First, for the most part, the number of White House staff trends up over the six decades analyzed here. (As we shall see, the lack of a fixed mean in the data can complicate statistical analysis.) The second interesting pattern is that the growth is not smooth; there is a small jump beginning with Eisenhower's first term in 1953, and then relatively large jumps under Nixon in 1969, and again under Reagan in 1981, and finally a third large jump under Clinton in 1993. After the first three increases, staff size tends to level off and even decrease slightly. Whether this pattern will repeat itself after Clinton's administration remains to be seen. But the patterns of growth raise key questions: What caused these jumps? What explains variations in staffing patterns more generally? The next section explores these issues.

A THEORY OF WHITE HOUSE STAFF INSTITUTIONALIZATION

Having defined the salient features of White House staff growth, we are now positioned to examine its causes. Recall that I argue, following Neustadt, that presidential power – a president's effective influence on policy and political outcomes – is primarily a function of bargaining effectiveness. To bargain effectively, however, presidents must acquire information regarding the likely impact of bargaining choices on preferred outcomes. To simplify the analysis,

---

[10] See, for example, Ragsdale and Theis (1997). Because the budgeted positions do not include those detailed to work in the White House, they probably underestimate actual staff size.

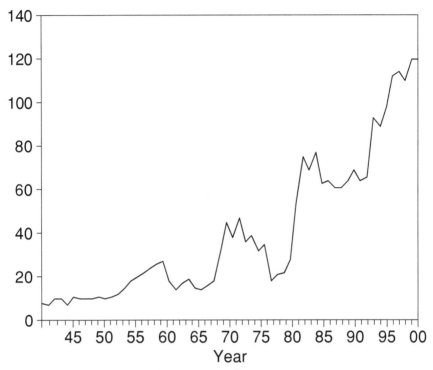

FIGURE 1.1. Growth in the White House Staff, 1941–2000

I distinguish between two key bargaining arenas: electoral and governing. In each arena, I argue, bargaining became an increasingly uncertain process, politically speaking, in the period 1940–2000. The growth in uncertainty not only occurred incrementally but also as a result of exogenous "shocks" to the bargaining arenas that raised information costs across a relatively short period of time.

I begin with the electoral arena, which I further subdivide into the nominating process and the general election. As Hagen and Mayer (2000) document, from 1940 through 1968 party organizations and party leaders dominated the process by which presidential candidates were nominated. For the most part, candidates seeking their party's nomination had to broker a deal with the handful of party leaders who controlled blocs of delegates. By 1972, however, this system had all but collapsed, to be replaced by a media-dominated, primary-based nominating process in which candidates could no longer rely on the party elite to deliver delegates' votes. Instead, candidates competed for delegates through a media-dominated primary process. To survive this gauntlet, candidates were forced to start campaigning much earlier, and to tailor their message to appeal to the more issue-oriented party activists who tend to vote in primaries. Devising a winning primary strategy required a media-savvy staff proficient in polling and media relations. Moreover, the advent of campaign finance reform in the period 1971–4 further complicated the nominating process, by forcing candidates to put together a fundraising infrastructure to qualify for taxpayer subsidies, and to negotiate the labyrinth of campaign finance rules and regulations. Again, this required candidates to recruit additional staff with the requisite expertise.

Changes also were underway during this period that affected the general election process. In hindsight, it is now clear that the importance of party as a cue to voting began declining as early as the 1950s. But the process of party decay accelerated after 1964 as manifested by an increase in split-ticket voting, and a rise in the proportion of voters who described themselves as independents. Moreover, there is some evidence that issues became progressively more important in this period in determining how the electorate cast their presidential ballot. By most accounts, then, the post-1964 period witnessed a period of electoral "dealignment" in which the party became a less useful means of predicting the vote. Presidential candidates could no longer count on a relatively stable voting coalition based on party identification to support them at the polls. Instead, they had to devise ways to exploit the new campaign finance laws and devise media strategies to actively court the increasingly larger bloc of uncommitted voters.

The situation was further complicated, however, because even as the size of the "moderate" middle of uncommitted voters grew larger, the two parties also began reconfiguring their constituencies. In particular, the Democrats lost their more conservative voters as the South went progressively Republican, and Republican moderates decreased in numbers as the Northeast became increasingly Democratic. By the 1980s, the median voter in each party was now located further apart along the ideological spectrum, making interparty coalition building by presidential candidates a more difficult task.

We see, then, a sharp durable shift in the electoral process in the period 1968–76 from a relatively closed system dominated by the party elite to a much more permeable and increasingly specialized process. Moreover, this shift takes place against the backdrop of long-term decline in the importance of party and an increase in the importance of issues as influences on electoral outcomes.

These changes in the electoral process spilled over into the governing arena. Most noticeably, the mid-1960s witnessed the rise of the incumbency advantage, in which House and, to a lesser extent, Senate members became increasingly adept at using the perquisites of office to make themselves less vulnerable during elections. Presidential "coattails," never large to begin with, began to diminish and legislators felt less electorally indebted to their nominal party leader (Erikson and Wright 2001). The upshot was the beginning of persistent divided government, in which presidents are as likely to face an opposition Congress as they are one controlled by their own party. And, as the constituency base of each party grew increasingly "pure," the number of conservative Democrats and liberal Republicans in Congress who once provided a means for bridging party differences rapidly diminished, increasing the likelihood of partisan gridlock on Capitol Hill. The most obvious manifestation was a greater tendency to engage in "politics by other means," including the use of independent prosecutors by the majority party in Congress to investigate the president of the opposing party.

At the same time, the influence of party leaders in Congress also diminished, due to internal reforms that "democratized" proceedings by providing rank-and-file legislators with more visible political platforms via subcommittee chairs and more extensive staffs with which to engage in casework and constituency service (Rohde 1991). Moreover, a revived party caucus became a useful tool through which party members in Congress could exercise influence over the party leadership. From the presidents' perspective, then, coalition building became a more time-consuming, less certain process in part because of growing number of legislators with increasingly polarized political views with whom they had to bargain, and the inability of party leaders to broker deals on their party's behalf.

In response, presidents were tempted to take their case to the public, utilizing new communications technologies, particularly the rise of television, and capitalizing on their standing as the only elected leader in American politics with a national constituency (Kernell 1997). But others could and did play this game. Members of Congress became increasingly adept at "going public" as well, using media strategies often supported financially by the single-issue interest groups that proliferated in the 1960s and 70s (Corrado 2000). The growth of political action committees in the wake of the 1974 campaign finance reforms was only the most obvious manifestation of this fracturing of public discourse into a cacophony of political voices. And with the advent of cable and twenty-four-hour news services, narrow casting replaced broadcasting as the primary means of disseminating the news to an increasingly fragmented viewing audience (Hess 2000). As a result, presidents found it harder to mobilize a "national constituency" to support their policies, and instead began focusing their message to targeted audiences, depending on the issue at hand. To do so effectively, they increasingly relied on polling and media consultants.

The upshot of these developments is that the process of constructing coalitions in the electoral and governing arenas became a politically more uncertain process for presidents. In the era of institutionalized pluralism," presidents could rely on a party elite who generally shared their political interests to provide bargaining information. To build winning coalitions in an era of party decay and "individualized pluralism," however, presidents now required specialists with knowledge pertaining to campaign finance regulations, public opinion trends, interest group politics and media relations, not to mention a more contentious set of Congressional preferences (see Kernell 1997; Ornstein and Mann 2000). By relying on outside experts, however, presidents risked mortgaging their political future to individuals who might exploit their information asymmetry for their own gain, particularly if they had a stake in the bargaining outcome. To forestall this, presidents sought to recruit these experts and place them within the WHO, where they would be more responsive to presidential direction. In effect, then, when confronted with high information costs associated with an increasingly uncertain and more specialized bargaining process, presidents substituted internal hierarchy for the political marketplace. The result through time is a larger, more functionally specialized WHO.

Fully documenting this argument is beyond the scope of this chapter. In the rest of this section, however, I provide a preliminary test of the underlying logic. I begin by presuming that, as conventional wisdom suggests, much of the growth in the presidential staff size is linked to the increased size and complexity of the programs pursued by presidents during the last six decades. To capture this growth in "policy uncertainty" I utilize a variety of proxy measures, including the number of federal employees, changes in the federal budget (measured in constant dollars) and the number of pages in the Federal Register, a crude measure of the size and complexity of the policy agenda. If functional explanations are correct, these all ought to be positively correlated with a growth in White House staff. At the very least, these measures serve as controls for the impact of government growth.

I then turn to the "political" variables related to the informational cost of bargaining and coalition building in the electoral and governing arenas. One of the most critical electoral variables, I argue, is the strength of the president's popular support, as indicated by the percent of the popular vote he received in the most recent presidential election. The higher the vote, I argue, the easier it will be for the president to predict the electorate's likely reaction to his policy choices and other actions, and therefore the smaller the staff requirements.[11]

A second electoral change is the breakdown of party control over the nominating process, and the concomitant rise in the importance of single-issue groups and other electoral "factions." To win the party's nomination for the presidency, presidential candidates must mobilize the support of these groups. A key source of campaign funds is the political action committees (PACs) that have proliferated since 1974. As a crude measure of the complexity of campaigning in an era of issue-oriented group-based funding, then, I count the number of PACs in existence each year. As PACs become a more important element in the electoral landscape, presidents will react by hiring specialists to deal with these groups (Corrado 1997).

A related campaign change is the growing importance of the media. As party control over the nominating process and general election has

---

[11] I assume the impact of the vote is felt through the four-year period until the next election.

weakened, the press has stepped in as the primary mediator between the candidates and the public. Devising effective media strategies has become critical for raising money and winning office. Presidents have reacted by hiring pollsters and other media strategists to advise them in dealing with the press. But the significance of the growing importance to presidents of interest group and press relations does not end with electoral victory; they also are crucial to a president's governing effectiveness as well (Ginsberg, Mebane, and Shefter 1995). In an era of the "permanent campaign," presidents are more dependent on media advisers and issue specialists than ever.

The proliferation of PACs described above serves as a proxy measure for the growing importance of issue-oriented interest groups to a president's governing effectiveness. However, to measure the evolving impact of the media on the White House staff, I also include a variable that accounts for the number of radio and television reporters accredited to cover Congress each year. This is an indicator of the growing pervasiveness of telecommunications coverage of government more generally.[12] As this number increases, so too should the size of the White House staff.

Along with the press and the public, the president's most critical governing relationship is with Congress. Again, the larger the president's political coalition the more predictable presidential bargaining with Congress should be (Kernell 1997). The simplest indication of the size of the president's congressional support is the number of seats his party controls in both chambers. To simplify the analysis, I take the average percent of the seats in the House and the Senate controlled by the president's party for each two-year period. As the averaged party support goes up, the president's staff requirements should lessen.

Even with majority support, however, bargaining can be costly to presidents if the two parties are ideologically at loggerheads. To control for the growing polarization of party politics in Congress, I take the average difference in the two parties' median ideological points in the House, for each Congressional session, based on Poole-Rosenthal first dimension DW-NOMINATE scores.[13] These provide an approximate measure of the median ideological preference for each party as a whole. The larger the ideological gap between parties in the House, the more difficult it will be for presidents to put together a winning coalition, and the larger the staffs they will recruit to assess and mobilize congressional support.

---

[12] I do not use White House press accreditation, because recent presidents have consciously sought to limit the number of media covering the White House.

[13] I use only the House DW-Nominate first dimension median scores, because the ideological measures cannot be compared across chambers, and thus averaging the House and Senate party median gaps is not appropriate. Moreover, in the time period under study, the House has been more ideologically divided than the Senate, and more likely to be controlled by the president's opposition party. For a description of these measures see Poole, Rosenthal, and McCarty (1997).

A final bargaining arena within the governing realm takes place between the president and the career civil service. Presidents can be expected when possible to saturate the permanent bureaucracy with party loyalists as a means of extending their administrative reach (Light 1995; Moe 1985). Their opportunities to do so depend in part on the number of Senate-confirmed political appointments (PAs) they make to the executive branch. It is likely that as the number of PAs appointment opportunities increase, a larger White House staff is required to recruit potential candidates and lobby for their appointment (Weko 1995).

In summary, the theory predicts that the annual size of the White House staff, as defined here, ought to be positively correlated with the size of ideological gap separating the two parties in Congress, the number of PACs, the number of Senate-confirmed presidential appointments to the executive branch and the size of the Congressional telecommunications corps. It should show a negative relationship with the size of the president's popular vote in the general election, and the percentage of the congressional seats controlled by the president's party. To control for a growth in the size of the public sector more generally, the analysis includes measures for federal personnel, the federal budget in constant dollars, the number of state employees and the number of pages of the Federal Register.

In any time series analysis, it is important to determine whether the variables are stationary.[14] Modeling a relationship using two or more series, such as White House staff size and any of the variables described above, and treating them as stationary when in fact they contain unit roots indicating they were generated by a "random walk" lead to spurious regression results (Granger and Newbold 1974). Before running the regression, then, each of the variables was tested for stationarity using an Augmented Dickey-Fuller (ADF) test.[15] The results indicated that in all but one case – percent party support in Congress – the existence of a unit root signifying a nonstationary variable could not be ruled out. Additional testing indicated that the variables are fractionally integrated to varying degrees, that is, correlations exist between distant time periods for each of the variables.[16] Stated another way, none of the variables in the model are perfectly stationary (implying reversion

---

[14] A stationary variable is one that returns to a constant mean. When affected by an external disturbance, the impact of that event will be "forgotten" over time at a constant rate. Nonstationary variables, in contrast, are "long-memoried"; external events have a cumulative impact and are not "forgotten."

[15] All statistical tests used a version of RATS statistical program. The ADF test involves regressing a variable against its lagged value and a series of lagged values in differenced form and examining the residuals for serial correlation. Testing procedures for time series are discussed more generally in Lebo, Walker, and Clarke (2000).

[16] Testing for fractional integration was done using Robinson's Gaussian Semi-Parametric estimation routine in RATS. See Lebo, Walker, and Clarke (2000) for a discussion of different methods of testing for fractional integration.

to the mean) or purely nonstationary (implying long-memory). Thus, they are most accurately modeled in their fractionally differenced form.[17] Moreover, at least two of the time series – the growth in White House staff and the lagged size of the congressional radio and television press pool – appear to be fractionally cointegrated. In their fractionally differenced state they are locked in a long-term relationship in which changes in the size of either tend to coincide.[18] To address both the fractionally differenced nature of the variables, and the long-term relationship between the press and White House staff, the final equation took the form of an error correction model, with the fractionally differenced form of the White House staff regressed against the fractionally differenced explanatory variables, and the lagged levels of the White House staff and the White House press included as a fractionally differenced error correction component of the equation.

As Table 1.1 indicates, the model explains about 57 percent of the overall variance in the number of White House staff in the period 1941–98. The impact measures in column 2 indicate the average annual impact of each variable on White House staff growth. Although the annual impact for most variables is small, the cumulative impact over five decades is substantial. As expected, increases in the president's party support in Congress, and an amelioration of the ideological distance between the two parties in Congress are both correlated with lower staff sizes. On average, for approximately every 2 percent gain in party seats White House staffs decline by a little less than one presidential aide. Similarly, a reduction in the median preferences between the two parties in the House of two points on the Poole-Rosenthal DW-NOMINATE scale will also decrease staff size by one.

Also as predicted, as the president's popular vote in the general election goes up, staff size also decreases. On average, an increase of a little more than 2 percent in the president's vote will lower the White House staff by one aide. An increase in the number of PACs, by contrast, is positively correlated with White House staff size; for every fifty PACs established, the White House staff will increase by one aide.

Changes in the size of the White House telecommunications press corps are also, as expected, positively correlated with a growth in the White House staff. An increase of fifty accredited radio or television media adds one additional aide to the White House, on average. Moreover, the error correction component suggests that whenever the two fall out of equilibrium, their relationship does readjust at a rate of 17 percent of the total disequilibrium the first year. It appears, then, that much of the long-term growth in the White House staff is a response to the expansion in radio and television coverage.

---

[17] For a discussion of fractional differencing see Box-Steffensmeier and Tomlinson (2000) and Lebo, Walker, and Clarke (2000).

[18] A system of variables is "cointegrated" if each of the variables is nonstationary, and some linear combination of them is stationary (Engle and Granger 1987).

TABLE 1.1 *Error Correction Model of White House Staff Growth,*
1941–1998

Explanatory Variable	Coefficient (Standard Error)	Impact
Senate-Confirmed Political Appointees	.03** (.01)	.94
Party Support in Congress	−.41*** (.10)	−.45
Gap in Median Party Positions (House)	.51* (.28)	.15
Political Action Committees	.02*** (.00)	.15
Presidential Vote	−.41** (.17)	−.25
Pages in Federal Register	−.0004*** (.0001)	−.50
Growth of Congressional Telecommunications Press	.02** (.01)	.39
Error Correction Component	−.16** (.07)	.00
Constant	−.41 (.86)	
Number of Cases (After adjusting endpoints)	57	
Adjusted R^2	.57	
Durbin-Watson	2.21	

Notes: Dependent Variable: Annual Change in Number of White House Staff
All variables are fractionally differenced. Entries are unstandardized OLS coefficients. "Impact" indicates change in White House staff caused by annual one unit change in explanatory variable. Calculated by multiplying mean annual change of fractionally differenced variable across fifty-seven observations with its regression coefficient.
*** $p < .01$, ** $p < .05$, * $p < .10$ (two-sided test).

As noted at the outset of this chapter, many scholars link the growth in the White House staff to a more "activist" federal government. Interestingly, neither federal budget nor federal employment is a statistically significant predictor of a change in White House staff size, and consequently I do not include them in final regression equation. More interesting still, a growth in government policy size and complexity, as reflected in the number of pages in the Federal Register, is *negatively* correlated with staff size. For every additional one thousand pages in the Register, White House staffs *decrease* by four aides. Annual changes in the White House staff size are evidently not driven by a general growth in government size, although it may well be the case that a change in the size of the EOP is linked to a more activist government.

TABLE 1.2 *Staff Size by Presidential Party, 1933–2001*

President's Party	Years	Mean	Standard Deviation
Republican	28	46.1	21.2
Democratic	40	30.9	31.2
TOTAL	68	37.3	33.5

In summary, it appears that the growth of the White House staff is positively associated with an increase in political bargaining uncertainty, as defined here. It bears repeating that this growth refers only to aides whose title includes the phrase "to the president." It is likely, however, that the number of lower-level aides performing primarily clerical functions also increases in concert with increases in the number of aides with more substantive duties.

ADDITIONAL IMPLICATIONS: PARTISAN DIFFERENCES IN WHITE HOUSE STAFFING?

In addition to explaining an empirical pattern, an effective theory also ought to help address other empirical puzzles that might not be immediately related to the original inquiry. One such puzzle is the apparent partisan difference in approaches to staffing the White House. A number of scholars point out that Republican presidents' White House staffs are typically larger, more hierarchical and more functionally specialized than are Democratic presidents' staffs (Hess 1988; Johnson 1974; Neustadt 1990). The empirical data gathered here supports that observation. The mean levels of White House staff size for Republican and Democratic presidents from 1933 to 2001 are significantly different, with Republicans' staffs 50 percent larger on average than Democrats' staffs.[19]

To what can we attribute this difference? Most scholars suggest a difference in management styles rooted in presidents' backgrounds and temperament, as well as the incumbent president's tendency to emulate the staffing approaches of previous presidents who share the same party affiliation. However, the findings here suggest an alternative explanation. It could be that the partisan difference in the size of White House staffs is rooted less in individual president's management styles and more in the different bargaining circumstances they confronted. Simply put, during the 1933–69 era of party-based "protocoalitions" Democrats dominated the presidency. Thereafter, as these bargaining protocoalitions dissolved, Republican presidents were more frequently in the Oval Office. Historically, then, Democratic presidents utilized smaller staffs because they presided in periods of lower political uncertainty. As evidence in support of this claim, note that Clinton, a Democratic

---

[19] A difference of means test indicates that the null of no difference is rejected with a probability of .06.

president with a small margin of victory in 1992 and who, after 1994, confronted an opposition-controlled and deeply polarized Congress, did not revert back to his party's norm of smaller White House staffs.

CONCLUSION

We are now ready to address the question with which the chapter began: What explains variations in White House staff size since 1940? The answer, I argue, is rooted in changing contextual circumstances that have collectively increased the political uncertainty associated with presidential bargaining. In the period 1940–68, presidential bargaining took place among durable party-based coalitions of Congressional leaders, party elites, broad-based interest groups, and a public largely organized along party lines. The slight increase in White House staff under Eisenhower, particularly after 1956, is in part caused by divided government and his need to take some control over an executive branch dominated by his New Deal appointees. But, for the most part, White House staff totals do not vary much in this era. The first significant staff increase begins with Nixon on the heels of his narrow 1968 electoral victory as he confronts an opposition-controlled Congress and the growing evidence of the partisan dealignment then underway. Ford largely continues Nixon's precedents. Carter, who enjoys four years of unified government, somewhat reduces the White House staff, but staff levels jump again beginning with Reagan's presidency in 1981, under the cumulative impact of a divided Congress, the increased polarization of the Republicans and Democrats in the House, a growing media presence and the proliferation of political action committees. Finally, a third significant jump occurs in 1993 on the heels of Clinton's narrow victory in a three-way presidential contest against George H. W. Bush and Ross Perot. Two years later, his party loses control of Congress to the Republicans, and soon after he is embroiled in the bitter partisan disputes that lead to his impeachment by the House and trial in the Senate.

This story, if accurate, is of more than academic interest. Beginning with the Brownlow Report's celebrated warning in 1937 that the "president needs help," presidency scholars through the mid-1960s generally believed that the expansion of the presidential staff provided presidents with a sporting chance to fulfill their growing obligations. But, after revelations regarding the role advisers played in presidential decisions pertaining to Vietnam, Watergate, and the Iran-Contra affair, not to mention lesser staff-related pratfalls, scholars' views began to change. Rather than providing presidents with "help," the larger, more politicized White House-centered presidential staffs of the 1970s and later seemed as likely to undercut presidential influence as to extend it.

In response, some critics proposed a number of reforms, including reducing White House staff size, making presidential assistants accountable to Congress, regularizing decision procedures and reinvigorating the traditional presidential cabinet as the primary locus of presidential administrative support. For the most part, these suggestions received only lip service from presidents. In the few instances in which presidents did seriously try to scale back White House staff influence, they soon discovered that no other administrative entity existed that could provide the same services. As a result, the reforms went nowhere, and today the White House is as large and as influential as ever.

Implicit within the post-Watergate "reform" school of thought was the presumption that if presidents only had the political will, they could reduce White House staff size. That they failed to do so offers a cautionary lesson: prescription should not proceed without proper diagnosis. One cannot hope to reverse the White House staff's growing influence without first understanding why it has acquired that influence in the first place. In this chapter, I have tried to show that the growth of the White House staff is rooted in an increase in presidential political uncertainty related to presidential bargaining. A variety of developments in the American political system – weakening party influence in the electorate, the growth of the candidate-centered campaign, the rise of the adversarial media, the devolution of power in Congress from the party leadership to the rank-and-file members – have collectively made it harder for presidents to predict the likely outcome of their bargaining choices. In response, they have hired staff experts to provide the requisite information and advice.

What, then, is the likelihood of significantly reducing the influence of the White House staff? The chances are not great, barring some reversion to a previous era, in which bargaining once again becomes largely the province of political elites with predictable preferences. For the near future, then, presidents will likely continue to see their bargaining options shaped by a polarized Congress, numerous narrowly focused and clashing interest groups, an adversarial media, and a wary public. Faced with this ongoing political uncertainty, presidents will continue to seek help – and to find it within their own hand-picked White House staff.

References

Box-Steffensmeier, Janet M., and Andrew R. Tomlinson. 2000. "Fractional Integration Methods in Political Science." *Electoral Studies* 19:63–76.

Burke, John P. 1995. "The Institutional Presidency." In *The Presidency and the Political System* 4th. ed., ed. Michael Nelson. Washington, DC: CQ Press.

Corrado, Anthony. 1997. "Financing the 1996 Elections." In *The Election of 1996*, ed. Gerald M. Pomper. Chatham, NJ: Chatham House Publishers.

Corrado, Anthony. 2000. "Running Backward: The Congressional Money Chase." In *The Permanent Campaign and Its Future*, ed. Norman J. Ornstein and Thomas E. Mann. Washington, DC: AEI and Brookings.

Cronin, Thomas. 1975. *The State of the Presidency*. Boston, MA: Little, Brown.

Dickinson, Matthew J. 1996. *Bitter Harvest: FDR, Presidential Power and the Growth of the Presidential Branch*. New York: Cambridge University Press.

Dickinson, Matthew J., and Katherine D. Tenpas. 2002. "The Revolving Door at the White House: Explaining Increasing Turnover Rates Among Presidential Advisers, 1929–97." *Journal of Politics* 64:434–48.

Engle, Robert F., and Clive W. J. Granger. 1987. "Cointegration and Error Correction: Representation, Estimation, and Testing" *Econometrica* 55:251–76.

Erikson, Robert S., and Gerald C. Wright. 2001. "Voters, Candidates, and Issues in Congressional Elections." In *Congress Reconsidered* 7th ed., ed. Lawrence C. Dodd and Bruce I. Oppenheimer. Washington, DC: CQ Press.

Gilmour, Robert S. 1975. "The Institutionalized Presidency: A Conceptual Clarification." In *The Presidency in Contemporary Context*, ed. Norman Thomas. New York: Dodd, Mead.

Ginsberg, Benjamin, Walter R. Mebane, Jr., and Martin Shefter. 1995. "The Presidency, Social Forces and Interest Groups: Why Presidents Can No Longer Govern." In *The Presidency and the Political System* 4th. ed., ed. Michael Nelson. Washington, DC: CQ Press.

Granger, Clive, and Paul Newbold. 1974. "Spurious Regression in Econometrics." *Journal of Econometrics* 2:111–20.

Hagen, Michael, and William G. Mayer. 2000. "The Modern Politics of Presidential Selection." In *In Pursuit of the White House 2000*, ed. William G. Mayer. New York: Seven Bridges Press.

Hammond, Thomas H. 1986. "Agenda Control, Organizational Structure, and Bureaucratic Politics." *American Journal of Political Science* 30:379–420.

Hammond, Thomas H., and Gary J. Miller. 1985. "A Social Choice Perspective on Expertise and Authority in Bureaucracy." *American Journal of Political Science* 29:1–28.

Hart, John. 1995a. "President Clinton and the Politics of Symbolism: Cutting the White House Staff." *Political Science Quarterly* 110:385–403.

Hart, John. 1995b. *The Presidential Branch*. 2nd ed. Chatham, NJ: Chatham House Publishers.

Hess, Stephen. 1988. *Organizing the Presidency*. Rev. ed. Washington, DC: Brookings.

Hess, Stephen. 2000. "The Press and the Permanent Campaign." In *The Permanent Campaign and Its Future*, ed. Norman J. Ornstein and Thomas E. Mann. Washington, DC: AEI and Brookings.

Johnson, Richard Tanner. 1974. *Managing the White House: An Intimate Study of the Presidency*. New York: Harper and Row.

Kernell, Samuel. 1989. "The Evolution of the White House Staff." In *Can the Government Govern?*, ed. Paul E. Peterson and John Chubb. Washington, DC: Brookings.

Kernell, Samuel. 1997. *Going Public: New Strategies of Presidential Leadership*. 3rd ed. Washington, DC: CQ Press.

Lebo, Matthew J., Robert W. Walker, and Harold D. Clarke. 2000. "You Must Remember This: Dealing with Long Memory in Political Analysis." *Electoral Studies* 19:31–48.

Light, Paul C. 1995. *Thickening Government*. Washington, DC: Brookings.

Miller, Gary J. 1992. *Managerial Dilemmas: The Political Economy of Hierarchy.* New York: Cambridge University Press.

Moe, Terry. 1985. "The Politicized Presidency." In *New Direction in American Politics*, ed. Paul Peterson and John Chubb. Washington, DC: Brookings.

Neustadt, Richard E. 1990. *Presidential Power and the Modern Presidents.* New York: The Free Press.

Ornstein, Norman J., and Thomas E. Mann, ed. 2000. *The Permanent Campaign and Its Future.* Washington, DC: AEI and Brookings.

Patterson, Bradley H., Jr. 2000. *The White House Staff: Inside the West Wing and Beyond.* Washington, DC: Brookings.

Polsby, Nelson W. 1968. "The Institutionalization of the House of Representatives." *American Political Science Review* 62:144–68.

Polsby, Nelson W. 1983. "Some Landmarks in Modern Presidential-Congressional Relations." In *Both Ends of the Avenue*, ed. Anthony King. Washington, DC: AEI.

Poole, Keith T., Howard Rosenthal, and Nolan McCarty. 1997. *Income Redistribution and the Realignment of American Politics.* Washington, DC: AEI.

Ragsdale, Lyn, and John Theis. 1997. "The Institutionalization of the American Presidency, 1924–92." *American Journal of Political Science* 41:1280–1318.

Rohde, David W. 1991. *Parties and Leaders in the Postreform House.* Chicago: The University of Chicago Press.

Rossiter, Clinton L. 1949. "The Constitutional Significance of the Executive Office of the Presidency." *American Political Science Review* 43:1206–17.

Rourke, Francis. 1991. "Presidentializing the Bureaucracy: From Kennedy to Reagan." In *The Managerial Presidency*, ed. James Pfiffner. Pacific Grove, CA: Brooks-Cole Publishing.

Seligman, Lester G. 1956. "Presidential Leadership: The Inner Circle and Institutionalization." *Journal of Politics* 18:410–26.

Walcott, Charles E., and Karen M. Hult. 1995. *Governing the White House.* Lawrence: University Press of Kansas.

Weko, Thomas J. 1995. *The Politicizing Presidency.* Lawrence: University Press of Kansas.

Wyszomirski, Margaret Jane. 1991. "The Discontinuous Institutional Presidency." In *Executive Leadership in Anglo-American Systems*, ed. Colin Campbell and Margaret Jane Wyszomirski. Pittsburgh, PA: University of Pittsburgh Press, 1991.

2

Political Uncertainty and Administrative Procedures

Richard G. Vanden Bergh
Rui J. P. de Figueiredo, Jr.

Free elections are central to the institutional structure of democratic governments. As Hamilton noted in the *Federalist Papers*, elections create "an immediate dependence on, an intimate sympathy with, the people" (Hamilton,
Jay, and Madison 1961, 165). Although elections establish an ongoing
connection between representatives and citizens, their impact on policy implementation is less clear. Regular elections create *uncertainty* about who
will hold office and for how long. They therefore introduce an additional set
of considerations for those who design the structure of government agencies
beyond simple organizational effectiveness. In this chapter, we explore the
relationship between electoral uncertainty and the adoption of a particularly important aspect of agency structure: the *administrative procedures*
public officials require government agencies to follow when agencies issue
policies.

There are two literatures that address the issue of why public organizations are structured in particular ways. The first addresses the problem of
how elected officials can use structure to control agencies. A number of scholars have shown that organizational design, administrative procedures, and
other aspects of organization structure can provide elected officials with a
means of overcoming agency problems. According to this scholarship, structural choices are the product of a struggle between independent-minded bureaucrats and their political fathers (Bawn 1995; de Figueiredo, Spiller, and
Urbiztondo 1999; Epstein and O'Halloran 1994, 1996, 1999; Fiorina 1983;
Ferejohn and Shipan 1990; Lupia and McCubbins 1994; McCubbins, Noll,
and Weingast 1987; Weingast and Moran 1983). Importantly, one of the
key insights in this literature is that the nature of control, and thus delegation, will depend on the degree of political homogeneity: when control over

The authors thank Barry Burden, Pablo Spiller, Barry Weingast, and Oliver Williamson for
helpful conversations. In addition, the section discussing Broadcast Radio Regulation draws
heavily, and in some cases verbatim, from de Figueiredo (2002).

political institutions is unified, delegation to executive agencies will be less constrained by thick administrative requirements and procedures.

This vein of the scholarship on delegation suffers from an important shortcoming, however. Whereas all of this literature demonstrates the way in which a legislature or president can overcome basic moral hazard problems – either a lack of effort or implementation of a new policy position – the actors in these models are static. In democracies, however, elected officials and the interests they represent will change. This means that agencies are not the only actors who threaten the future implementation of the officials' or group's target policy. In addition, *current* officials must be concerned that *future* holders of public authority will undo what has been accomplished in the present period. Unfortunately, because the actors never change in most of the control and delegation models, these studies leave this fundamental design problem largely unexplored.

A second literature adds such a dynamic perspective. A number of scholars, including Moe (1989, 1990), Rothenberg (1994), Horn (1995), and McCubbins, Noll, and Weingast (1987, 1989), argue that elected officials are keenly aware of the likelihood of their own demise. Thus, the policies they enact are subject to possible sabotage by future winners (Horn 1995; Moe 1991; Rothenberg 1994). The potential for such destructive behavior means that today's winners must install protective mechanisms against the future actions of one's opponents (Moe 1989). In the context of American bureaucracy, this means that prevailing groups will legislate a number of "insulation mechanisms" to ensure that their creation is not undermined. As Moe explains:

The driving force of political uncertainty, then, causes the winning group to favor structural designs it would never favor on technical grounds alone: designs that place detailed formal restrictions on bureaucratic discretion, impose complex procedures for agency decision making, minimize opportunities for oversight, and otherwise insulate the agency from politics. The group has to protect itself and its agency from the dangers of democracy, and it does so by imposing structures that appear strange and incongruous indeed when judged by almost any reasonable standards of what an effective organization ought to look like. (Moe 1990, 137)

In this context, organizational design can be seen as a product of the political uncertainty with which political actors live (Horn 1995; Moe 1989, 1991). In sum, this literature makes two claims about the relationship between such uncertainty and the structure of government: first, that political uncertainty leads to structural insulation of government agencies, and second, that this structural insulation leads to greater inefficiency of agency outputs.

For students of public organizations, however, the existing dynamic theory also requires expansion. In particular, the theory has two shortcomings. First, the dynamic theory assumes that control is complete. This ignores the possibility that administrative procedures will be the outcome of a bargain, a bargain that must itself be the result of political negotiation. As the literature on static delegation points out, the outcome of such bargains will depend on the political homogeneity, or heterogeneity, of the actors controlling various political institutions. Second, the dynamic theory ignores the possibility that electoral uncertainty itself is a *variable*. In fact, at different times in the history of the federal government *and* the state governments, uncertainty about who would hold elected office has varied greatly. In some cases, outcomes are highly volatile from election to election. In others, electoral outcomes are stable, and virtually preordained.

In this chapter, we develop a model that brings together these central features of the design of administrative procedures, combining insights about political feasibility and political incentives in a static delegatory environment, with insights about political uncertainty and the dynamic considerations implied by electoral volatility. The model proceeds in two parts. The first component is a formal model that captures the interaction between a legislature, an elected executive, and a representative executive-branch agency. The model establishes a benchmark case in which actors are only concerned about current period outcomes. In the model, the players must interact to determine both the administrative constraints placed on the agency and an agency's implementation of policy under these procedural guidelines. This approach highlights that implementation of administrative procedures might be politically infeasible in environments in which the legislature would want to propose them. Additionally, when such procedures are politically feasible, the legislature and governor might not find them beneficial. Only under specific conditions will implementation of administrative procedures be *both* beneficial *and* politically feasible.

In the second part of the model, we extend this *static* analysis to explicitly take into account the *degree of uncertainty* about future political environments. We do this using a decision-theoretic model incorporating expectations. The model serves to generate a number of important insights – and testable hypotheses – about when and where electoral uncertainty can lead to the use of administrative procedures. First, incorporating expectations into the decision-making calculus, the executive and legislature both benefit from thicker procedures in a greater number of environments. In this sense, the model shows how the introduction of electoral uncertainty expands the set of cases under which agency structure will be used to insulate policy decisions. Second, the model points to an important revision to the existing theory on when electoral competition will lead to thick procedural guidelines. One of the central claims in the extant literature is that *uncertainty* leads to procedural richness. This would imply that when future election outcomes are expected to be close – in other words when uncertainty is maximal – public officials will be most likely to impose such procedures. Our model predicts, however, that political parties, and the interest groups that support them, must feel that their future prospects are *weak* in order to be willing to bear the costs of reduced agency flexibility. The reason is that they will be the most willing to pay the costs of "insulation" by procedures since they will frequently be out of power. In this sense, it is under conditions of greater certainty, when the likelihood that one side will win is high, that we are most likely to see such procedures. Finally, by bringing in political *feasibility*, the model provides an important redefinition of the relationship between divided government and future expectations by showing how the two interact to determine when and where we are likely to see more robust procedural restrictions placed on agencies.

The chapter proceeds as follows. In the following section, we lay out the static model, which provides intuition for the relationship between political incentives and political feasibility. We then turn to dynamics, exploring how uncertainty about future control over political institutions affects the results from a model with no uncertainty. Importantly, the results of this analysis point to the need to alter our current understanding of how political uncertainty relates to agency insulation. We next illustrate the most important result in the chapter by discussing two cases: the origins of the Consumer Product Safety Commission (CPSC), and the emergence of the Federal Communications Commission (FCC) and broadcast radio regulation. These two cases serve to emphasize how electoral strength and not uncertainty is the key to understanding when thick procedural requirements will be placed on agencies. When groups are confident they will be out of power, they tend to protect their policies from future drift with thick procedures, but when they are not worried about their future prospects of control, agencies will be relatively unencumbered by such procedural mechanisms. Finally, we offer some concluding thoughts.

CURRENT INCENTIVES AND AGENCY COSTS

Consider a single dimensional policy space with each actor's preferences being single peaked on the real line. Assume, that utility functions are given by $U^i = -|x - i|$, where x is the relevant policy and i is actor i's ideal point. Let L, G, and A represent the ideal points of the current legislature, elected executive, and representative agency, respectively. Note that we use the acronym G to indicate the elected executive and will use the term "governor" to refer to her. Assume, for the moment, that the governor is able to appoint agency heads with similar preferences (i.e., $A = G$).

We analyze a three-stage game. In the first stage, the legislature proposes a statute to impose procedural complexity on the representative agency. Adopting administrative procedures imposes decision costs on agencies.[1] Thus, the legislature proposes to impose an exogenously determined level of

---

[1] See the following articles for support for this modeling simplification: Benjamin (1942); Bonfield (1986); Cooper (1965); Davis (1978); Gifford (1977); Heady (1952); Horn (1995); Kleps (1947); Riegel and Owen (1982); Spiller and Tiller (1997); Tiller and Spiller (1995, 1996).

cost T^A on agencies, or the legislature imposes no cost, indicated by $T^A = 0$. To propose T^A, the legislature pays a cost $C(T^A)$.[2] The governor either supports or vetoes the proposal. In stage two, the agency examines the status quo policy (x^0) and chooses to support it at no cost or to promulgate a rule $x^a \in \mathbf{R}^1$, in accordance with the administrative procedures, at a cost to the agency equal to T^A. In stage three, the legislature observes the agency's decision and chooses to support the agency at no cost or to propose a new statute x^S at cost T^L.[3] Again, the governor will support or veto the proposal.

Without loss of generality, assume that the current legislature's ideal point $L = 0$. Also assume that $G = A \leq L$. As such, there are three cases to consider capturing the relative position of the status quo policy relative to G, A, and L: first, $x^0 < A$; second, $x^0 \notin [A,L]$; and finally, $x^0 > L$. We refer to these three cases as the "aligned preferences," "zero-sum," and "radical agency" game, respectively.

Individual rationality, subgame perfection, and complete and perfect information are assumed throughout. Thus, we solve the game by backward induction. In order to gain both intuition and insight about the equilibrium to the model, in the following subsections, we take each stage of the game in turn to discuss the outcomes. We provide a formal proof of the results in the Appendix.

Overturning the Agency

We begin by analyzing the behavior of the legislature and governor given the agency's decision in stage two. For the "aligned preferences," "zero-sum," and "radical agency" game, the behavior of these two actors in stage three will be the same. The intuition is straightforward. Whether the agency maintains the status quo or promulgates a new rule, the legislature and governor have an option to revise the statute. The legislature will want to revise policies that are far from their ideal point relative to the cost of the revision. To propose a revision to policy is costly. The legislature will therefore only propose a revision if the benefit outweighs the proposal cost *and* the governor

---

[2] The source of the proposal costs come from effort to form a majority coalition. Additionally, we assume that the legislature alone pays the proposal costs and that the governor does not have to incur costs in proposing statutes. As such, only the legislature proposes legislation. Also, assume that $C(T^A)$ is equal to zero for $T^A = 0$, and strictly positive for all $T^A > 0$.

[3] The current legislature could revert the agency policy (x^a) back to the status quo or enact a new statute x^S. We assume that the cost to the legislature is the same, T^L. This assumption is consistent with McCubbins, Noll, and Weingast (1989). They say, "...The outcome of a legislative attempt to rectify an act of noncompliance by an agency will not, *in general*, reproduce the policy outcome that was sought by the winning coalition, even if the preferences of the members of the legislative body remain unchanged" (433, emphasis added). If the legislature chooses to overturn an agency rulemaking via statute, then no matter where the new policy is relative to the agency rule, the legislature realizes cost T^L.

supports the proposal. The governor will only support revisions that move policy closer to its ideal point. Of course, with supermajority support, the legislature can override a gubernatorial veto and will propose a revision.

Agency Rulemaking

The agency makes its decision given the behavior of the legislature and governor in stage three. The agency will take into account several factors: the cost to the agency of rulemaking, the cost to the legislature of proposing a revised statute, the size of the legislative coalition that proposes a revised statute, and the governor's support for a proposed statute.

Aligned preference environment. Recall that in this environment, the preferences of the governor, agency, and legislature are aligned relative to the status quo. If the legislature's proposal costs are large relative to the status quo, then the agency will be able to promulgate rules equal to its own ideal point, because the legislature does not realize a net benefit from proposing a revision.

The interesting action, however, occurs when the current legislature's statutory costs are relatively small. In that case, the legislature might have an incentive to propose a revision to the status quo policy. Additionally, the legislature will want to overturn an agency rule if it is far from the legislature relative to the proposal cost. Whether the legislature actually proposes a revision will depend on its *political feasibility*, that is, gubernatorial support or their ability to override a veto. Foreseeing this, the agency will rule such that the current legislature either supports the rule or the legislature cannot override a gubernatorial veto. If the cost of rulemaking is small enough, the agency will rule as close to its ideal point as possible without triggering legislative action that either garners the support of the governor or can override a gubernatorial veto.[4] Because the governor and agency's ideal points are the same, the agency is only concerned with the legislature if it has supermajority support for a revision. In any event, policy made by the agency, in this *aligned preferences environment*, will make all parties better off.

Zero-sum environment. In this environment, the preferences of the governor/agency are in opposition to the desires of the legislature relative to the status quo. In contrast to the "aligned preferences environment," any movement of policy away from the status quo makes either the legislature or the governor/agency worse off. In this case, as before, the agency will set policy taking into account costs and veto points. Unlike before, any agency

---

[4] This result is consistent with other important insights that elected officials can only partially mitigate the risk of bureaucratic arbitrariness (McCubbins, Noll, and Weingast 1987; McCubbins, Noll, and Weingast 1989; Moe 1987; Wilson 1989).

decision is likely to decrease the utility of the legislature and increase the utility of the governor/agency.

Radical agency environment. In this environment, the status quo is to the right of the legislature's ideal policy and the governor/agency would like to see (from the legislature's perspective) *radical* moves in policy to the left (i.e., decreases legislature's utility relative to status quo). Similar to the "zero-sum environment," there are potential agency rulings that will make the legislature worse off. The agency will have an incentive to make this type of ruling when it has radically different preferences than the legislature, the cost of rulemaking is small enough, and the cost of proposing revised statutes that receive supermajority support is relatively high.

The Choice of Procedures

The legislature and governor impose costs T^A on the agency given the agency's incentive to promulgate rules and the governor and legislature's incentives to revise agency decisions. Whereas the elected actor's behavior in stage three is the same in all environments, the agency will behave differently depending on the relative location of the status quo, veto considerations, and the magnitude of the costs of both rulemaking and legislating. Thus, we examine the decision to impose costs on agency decision-making in each environment.

> **Proposition 1:** *In an "aligned preference environment," the equilibrium cost imposed on the agency by the legislature and governor is $T^{A*} = 0$.*

Proposition 1 provides an intuitive result. The actors' preferences are aligned relative to the location of the status quo. Any movement in policy via rulemaking will make the legislature, governor and agency better off. While there are instances where a *majority* of the legislature would like the agency to make policy even closer to its ideal policy, any proposed revision will be vetoed by the governor. As a farsighted actor, the legislature will impose no additional rulemaking costs on the agency ($T^A = 0$). For all values of the proposal cost (T^L), the agency will promulgate rules in a manner consistent with the legislature's preferences, at the least possible cost to the legislature. The legislature does not have to act to achieve this outcome.

> **Proposition 2:** *In both "zero-sum" and "radical agency" environments, the legislature will impose durable costs on agencies only when a supermajority supports the statute.*

Figure 2.1 illustrates Proposition 2 for the zero-sum environment. The policy space is single dimensional as illustrated by the horizontal line, with the utility or payoff of the actors indicated on the vertical axis. L represents the ideal point for the legislature. In this model, we simplify the analysis by

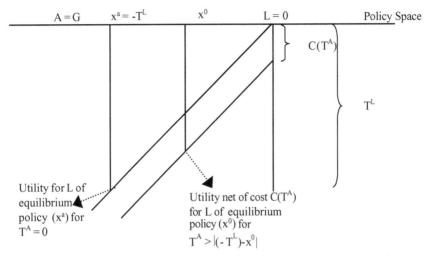

Zero-Sum Environment:

Impose cost on Agency of $T^{A}* > |(-T^{L})-x^{0}|$ to discourage rulemaking

FIGURE 2.1. Zero-Sum Environment

setting $L = 0$. The utility that L receives for a given policy x in the policy space is graphically illustrated by the downward sloping line. As one can see, L's utility declines linearly as the location of a policy outcome moves away from L's ideal point of zero (0). That is L's utility is equal to $-|x|$ for all potential policy outcomes. In this example, the agency's (A) ideal policy is assumed to be to the left of the legislature's and equal to the executive's (G) ideal point. As discussed, the model explains the legislature's choice to impose costs on agency rulemaking (T^{A}). To impose these costs, however, the legislature considers three exogenous factors: the cost to overturn agency rules through a statute (T^{L}), the cost to impose rulemaking costs on the agency $C(T^{A})$, and the location of the status quo policy (x^{0}).

The legislature (L) will impose costs on the agency only if the cost to the legislature ($C(T^{A})$) of imposing T^{A} on the agency is small enough. A farsighted agency, with sufficiently low rulemaking costs, will account for the legislature's cost to revise the status quo (T^{L}) and, thereby, promulgate rules further from the legislature's ideal point. For example, if $T^{A} = 0$, then A can promulgate a rule at the point in the policy space ($x^{a} = -T^{L}$) where L is indifferent between the agency's rule and overturning the agency at a cost of T^{L} to achieve its ideal policy. The legislature may prevent this "policy drift" by imposing rulemaking costs (T^{A}) on the agency that are large enough to discourage agency action. That is, the agency will be indifferent to the status quo policy (x^{0}) and promulgating a new rule at a cost T^{A} to achieve policy x^{a}.

The legislature is only willing to incur $C(T^A)$ to impose rulemaking costs on the agency if the legislature realizes a net benefit of maintaining the status quo. This will happen only if the legislature's cost of imposing structure on the agency is small enough $(C(T^A) < |(-T^L) - x^0|)$ and it can override a gubernatorial veto. In this case, the net payoff from imposing costs on the agency and maintaining the status quo $(U^L(x^0) - C(T^A))$ is greater than the payoff from the agency moving policy close to its ideal point $(U^L(x^a))$.[5]

An interesting implication of the above analysis is that in no instance will the governor support legislative proposals to impose costs on agencies for the *current legislative session*. In those environments in which the legislature might have an incentive to enact procedural legislation, the governor will veto any such proposal. Even in an environment in which the preferences of the legislature and governor are aligned, procedural legislation will not obtain, because the legislature's net benefit is greatest from not imposing costs on agencies. Thus, when net benefits accrue to a *majority* of the legislature, passage of procedural legislation is not *politically feasible*. When the governor and legislature are aligned so that imposing costs on the agency is politically feasible, such legislation does not provide net benefits to the legislature. Political feasibility and net benefits *both* obtain only when the legislature and governor have opposing interests *and* a supermajority of the legislature supports imposing costs on the agency.[6] This result reflects, in part, behavior confined to the current legislative session. As we will now show, incorporating expectations into the decision-making calculus, expands the set of political environments in which a statute imposing costs on agencies is both politically feasible and provides net benefits to the legislature and governor.

FUTURE EXPECTATIONS AND AGENCY COSTS

The above model highlights an important tension that exists between the governor and legislature. This tension reflects, in part, that there is a time-inconsistency between the durability of the decision costs and the

---

[5] The intuition for the radical agency environment is similar and is provided in the Appendix. Note that when the cost of revising the status quo is small for a supermajority legislature, then the agency (no matter how "radical") is restricted by this low cost. In this instance the legislature will not have to incur any cost to realize a greater payoff. In the "zero-sum" environment and the "radical-agency" environment the agency will make a ruling so that the supermajority legislature is indifferent between the ruling and a revision. In any event, for low revision costs, the legislature benefits from this ruling without incurring any cost.

[6] The model generates qualitatively equivalent results when we relax the assumption about the preferences of the agency, that is, when $\alpha < 1$. In this situation, there are political environments in which the governor would benefit from imposing costs on agencies. A majority of the legislature, however, would not benefit in those environments and will therefore not propose legislation. In environments in which a majority of the legislature would benefit from imposing costs on the agency, the governor will oppose. As above, political feasibility and net benefits obtain only when the legislature has supermajority support for a proposal.

information the legislature uses to make its decisions. The durability of statutes, which survive beyond the current legislative session, suggests that the legislature and governor will take into account expectations over future political preferences when designing administrative procedures. Incorporating *political expectations* into the model changes the calculus of the legislature and governor in important ways. Therefore, while the legislature might not be able to gain gubernatorial support for decision costs imposed on the *current* bureaucracy, the governor and legislature might have an incentive to enact durable decision costs, if they expect that future agencies will have divergent preferences. Additionally, the risk of future policy drift will vary over time and across political environments. Accordingly, the opportunities for elected actors to impose costs on agencies will also vary across polities and over time.

To incorporate expectations of the legislature and governor about future agency preferences into the analysis, we characterize two potential political outcomes for each elected official. We assume that the governor and legislature have the same information and thus symmetric expectations. To fix the intuition for the dynamics, we will refer to the groups in terms of parties. The public officials thus have expectations over which political party will control the legislative and executive branch in the future. Notably, although we refer to these as parties, it is important to note that the main literature that we use takes interest groups as the main actors in the politics of structural choice. Following this literature, our model speaks primarily to interest group competition, as mediated by parties (Moe 1990). To fix concepts for later empirical work that test the propositions laid out here, in which parties will be a proxy for interest group representation (see de Figueiredo forthcoming), as we develop predictions here we will refer to parties.

There are two political parties (Republican or Democrat) and four potential outcomes. Figure 2.2 outlines the political expectations of the current governor and legislature. The probability that the Republicans (Democrats) will control the legislature is $p(1 - p)$. For future governors, $q(1 - q)$ is the probability of Republican (Democratic) control.

By characterizing the current political environment similarly (i.e., four environments representing party control of the legislature and governor), we can analyze the current political actor's incentive to impose costs on future agencies, *given their expectations* over future outcomes.

Table 2.1 lays out the sixteen potential environments. Each cell of the table represents a "current political environment." Note, for example, the environment called "stable homogeneity" the legislature and governor are currently aligned and they expect to continue to be aligned (and of the same party) in the future. In this type of environment, there is negligible risk of future agencies promulgating rules that drift far from the current preferences of the legislature and governor. This is qualitatively similar to the "aligned

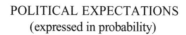

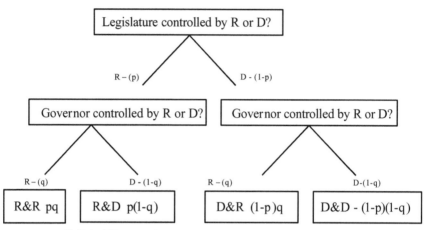

FIGURE 2.2. Political Expectations

preference environment" in the model in the previous section. A statute might be politically feasible but it does not provide a net benefit to the legislature. As such, there is little incentive for the legislature (and governor) to impose long-run decision costs on the bureaucracy.

Contrast "stable homogeneity" with the two cells labeled "stable heterogeneity." This environment is equivalent to the "zero-sum" model derived above. In this environment, the legislature and governor have opposing preferences and expect the same relative preferences in the future. The legislature thereby perceives some risk that the bureaucracy will promulgate rules that drift away from the legislature and will want to impose long-term costs on the bureaucracy to insure against that drift. The governor, however, will want to oppose implementation of the statute. Thus, enactment of legislation is politically feasible and provides a net benefit only when the legislature has a supermajority to override a gubernatorial veto.

Finally, note the six examples of "unique homogeneity." In the unique homogeneity environment, the legislature and governor are currently aligned and they expect the agency to have substantially different preferences in the future. Here, there is an incentive to impose long-term costs on the agency. The current legislature and governor both perceive net benefits accruing to them if they protect against future rulemaking by a bureaucracy with substantially different preferences. Thus, the legislation is now both politically feasible and provides a net benefit to all of the political actors.

TABLE 2.1 *Configurations of Current and Expected Political Control*

		Current Party Control – Legislature/Governor			
		R/R	R/D	D/R	D/D
Expected Future Party Control – Legislature/Governor	R/R	Stable Homogeneity (−)	Unstable Heterogeneity (0)	Unstable Heterogeneity (0)	Unique Homogeneity 3 (++)
	R/D	Unique Homogeneity 1 (+)	Stable Heterogeneity (+)*	Unstable Heterogeneity (0)	Unique Homogeneity 2 (+)*
	D/R	Unique Homogeneity 2 (+)*	Unstable Heterogeneity (0)	Stable Heterogeneity (+)*	Unique Homogeneity 1 (+)
	D/D	Unique Homogeneity 3 (++)	Unstable Heterogeneity (0)	Unstable Heterogeneity (0)	Stable Homogeneity (−)

* Supermajority in legislature increases probability of enacting statute.

This analysis suggests a number of testable "all things equal" hypotheses about the use of administrative procedures to constrain agency policy making. First, the probability of observing a statutory policy enacted that imposes long-run decision costs on the bureaucracy is lower when the legislature and governor have stable aligned preferences. Second, this probability is higher when the legislature and governor have stable opposing preferences *and* the legislature currently holds a supermajority of the seats. And, finally, this probability is higher when the legislature and governor are currently aligned *and* the governor and/or legislature are expected to have opposing preference in the future.

TWO EMPIRICAL ILLUSTRATIONS: STRONG VERSUS WEAK GROUPS AND PROCEDURAL INTENSITY

In the preceding analysis, we examined the effect that uncertainty about electoral outcomes has on the nature of procedural requirements placed on agencies by public officials. One of the most important findings was that the focus in the literature should not be on uncertainty per se, but on the difference in strengths between groups. The formal analysis indicated that while it is true that groups who gain a "moment in the sun" – the opportunity of unified control of public authority, something akin to Kingdon's notion of a "policy window" – will logically place thick procedural requirements on agencies as a means of insulating them from future sabotage, the opposite does not necessarily hold (Moe 1989; Kingdon 1984).

While a deep empirical analysis is beyond the scope of this paper, a few stylized examples are instructive. As noted earlier, the work of Moe (1989, 1990, 1991) and others (e.g., Horn 1995) provides consistent evidence that groups with a tenuous hold on public authority, such as environmentalists and consumers, will saddle government agencies and the policy implementation apparatus with mechanisms that at once reduce the agency's ability to carry out its mandate, but also protect it from future interference. Importantly, however, these two cases are outliers, in that groups that are only occasionally in power temporarily gain control of public authority (which is by definition a rare event). The models developed herein, however, provide a more general understanding of the politics of structural choice.

In the rest of this section, therefore, we describe two examples that illustrate the results from the above models and supplement the previous analysis. First, we briefly recapitulate the case of consumer safety regulation, emphasizing that the case was indeed one in which a weak, vulnerable group had temporarily gained control. The second case – early broadcast radio regulation and the origins of the Federal Radio Commission (FRC) and later the Federal Communications Commission (FCC) – is an example of the more common one left out by Moe and his colleagues: one in which a strong group erects a thin and flexible administrative apparatus.

Consumer Product Safety Regulation

As argued by Moe (1990), understanding the politics surrounding the erection of the Consumer Product Safety Commission (CPSC) is crucial to understanding its structure. Despite being ensconced in a complex policy environment in which relatively arcane scientific requirements might have favored a flexible, discretionary agency, when erected, the CPSC was an agency whose structure was intentionally burdensome on regulators.

A number of features of the CPSC's initial structure illustrate the structural choice of an agency with limited flexibility. First and foremost, the agency was organized as an independent commission, rather than as an executive agency. Although this would come with all of the pathologies of earlier independent commissions, it would serve to provide a modicum of protection from future drift relative to placement in the executive (Moe 1990). As Lemov (1983) notes, even an attempt to set up a very limited product safety office in the executive Department of Health, Education, and Welfare was defeated on the Senate floor, as it was feared that from its innocuous beginnings, such an office would coopt the CPSC's mandate. Second, the agency was burdened with a number of restrictions on what standards it could promulgate and how they could be enforced. As a case in point, in many areas the CPSC was not given discretion to choose between bans and more limited "work through" remedies in response to noncompliance (Lemov 1983).[7] Finally, the standards that were to be developed were based on a process in which the agency was beholden to standard-seeking private parties and outside groups. On the one hand, rule making was to be initiated by petitions from the public. On the other hand, specific standards were to be developed not by the agency by itself but through a process in which private parties would be enjoined to develop precise standards. As Moe (1990, 293) summarizes, "... [Its creators] loaded the [CPSC] down with cumbersome procedural requirements and checks on its behavior and discretion. These structural choices made it difficult for the agency to do anything very effectively."

The crucial question that arises is why would its creators design such an ineffective agency? The model illuminates two conditions necessary to observe insulation of policies. First, a group has to have been previously shut out of complete control of public authority, which answers, "Why then (and not earlier)?" Second, a group has to be fearful that its newfound control will not persist, which answers, "Why at all?" Consistent with Moe's story, then, the reason the agency was so hampered was a combination of the past, present and future of the consumer movement. Historically, the

---

[7] One example of such restrictions on discretionary enforcement was that private parties could enjoin litigation to enforce agency standards. Another was that bans were made mandatory for all violating imported products. (*Congressional Quarterly Weekly Report* 1972; Lemov 1983; Moe 1990).

consumer movement went from being nonexistent to weak. Prior to the 1960s, consumers were largely unorganized, with protections limited primarily to food, medicine, and trust regulation (Mayer 1989). Organizations such as the Consumer Union, the National Consumers Leagues, and the rural electrical cooperatives were limited in scope and political power. As Nadel (1971, 32) describes of the period from the Progressive Era to the 1960s, "While *Consumer Reports* began to run articles on chemicals in foods, meat inspection, and finance rackets, it was largely a voice in the wilderness and the period was one of general quiescence for consumer protection (as many other later reform issues) until the early 1960s." In the 1960s, however, an organized, politically powerful consumer movement began to emerge. A combination of conditions – rising prices, increasing depersonalization and increasingly national and even international scale in product markets, increasing complexity of consumer choice, strong political entrepreneurship and decreasing costs of organization – all led to the development of a strong consumer movement (Mayer 1989; Nadel 1971; Pertschuk 1982). By the early 1970s, "in Congress, consumer groups were dominant" (Moe 1990; see also Nadel 1971; Vogel 1996).

But while the emergence of a "newfound" political power was necessary to lead the creators to erect an agency that was procedurally constrained, it was not sufficient. In addition, consumer leaders also feared that their current preeminence would give way to the old situation of political dominance by other groups. There were a number of reasons consumer groups feared their loss of power. First, in the late 1960s and early 1970s, consumers were already faced with a hostile executive branch which was at best interested in coopting and modifying their agenda and at worst subverting it. Second, as Moe (1990) argues, these groups were uneasy for historical reasons. While the groups enjoyed their current dominance, they were fully aware of their previous difficulties in gaining control. Third, the emergence of the movements for social regulation had created a mission among opponents, business groups, which became increasingly organized in response (see Vogel 1996, Ch. 6). Finally, the coalition that had pushed the consumer agenda had already begun to show signs of weakness. As the movement moved from general to specific policies, the unified strength of the movement began to weaken (Vogel and Nadel 1976; see also Pertschuk 1982; Vogel 1996). For all of these reasons, "it was unclear how long consumer dominance was going to last...[and] the next fight might well come out differently" (Moe 1990).

As Moe argues, the consumer movement and the emergence of the CPSC was a case in which a vulnerable group, enjoying a "moment in the sun," had found itself in control over public authority. This gave the movement an opportunity to pass a program of consumer protection that was far-reaching. The group, however, fearful of its future position, did so in a way that ultimately limited the ability of the agency to implement vigorous product safety regulation. The importance of this case, therefore, is twofold. On the one hand, it illustrates the consistency of the model with the effect that Moe describes for vulnerable groups. On the other, it illustrates that these conditions are perhaps rare and unique: the groups that achieve their position occasionally and therefore, by definition, rarely, will take these actions. Cases of agency insulation described in the literature, therefore, are selective and outlying, not typical.

Broadcast Radio Regulation

The origins of radio regulation present a different set of political conditions to the case of consumer product regulation. The main difference in the political environment was that in this case, regulation was being pushed for by the dominant coalition, with very little opposition. In this context, an administrative structure was erected that was much less constrained but also much more subject to future interference. (Note: The remainder of this section draws heavily from de Figueiredo [2002].)

Broadly speaking, the two major pieces of legislation that created a formal administrative apparatus for radio regulation were the 1927 Radio Act, which created the FRC, and the 1934 Communications Act, which created the FCC, folding the FRC into the new agency. Prior to 1927, federal policy toward radio frequency regulation was governed by a series of legislative acts – 1887 Interstate Commerce Act, 1910 Mann-Elkins Amendments to the Interstate Commerce Act, 1910 Wireless Ship Act, and 1912 Radio Act – that were designed for the management of commercial shipping frequencies and not commercial broadcasting. The latter did not emerge as a viable economic business until after World War I.[8] With the emergence of broadcast radio, the courts began to rule against the applicability of previous legislation to management of the broadcast frequencies. In a series of court and executive decisions, it became increasingly clear that extant statutes would not be sufficient to manage the new technology.[9]

---

[8] Wollenberg (1989, 62) reports that at the beginning of 1919, there were no broadcast radio stations. By 1922, there were 564.

[9] Immediately following the passage of the 1912 Act, for example, the Attorney General opined that the executive could not *manage* licenses under the Act; instead it must issue to all falling within the aegis of the Act. In the 1923 Court of Appeals decision in *Hoover v. Intercity Radio*, the Court ruled that under the 1912 Radio Act, the Secretary of Commerce (Herbert Hoover) did not have discretion to withhold licenses, effectively eliminating the ability of the government to manage the common pool congestion problem or to coordinate the allocation of frequencies. A 1926 District Court ruling in *United States v. Zenith Corporation* further strengthened this decision, where it was ruled that the Secretary could not promulgate any rules under the aegis of the Act. After *Zenith*, the Secretary essentially withdrew from involvement, setting up a bureau in the department strictly to act as a registration and recording service with no administrative authority (Emery 1971; McMahon 1979; Wollenberg 1989).

This gap in the regulatory framework created a strong alignment of interests in the mid-1920s behind the erection of an agency to manage radio frequencies. The relatively unopposed coalition was led by existing or aspiring broadcasters, who saw regulation as a boon in two senses: on the one hand, it was sorely needed to eliminate negative externalities from congestion and lack of coordination; on the other, it provided stations with a way to maintain a strong position in growing and potentially competitive markets. These broadcasters who were demanding regulation had little to fear from opponents in the future, both in the short and long term. In the short term, the growing disorganization of the industry, with no coordination, meant that all segments of interests were clamoring for the government to step in and more actively organize the use of the airwaves: the nascent broadcasters, listeners, religious groups, content providers, and commercial radio operators all had a common and intense interest in limiting congestion, interference and a lack of coordination.[10,11] Even in the future, consumer interests were unlikely to play much role, as they were largely unorganized. Alternatively, the broadcast industry, as it evolved, was very quickly extremely organized, with the National Association of Broadcasters becoming an important force driving the development of legislation in the four National Radio Conferences in the 1920s and 1930s.

The lack of opposition, a situation that was likely to maintain for the foreseeable future, was reflected in the focus on efficiency rather than insulation. As noted earlier, the sincere interest in solving this problem meant that almost all parties supported removing any jurisdiction from the Interstate Commerce Commission (ICC), which was perceived as more interested in other domains and lacked sufficient focus. Given that a separate regulatory agency was to be set up, the question was how to structure its powers.

---

[10] As Wollenberg (1989, 62) notes, "[In 1927,] virtually all interested segments of the public, notably including the broadcast industry, sought legislation as reflected in the recommunications of the fourth radio conference in 1925." This view was seconded by Hoover who stated, "It [radio regulation] is one of the few instances that I know of where the whole industry and country is earnestly praying for more regulation." (cited in Krasnow 1982, 17)

[11] Indeed, unlike in some other regulatory domains, their interest extended to common views on the exact nature of the policy: because the economic impact on individual consumers of broadcast regulation was indirect, since the stations did not charge for their use, most of the policy proposals that limited competition were supported by the public and the broadcasters. As Robinson (1989, 11) notes, for example, the issue of content regulation, in which certain portions of programming were required for "public service" uses were not objected to by industry. This at once served as an entry barrier for the industry and served the public interest in voters' minds. As he states, "The broadcast industry did not dissent to this imperative of public obligation; they embraced it." Mahan (1982, 165–6) makes a similar point: "What the Radio Act did by justifying regulation of the radio interest in the name of the radio industry in the name of the public interest was, in essence, to identify the interests of the industry with those of the public at large, and thus, the protection of radio business interests with the protection of radio audiences."

This classic structural choice, however, was resolved in a way much different than the debate over the organization of the Environmental Protection Agency (EPA) or CPSC discussed by Moe. In this case, the agency was, in almost every area, given leeway, discretion, and a very wide range of motion. Rather than giving the FRC a very specific statute to implement, in the 1927 Act, "Congress turned essentially all radio regulation over to the new agency, whose discretion was limited mainly by a new requirement that its actions serve the public interest" (Wollenberg 1989, 65; see also Emery 1971, 45–49). Indeed, specific procedures that were considered and summarily discarded highlight the nature of this debate. One issue was how to structure the Commission's decision-making authority over licenses. One possibility was to house decisions over license appeals in the full body of the agency, which would have served to lessen the impact any single commissioner might have had on the implementation of policy. Instead, however, Congress arranged that the each commissioner would have full authority over licensing decisions in five regional zones (Radio Act of 1927 §29). Although this enhanced the speed and efficiency in which licenses were granted, it made it more susceptible to future appointments by potential rivals. Furthermore, unlike the previous statutory regime, now the courts supported the broad powers granting the executive wide latitude to implement restricting and coordinating license policies.[12] This broad mandate meant that in the period from 1927 to 1934, there was a sea change in the implementation of radio policy, primarily by a largely unfettered Radio Commission.

The other significant piece of legislation concerning regulation of radio was the 1934 Communications Act. It was prompted by the desire to integrate regulation of all communications into a single agency. The 1927 Act had divided control over communications policy between the FRC, which regulated radio, and the ICC, which retained control over common carriage. The 1934 Act eliminated the FRC, but transferred all control over radio to the newly created FCC. The broad discretion granted to the FRC in 1927 might have been altered in 1934, with the passage of the Communications Act of 1934; in fact, with respect to radio regulation, the procedural constraints remained muted, only in some limited sense becoming more stringent (Krasnow 1982, 10). Title III of the 1934 Act, which governed the licensing of broadcast radio operators, added a number of provisions to the previous statute, but all were innocuous and did not provide much constraint on the implementation of policy.[13] If anything, the 1934 Act maintained the

---

[12] In both the *KFBK Broadcasting Association v. Federal Radio Commission* (1931) and *Trinity Methodist Church, South v. Federal Radio Commission* (1932), the District of Columbia Circuit Court upheld the FRC's right to deny licenses. In these cases, the courts gave the FRC broad latitude to interpret and implement the public interest standard contained in the statute.

[13] As Wollenberg (1989) outlines, these three were that the FRC had to provide a public announcement and hearing when there were changes to existing licenses; limited transfers

executive's discretion while expanding its reach. Under the same discretion as before, the FCC was to "have the authority to suspend the license of any operator" in addition to the authority to revoke it (Communications Act of 1934, §303[m]). Similarly, Section 302 of the Act included additional rulemaking powers for the FCC to govern chain broadcasting, again with no constraint on the agency's interpretation or implementation except that it is in the public interest.[14] More generally, the issue of the extent of judicial review was also debated as a potential constraint on the agency. During hearings about the Act, a number of radio broadcasters who had had their licenses revoked objected to the limited extent of review and appeal granted in the 1927 Act (Cass 1989, 86–7; United States Congress 1934, 56–7). In the end, review powers were limited as Congress decided to limit the review powers of the courts and leave discretion to the agency.[15] Furthermore, the Act provided strong, discretionary powers for enforcement, allowing for fines and penalties, in addition to revocation of licenses. Importantly, the use of these powers was left largely to the FCC's discretion.[16] The main limitation on the FCC was, as with the 1927 Act, a stricture to regulate in the "public interest." This standard was broadly interpretable, and meant that the agency was granted a great degree of discretion to manage licenses and promulgate regulations.[17]

according to the same broad public interest provision for new licenses; and required construction permits to have been granted for the existing licenses. The first of these three is probably the most constraining, although the public hearings were not construed as they are today to be a significant restriction on the agency. The hearing did not grant standing, for example, to potential interested parties, a universal procedure governing administrative rulemaking under the Administrative Procedure Act of 1946.

[14] Indeed, when this power was challenged in the courts, the Supreme Court reaffirmed the FCC's broad powers, stating, "... [Although] the Act does not explicitly say that the Commission shall have the power to deal with network practices found inimical to the public interest.... Congress was acting in a field of regulation which was both new and dynamic.... In the context of the developing problems to which it was directed, the Act gave the Commission not niggardly but expansive powers." (*National Broadcasting Co. v. United States* 319 U.S. 190, 218–219 [1943])

[15] As Representative Beck commented, "I am certain it is true – that the present commission has made many mistakes, yet we are of the opinion that there would be less abuse by reason of lodging that discretion to them than there would be to some court [that discretion]" (United States Congress 1932, 3683).

[16] According to the Act, the FCC has the power to initiate investigations "concerning which any question may arise under any provisions of the Communications Act. Following such an inquiry, the FCC is authorized to take any action within its general authority it deems appropriate." (Communications Act of 1934, §402) As Cass (1989, 88) comments, "Together with the specific rule-making authority granted elsewhere, this [Section 402] power constitutes a strong tool for promoting coherent regulation of communications."

[17] As Krasnow (1982, 19) concludes: "The flexibility inherent in this elusive public interest concept can be enormously significant to the FCC... as a means of modifying policies to meet changed conditions and to obtain special support."

The history of early regulation of radio broadcasting is a balancing example to regulations initiated by groups that perceive themselves as enjoying only a "moment in the sun." Both in the 1927 Radio Act and further in the 1934 Communications Act, regulation was not initiated by such a constellation of interests but by groups who did not fear loss of power in the future. The result was legislation that culminated in the 1934 Act that enabled the agency to act on its own. As Cass (1989, 90) notes, "The Commission's capacity to shape policy in a manner that responds to changing circumstances and shifting interests is further advanced by the broadly worded authority delegated to the Commission in Titles II and III and by the limited scope of judicial review available." Indeed, Robinson (1989, 18) provides a similar assessment, "What is remarkable about the communications field is the degree of freedom permitted the agency not merely to adapt its powers to deal with new contingencies, but indeed to expand its jurisdictional reach to concerns wholly different from those that animated the regulation in the first instance." In this sense, the relaxed procedural and jurisdictional control was made possible precisely by absence of any fear that the agency would be captured in the future by politically opposed interests.

DISCUSSION

One of the key brands of uncertainty in politics is that created by elections. This uncertainty potentially has a profound effect on the nature of organizational structures in public bureaus. Unlike private organizations, public ones face the prospect of ever changing principals. In this chapter, with an eye to empirical examination, we develop a deeper understanding of how this electoral uncertainty affects the incentives behind and the structures created by elected officials when implementing policy.

The contribution of this chapter is twofold. First, we connect two streams of literature on delegation to government agencies: the static delegation literature, which emphasizes both how procedures can constrain agencies from drifting too far from political principals' wishes and that such constraint will be particularly imposed under conditions of divided control of political institutions; and the dynamic structural choice literature that emphasizes how electoral uncertainty leads to the insulation of agencies through administrative procedures. By connecting these two streams, we show how the choice of administrative procedures is a function not only of each of these factors separately, but that uncertainty and feasibility interact to lead to variation in the adoption of procedural constraints.

The second contribution, following de Figueiredo (2002, forthcoming), is to redefine the relationship between uncertainty and structural choice. In particular, the literature makes the general claim that uncertainty leads to insulation of government agencies through structure. Translating this claim in terms of electoral competition, this would imply that one should observe the greatest degree of constraint imposed when competition, and thus uncertainty, is most intense. Our model, and subsequent examination of two extreme cases, indicates that the focus on uncertainty per se is misplaced. Instead, it is in environments in which uncertainty is at its lowest that we are likely to observe the institution of such procedures. Furthermore, the analysis clarifies that the incentives of groups, or parties, in this situation are not symmetric. Weak groups, when temporarily in power, will be willing to bear the costs of both passing and living with relatively inflexible agencies; they are willing to do so to gain benefits when they are out of power regularly in the future. But stronger groups, who will not be hit as hard by future sabotage since their opponents will rarely have the opportunity to do so, will be less likely to bear such costs, and therefore will not have similar incentives.

This last point raises a final important consideration when we turn to the question of whether electoral uncertainty can be used as an explanatory of any perceived agency inefficiency. Notably, if as the model shows, the only groups that have an incentive to constrain agencies' flexibility through the use of thick procedural guidelines – and therefore their ability to adapt to changing circumstances, fully utilize their expertise, and set good policy – are the ones who are rarely in power, then by implication, observed structural inefficiency cannot be broadly attributed to political uncertainty. In fact, elections will only therefore rarely lead to bureaucratic sclerosis.

APPENDIX

Assume single-dimension, single-peaked preferences with well-defined ideal points. Assume, utility functions are given by $U^i = -|x - i|$ where x is the relevant policy and i is actor i's ideal point. L and A represent the ideal points of the current supermajority legislature and representative agency respectively.

In this three-stage game, the legislature proposes to impose a level of cost T^A on agencies at a cost $C(T^A)$.[18] In stage two, the agency examines the status quo policy (x^0) and chooses to support it at no cost or to promulgate a rule $x^a \in \mathbf{R}^1$ at a cost T^A. In stage three, the legislature supports the agency at no cost proposes a new statute x^S at cost T^L.[19] Individual rationality, subgame perfection, and complete and perfect information are assumed throughout. The game is solved via backward induction.

Without loss of generality, assume that $L = 0$, and that $A \leq L$.[20] As such, there are three cases to consider: first, $x^0 < A$; second, $x^0 \in [A,L]$; and

---

[18] See footnote 2.
[19] See footnote 3.
[20] The game in which $G = A \geq L$ is symmetric.

finally, $x^0 > L$. We refer to these three cases as the "aligned preferences," "zero-sum," and "radical agency" game, respectively. We explicitly prove the "radical agency" case here. Results for the other two cases follow directly, according to the same logic.

Stage Three

Define the payoff for player i as $\pi^i(x) = U^i(x) - T^i(x)$. If the agency maintains x^0, then the current legislature will also maintain x^0 if $\pi^L(x^0) \geq \pi^L(x^S)$, otherwise the legislature enacts a new policy x^S. Note if the current legislature were to revise x^0 in favor of $x^S \in \mathbf{R}^1$, it will rule $x^S = L$. This reflects that the supermajority legislature is the final player of the game. Thus, the legislature supports the status quo policy if $U^L(x^0) \geq U^L(x^S) - T^L$. This implies that the current legislature will support x^0 (enact x^S) only if $T^L \geq |x^0|$ ($T^L < |x^0|$). The calculus of the current legislature with respect to an agency rule (x^a) is similar. If the agency promulgates a rule x^a, then the current legislature will support x^a (overturn x^a in favor of x^S) only if $T^L \geq |x^a|$ ($T^L < |x^a|$).

Stage Two

The agency will either support status quo or promulgate a rule depending on the payoff. The payoffs depend on the magnitude of the legislature's cost of policy making (T^L). Examine two cases: $T^L \geq |x^0|$ and $T^L < |x^0|$.

Radical agency environment. That is $x^0 > L = 0 \geq A$. In this environment, the agency and legislature both prefer policy outcomes for any $x \in [-x^0, x^0]$. From the agency's perspective, any movement of policy to the left of x^0 is preferred. This is not the case for the legislature. The legislature prefers the status quo to any policy to the left of $-x^0$. Thus, when the agency's ideal policy $A \notin [-x^0, x^0]$, then the legislature knows that the agency will seek "radical" rulings relative to the legislature.

Consider the agency's behavior when the cost of legislating is small relative to the status quo. The agency knows that when $T^L < |x^0|$ that the legislature will revise x^0 in favor of $x^S = 0$. In that case, the agency's payoff would be $-|A|$. If the agency promulgates a rule $x^a = \min\{-T^L, A\}$, however, it avoids the statutory revision and worse outcome of $x^S = 0$. The agency's payoff, $\pi^A = -|x^a - A| - T^A$ means that the agency will rule if $-|x^a - A| - T^A > -|A|$. If $A \geq -T^L$, then the agency will rule if $T^A < |A|$. If $A < -T^L$, however, then the agency will only rule if $T^A < T^L$. Intuitively, this says that since the legislature will overturn x^0 in favor of $x^S = 0$, if the agency supports x^0, then the agency will only rule closer to its ideal if the distance from the ruling to x^S is large relative to the cost of rulemaking.

When the cost of legislating is large relative to the status quo, then the agency must compare its payoff from rulemaking to the payoff from the status quo policy. In this case, if $A \geq -T^L$ (i.e., the cost of writing a statute is large even relative to the agency's ideal policy), then the agency rules $x^a = A$ so long as $T^A < |x^0 - A|$. If $A < -T^L$, however, then the agency rules $x^a = -T^L$ if $T^A < |-T^L - x^0|$. In either case, the cost of rulemaking must be smaller than the distance that the agency can move the policy away from the status quo, to motivate agency action.

Stage One

Proposition 2.1: In a "radical agency environment," the legislature will impose costs on the agency as follows:

a.	$T^{A*} = 0$	for $T^L < |x^0|$
b.	$T^{A*} \geq |x^0 - A|$	for $T^L \geq |x^0|$, $A > -T^L$ and if $C(T^A) < |A - (-x^0)|$
c.	$T^{A*} \geq |(-T^L) - x^0|$	for $T^L \geq |x^0|$, $A < -T^L$ and if $C(T^A) < |-T^L - (-x^0)|$

Proposition 2.1.a states that when the legislature's cost of revising the status quo is small then the agency no matter how "radical" is restricted by this low cost. The agency will be willing to promulgate a rule closer to its ideal point and the legislature's. In this instance, the legislature will not have to incur any cost to realize a greater payoff.

Proposition 2.1.b says that the legislature will pass a statute limiting agency action if the cost of writing that statute is less than the distance the agency will move policy away from the legislature's utility from the status quo. Figure A.1 illustrates this result. Proposition 2.1.c is a similar result. It shows that the legislature will pass a statute to discourage agency action, and thereby maintain the status quo, if the cost of discouraging agency rulemaking ($C(T^A)$) is smaller than the distance that the agency would move policy

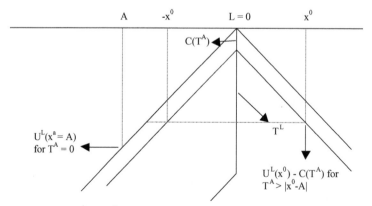

FIGURE A.1. $T^{A*} > |x^0 - A|$ to Discourage Agency Rulemaking

taking into account the cost to the legislature of overturning the agency's rulemaking.

References

Banks, Jeffrey S. 1989. "Agency Budgets, Cost Information and Auditing." *American Journal of Political Science* 33:670–99.

Bawn, Kathleen. 1995. "Political Control Versus Expertise: Congressional Choices about Administrative Procedures." *American Political Science Review* 89: 62–73.

Bawn, Kathleen. 1997. "Choosing Strategies to Control the Bureaucracy: Statutory Constraints, Oversight, and the Committee System." *Journal of Law, Economics & Organization* 13:101–26.

Benjamin, Robert M. 1942. "Administrative Adjudication in the State of New York." Governor of the State of New York, New York.

Bonfield, Arthur E. 1986. *State Administrative Rule Making*. Boston: Little, Brown, and Company.

Calvert, Randall L., Mathew D. McCubbins, and Barry R. Weingast. 1989. "A Theory of Political Control and Agency Discretion." *American Journal of Political Science* 33:588–611.

Cass, Ronald A. 1989. "Titles IV, V, and VI: Review, Enforcement, and Power under the Communications Act of 1934: Choice and Chance in Institutional Design." In *A Legislative History of the Communications Act of 1934*, ed. Max D. Paglin. New York: Oxford University Press.

Congressional Quarterly Weekly Report. 1972. "Product Safety: Stricter Law in Congressional Mill." 30(July 1):1614–15.

Cooper, Frank E. 1965. *State Administrative Law*. Indianapolis: Bobbs-Merrill.

Davis, Kenneth C. 1978. *Administrative Law Treatise*, vol. 1. San Diego: K.D. Davis.

de Figueiredo, Rui J. P., Jr. 2002. "Electoral Competition, Political Uncertainty and Policy Insulation." *American Political Science Review* 96(2):321–333.

de Figueiredo, Rui J. P., Jr. Forthcoming. "Budget Institutions and Political Insulation: Why States Adopt the Item Veto." *Journal of Public Economics*.

de Figueiredo, Rui J. P., Jr., Pablo T. Spiller, and Santiago Urbiztondo. 1999. "An Informational Perspective on Administrative Procedures." *Journal of Law, Economics and Organization* 15:283–305.

Dodd, Lawrence C., and Richard L. Schott. 1979. *Congress and the Administrative State*. New York: Wiley.

Emery, Walter B. 1971. *Broadcasting and Government: Responsibilities and Regulations*. Lansing: Michigan State University Press.

Epstein, David, and Sharyn O'Halloran. 1994. "Administrative Procedures, Information, and Agency Discretion." *American Journal of Political Science* 38:697–722.

Epstein, David, and Sharyn O'Halloran. 1996. "Divided Government and the Design of Administrative Procedures: A Formal Model and Empirical Test." *Journal of Politics* 58:373–97.

Ferejohn, John, and Charles Shipan. 1990. "Congressional Influence on Bureaucracy." *Journal of Law, Economics and Organization* 6:1–20.

Fiorina, Morris P. 1983. "Legislative Choice of Regulatory Forms: Legal Process or Administrative Process?" *Public Choice* 39:33–70.

Gifford, Daniel J. 1977. "The New York State Administrative Procedure Act: Some Reflections upon Its Structure and Legislative History." *Buffalo Law Review* 26:589–634.

Hamilton, Alexander, John Jay, and James Madison. 1961. *The Federalist Papers.* Selected and edited by Clinton Rossiter. New York: Penguin.

Heady, Ferrel. 1952. *Administrative Procedure Legislation in the States.* Ann Arbor: University of Michigan Press.

Hess, Stephen. 1988. *Organizing the Presidency.* Washington, DC: Brookings Institution.

Horn, Murray J. 1995. *The Political Economy of Public Administration: Institutional Choice in the Public Sector.* Cambridge: Cambridge University Press.

Huntington, Samuel P. 1973. *The Congress in America's Future,* ed. D. B. Truman. Englewood Cliffs, NJ: Prentice Hall.

Kingdon, John. 1984. *Agendas, Alternatives and Public Policies.* Boston, MA: Little, Brown.

Krasnow, Erwin G. 1982. *The Politics of Broadcast Regulation.* 2nd ed. New York: St. Martin's Press.

Lowi, Theodore J. 1979. *The End of Liberalism: The Second Republic of the United States.* New York: Norton.

Lemov, Michael R. 1983. *Consumer Product Safety Commission.* Colorado Springs, CO: Shepard's/McGraw-Hill.

Lupia, Arthur, and Mathew D. McCubbins. 1994. "Designing Bureaucratic Regulation." *Law and Contemporary Problems* 57:91–126.

Mahan, Mary Elizabeth. 1982. *Commercial Broadcast Regulation: Structures and Processes in Mexico and the United States.* Ph.D. dissertation. University of Texas at Austin.

Mayer, Robert N. 1989. *The Consumer Movement: Guardians of the Marketplace.* Boston, MA: Twayne Publishing.

McCubbins, Mathew D., Roger Noll, and Barry Weingast. 1987. "Administrative Procedures as Instruments of Political Control." *Journal of Law, Economics and Organization* 3:243–77.

McCubbins, Mathew D., Roger Noll, and Barry Weingast. 1989. "Structure and Process, Politics and Policy: Administrative Arrangements and the Political Control of Agencies." *Virginia Law Review* 75:431–82.

McCubbins, Mathew D., and Thomas Schwartz. 1984. "Congressional Oversight Overlooked: Police Patrols versus Fire Alarms." *American Journal of Political Science* 28:165–79.

McMahon, Robert Sears. 1979. *Federal Regulation of the Radio and Television Broadcast Industry in the United States, 1927–1959: With Special Reference to the Establishment and Operation of Workable Administrative Standards.* New York: Arno Press.

Mitnick, Barry M. 1980. *The Political Economy of Regulation: Creating, Designing and Removing Regulatory Forms.* New York: Columbia University Press.

Moe, Terry. 1987. "An Assessment of the Positive Theory of 'Congressional Dominance'." *Legislative Studies Quarterly* 12:475–520.

Moe, Terry M. 1989. "The Politics of Bureaucratic Structure." In *Can the Government Govern?* ed. John E. Chubb and Paul E. Peterson. Washington, D.C.: Brookings.

Moe, Terry M. 1990. "The Politics of Structural Choice: Toward a Theory of Public Bureaucracy." In *Organizational Theory from Chester Barnard to the Present and Beyond*, edited by O. E. Williamson. New York: Oxford University Press.

Moe, Terry M. 1991. "Politics and the Theory of Organization." *Journal of Law, Economics and Organization* 7(Special):106–29.

Nadel, Mark V. 1971. *The Politics of Consumer Protection*. New York: Bobbs-Merrill Company.

Niskanen, William A. Jr. 1971. *Bureaucracy and Representative Government*. Chicago: Aldine-Atherton.

Ogul, Morris S. 1976. *Congress Oversees the Bureaucracy: Studies in Legislative Supervision*. Pittsburgh: University of Pittsburgh Press.

Olson, Mancur. 1971. *The Logic of Collective Action: Public Goods and the Theory of Groups*. Cambridge, MA: Harvard University Press.

Peltzman, Sam. 1976. "Toward a More General Theory of Regulation." *Journal of Law and Economics* 19:211–48.

Pertschuk, Michael. 1982. *Revolt Against Regulation: The Rise and Pause of the Consumer Movement*. Berkeley: University of California Press.

Riegel, Stanley A., and John P. Owen. 1982. *Administrative Law: The Law of Government Agencies*. Ann Arbor, MI: Ann Arbor Science Publications.

Ripley, Randall B. 1979. *Congress: Process and Policy*. New York: Norton.

Robinson, Glenn O. 1989. "Title I: The Federal Communications Act: An Essay on Origins and Regulatory Purpose." In *A Legislative History of the Communications Act of 1934*, ed. Max D. Paglin. New York: Oxford University Press.

Rothenberg, Lawrence S. 1994. *Regulation, Organization and Politics: Motor Freight Policy at the Interstate Commerce Commission*. Ann Arbor, MI: University of Michigan Press.

Scher, Seymour. 1963. "Conditions for Legislative Control." *Journal of Politics* 25:526–51.

Seidman, Harold. 1975. *Politics, Position, and Power: The Dynamics of Federal Organization*. New York: Oxford University Press.

Spiller, Pablo, and Richard Vanden Bergh. 1997. "Toward a Positive Theory of State Supreme Court Decision Making." Unpublished manuscript.

Spiller, Pablo T. 1992. "Agency Discretion Under Judicial Review." *Mathematical Computer Modeling* 16:185–200.

Spiller, Pablo T., and Emerson H. Tiller. 1997. "Decision Costs and the Strategic Design of Administrative Process and Judicial Review." *The Journal of Legal Studies* 26:347–70.

Spulber, Daniel F., and David Besanko. 1992. "Delegation, Commitment, and the Regulatory Mandate." *Journal of Law, Economics, & Organization* 8: 127–54.

Stigler, George J. 1971. "The Theory of Economic Regulation." *Bell Journal of Economic and Management Science* 2:3–21.

Tiller, Emerson, and Pablo T. Spiller. 1995. "The Choice of Administrative and Judicial Instruments: Strategy, Politics and Decision Costs in the Administrative Process." Unpublished manuscript.

Tiller, Emerson H., and Pablo T. Spiller. 1996. *Strategic Instruments: Politics and Decision Costs in Administrative and Judicial Process.* Center For Legal and Regulatory Studies, Graduate School of Business, University of Texas at Austin.

United States Congress. 1927. *Radio Act of 1927.* Washington, DC: Government Printing Office.

United States Congress. 1934. *Communications Act of 1934.* Washington, DC: Government Printing Office.

United States Congress. 1932. *Congressional Record – House, February 10, 1932.* Washington, DC: Government Printing Office.

United States Congress. House Committee on Interstate and Foreign Commerce. 1934. *Hearings: Federal Communications Commission.* April 10. Washington, DC: Government Printing Office.

United States Congress. Senate Committee on Interstate Commerce. 1934. *Hearings: Federal Communications Commission.* March 9, 10, 13, 14, and 15. Washington, DC: Government Printing Office.

United States Department of Commerce, Bureau of the Census. 1975. *Historical Statistics of the United States: Colonial Times to 1970, Vols. 1 and 2.* Washington, DC: Government Printing Office.

Vogel, David. 1989. *Fluctuating Fortunes: The Political Power of Business in America.* New York: Basic Books.

Vogel, David. 1996. *Kindred Strangers: The Uneasy Relationship between Politics and Business in America.* Princeton, NJ: Princeton University Press.

Vogel, David, and Mark Nadel. 1976. "The Consumer Coalition: Dimensions of Political Conflict." In *Protecting the Consumer Interest: Private Initiative and Public Response,* ed. Robert N. Katz. Cambridge, MA: Ballinger Publishing Company.

Weingast, Barry, and Mark Moran. 1983. "Bureaucratic Discretion or Congressional Control? Regulatory Policymaking by the Federal Trade Commission." *Journal of Political Economy* 91:765–800.

Wilson, James Q. 1980. "The Politics of Regulation." In *The Politics of Regulation,* ed. James Q. Wilson. New York: Basic Books.

Wilson, James Q. 1989. *Bureaucracy: What Government Agencies Do and Why They Do It.* New York: Basic Books.

Woll, Peter. 1977. *American Bureaucracy.* New York: Norton.

Wollenberg, J. Roger. 1989. "Title III: The FCC as Arbiter of 'The Public Interest, Convenience, and Necessity.'" In *A Legislative History of the Communications Act of 1934,* ed. Max D. Paglin. Oxford: Oxford University Press.

3

Uncertainty and Legislative Capacity for Controlling the Bureaucracy

George A. Krause

INTRODUCTION

Are legislative oversight committees effective at influencing the behavior of administrative agencies? Before the early 1980s, the conventional wisdom among congressional scholars was that legislative committees were not successful at this task. This view was based on the observation that members did not invest much time and energy in the oversight function, because little electoral incentive existed to engage in such activities (Dodd and Schott 1979; Ogul 1976; Scher 1963; Wilson 1980). Relatedly, the information advantage enjoyed by administrative agencies made effective monitoring by legislative oversight committees highly impractical (Niskanen 1971).

This perspective, however, was directly challenged in a pair of seminal articles by Barry Weingast and Mark Moran (1982, 1983). The "legislative dominance" model developed by Weingast and Moran is based on the simple premise that changes in the ideological policy position of the median committee member will be positively associated with changes in agency behavior, in the form of either decision making or policy outputs.[1] The theoretical basis for this hypothesis is that administrative agencies' feasible set of policy-making activities are explicitly linked, and thus consistent, with the central tendency of legislator preferences for a

---

[1] In a refinement of the legislative dominance model, Woolley (1993) relaxes the unicameral assumption of Weingast and Moran by allowing for a bicameral legislature.

Associate Professor of Political Science, Department of Government and International Studies, University of South Carolina, Columbia, South Carolina 29208. *E-mail: George.Krause@sc.edu.* An earlier version of this chapter was presented at the 2001 annual meeting of the Midwest Political Science Association, Chicago, IL. April 20–22. The author thanks Barry Burden and John Mark Hansen for providing thoughtful comments on an earlier version of this essay, and Brad Gomez for a helpful conversation. The author appreciates the assistance of Bill Kemick, Michelle Dames, and Homer Steedly in reproducing the images appearing in Figures 1–4.

given oversight committee. They conclude that congressional influence over bureaucratic behavior is pervasive in a retrospective sense.[2] Numerous studies find corroborative empirical evidence in favor of this theoretical prediction (e.g., Faith, Leavens, and Tollison 1982; Grier 1991; Moe 1985; Morris and Munger 1998; Scholz, Twombly, and Headrick 1991; Wood and Waterman 1994). This body of empirical research concludes that legislative committees play an effective role in shaping the behavior of administrative agencies in a manner consistent with research by Weingast and Moran (1982, 1983).[3]

The main point of this chapter is simple. The theoretical conceptualization of legislative dominance models might not accurately capture the extent to which a legislative committee is capable of influencing the behavior of a bureaucratic agency, independent of any potential feedback relationships (see Krause 1996, 1999). The basis for this claim is twofold. First, a prerequisite for legislative control is the *capacity* of the oversight committee to accomplish this task in an effective manner. Legislative capacity for political control over an agency is distinct from the concept of control itself in that the former is a necessary precondition for the exercise of the latter. Thus, if a legislative committee fails to possess strong capacity for shaping bureaucratic behavior to begin with, then it cannot be expected to attain this goal successfully. Conversely, strong capacity for legislative control over policy administration should make it easier for the committee to adeptly shape agency behavior, ceteris paribus.

Second, existing scholarship on the subject of legislative influence over policy administration has only considered the effect of political signals emanating from the committee in the form of the mean or median policy preference. These signals, however, are part of a larger committee policy preference distribution that remains unexplored in existing research on legislative control of the bureaucracy. It is appropriate to infer that the degree by which committee policy preferences are diffuse within such a distribution will vary. Congressional scholars acknowledge that legislative committees differ based on the extent to which they reflect a unified view on policy matters under their jurisdiction. Richard Fenno's (1973) classic treatise on congressional decision making reveals varying degrees by which members disagree on policy matters across committees in the U.S. House of Representatives. For instance, Fenno finds that policy disagreement regarding committee reports among all House Education and Labor committee members is slightly more

---

[2] Because this study focuses on oversight monitoring behavior by legislative committees, this study pertains to *ex post* (retrospective) mechanisms of political control as opposed to *ex ante* (prospective) methods. The seminal treatise on the latter topic is by McCubbins, Noll, and Weingast (1987, 1989).

[3] This issue is separate from Moe's (1987) claim that top-down political influence over the bureaucracy is a multi-institutional phenomenon that does not solely rest with the legislative branch.

than double than it is among all House Foreign Affairs committee members for the 1955–66 period. Moreover, this policy disagreement gap is approximately five times (in percentage terms) larger within each partisan group for the Education and Labor committee vis-à-vis the Foreign Affairs committee (Fenno 1973, 83–4). Because the diffuseness of policy preferences within a given legislative committee is not identical across various committees and at all points in time, it is imperative to consider the uncertainty (or *noise*) corresponding to political signals that has been ignored in existing scholarship on democratic control over the bureaucracy.

This conceptual omission is addressed by advancing the proposition that the distribution of committee policy preferences must be considered when investigating the capacity of legislative control over the bureaucracy within the context of a "top-down" principal-agent model of political influence. The means by which noise variations can result in the distortion and clarification of policy signals emanating from a legislative committee, the substance of such signals, and its subsequent theoretical impact on the capacity for legislative control of the bureaucracy are investigated in this chapter. In addition, the marginal effects of signal and noise changes on legislative oversight capacity attributable to the shifting distribution of policy preferences for a hypothetical legislative committee are examined. The overarching aim of this chapter is consistent with the general theme of this edited volume – that students of American politics need to take uncertainty seriously in analyzing political phenomena. Next, the logical basis underlying the signal to noise approach used to understand legislative capacity for controlling the bureaucracy is discussed.

THE DISTRIBUTION OF LEGISLATIVE COMMITTEE POLICY PREFERENCES IN BUREAUCRATIC POLITICS

The focus of spatial models of legislative-agency relations are centered on the ideal point of the median legislator serving on an oversight committee. This is often translated in a statistical sense to refer to the median (or perhaps, mean) roll-call ideology of a legislative oversight committee. This ideal point is referred to as a political or policy signal, as it is a summary measure of the ideological policy composition of a legislative committee. The median voter theorem that serves as the basis for standard spatial theoretical models, such as the work of Weingast and Moran, predicts that responsiveness would mirror the policy preferences of the median legislator and that any noise corresponding to this signal is of no practical consequence in determining policy outcomes (Black 1958; Downs 1957). Such analyses ignore the importance attached to the uncertainty or diffuseness of committee policy preferences.

An alternative view of policy influence based on signaling under uncertainty suggests that this omission is critical because existing theoretical models of legislative-bureaucratic relations typically provide us with only a partial portrait of the *distribution* of policy preferences within a legislative oversight committee. Analyzing this phenomenon must involve both its signal (central tendency) and its noise (dispersion).

The main proposition contained in this chapter is straightforward. The degree of uncertainty corresponding to a policy signal is critical for understanding the capacity for political control over an administrative agency by a legislative oversight committee. Capacity for effective legislative control by a committee is a necessary precondition for it being successful in shaping agency behavior. This is distinct from addressing whether or not a legislative committee is influencing or controlling bureaucratic behavior. In general, capacity within the context of political control over the bureaucracy research refers to the capability of a legislative committee to influence agency behavior if it so desires. Thus, a legislative committee can possess considerable oversight capabilities in shaping policy but might find less need to utilize them (e.g., agriculture policy). Conversely, a committee may wish to exert notable oversight power yet has limited means to do so without taking monumental action that is often impractical (e.g., monetary policy).[4] Therefore, an agency may accrue greater discretion in one of two ways – either it has been explicitly granted such authority by political overseers, or it has been provided *de facto* authority where legislators purposefully act in a passive manner. The topic of capacity for legislative control is a critical substantive issue because a legislative committee that exhibits weak capacity in controlling agency behavior will be more apt to have a difficult time in actually shaping administrative behavior.

Two means exist by which diffuse committee policy preferences reduce legislative capacity for political control. One channel is that the legislative committee sends out noisy signals to an agency that dilute the force of its message. On an informational level, an agency will experience greater (less) difficulty in trying to ascertain what legislators prefer when committee preferences reflect policy disagreement (consensus), all else being equal. When policy disagreement abounds on a legislative committee, an agency will be unsure as to how to respond and thus they will move in a modest piecewise fashion, if at all. The other channel by which diffuse committee preferences decreased capacity for legislative control over the bureaucracy occurs through the strategic behavior of the agency with the intended purpose of obtaining greater autonomy (Bryner 1987; Dahl and Lindblom 1953; Hammond and Knott 1996; Wilson 1989). Under these circumstances, the agency will play committee members off against one another in order to acquire greater discretion in policy making and implementation. Either way, an agency will be

---

[4] Other factors may also affect capacity for legislative control (e.g., agency design, policy type). With this said, it is assumed that all else being equal, committee signals that are more proximate to the agency's location and/or less noisy will enhance its ability to shape administrative behavior.

less (more) subject to political control by a legislative committee when the uncertainty surrounding the latter's policy preferences is high (low), ceteris paribus. Therefore, determining the capacity of legislative committees to control bureaucratic behavior is essential for understanding the likelihood that it does occur.

The distribution of a legislative committee's policy preferences can be thought of as consisting of a *signal* (central tendency) and *noise* (dispersion). The signal represents the stimulus intended to elicit a response, while noise represents the distortion of the signal as it is transmitted. The signal and noise concepts are steeped in a deep intellectual tradition that covers the study of diverse subjects ranging from the acoustics of audio devices in electrical engineering to product quality in operations research to the quality of communication between individuals in communications studies. In the present study, these concepts are applied to understanding a legislative committee's capacity for controlling bureaucratic behavior.

A useful metaphor relating to understanding the importance of the signal and noise components in the distribution of legislative committee policy preferences comes from the seminal research on product quality in operations research developed by Genichi Taguchi (e.g., see Albright and Roth 1992; Taguchi, Chowdhury, and Taguchi 1999; Taguchi and Clausing, 1990; Taguchi and Konishi 1986). Taguchi's thesis is simple. If product quality is represented by the degree of customer dissatisfaction with a product based on its performance, then a quadratic loss function can characterize this dissatisfaction irrespective of whether the mean value equals the variance. Larger deviations from an intended target result in greater customer dissatisfaction with the product. Relatedly, Tunner (1990) sets forth an approximation of . . . mean loss that is given by:

$$\mu_{\text{Loss}} = k[\sigma^2 + (\bar{x} - x_{\text{Optimal}})^2] \tag{1}$$

where k is a scaling parameter (for simplicity purposes it can be set equal to unity), σ^2 is the amount of variance in customer dissatisfaction, $\bar{x}$ is the mean value of customer dissatisfaction, and x_{Optimal} is the target value where the customer is most satisfied. Mean loss from the distribution of customer responses rises when (1) the variance of product quality increases, or (2) the mean product quality deviates from its target of maximum consumer satisfaction or product quality. In the limiting case when average product quality is identical to the target value and all products are at this location in the distribution, then $\mu_{\text{Loss}} = 0$ by definition. Thus, the average loss in product quality is based on its mean quality relative to its target value of consumer satisfaction being maximized, as well as the amount of variance in product quality that is measured by customer satisfaction.

The logic underlying the Taguchi loss function is directly relevant for purposes of better understanding legislative committee oversight influence over the bureaucracy. The capacity for effective legislative control is enhanced when the mean or median committee policy preference is closer to the behavior of the targeted group (i.e., an administrative agency), and also committee policy preferences exhibit less variance or volatility. Thus, variations in the signal and noise component underlying the distribution of policy preferences can alter the capability of legislative control over the bureaucracy. This is because administrative agencies are neither capable nor willing to respond to noisy signals, and to expect that they do overstates the capacity legislative committees possess in molding agency behavior. Omitting the dispersion present in the distribution of a legislative committee's policy preferences can provide a misleading view of the true capability legislative efforts at controlling the bureaucracy. The subsequent sections provide both a conceptual and theoretical treatment of this issue and its relevance for democratic accountability.

SIGNALS, NOISE, AND LEGISLATIVE CAPACITY FOR CONTROLLING ADMINISTRATIVE BEHAVIOR

Existing research on congressional control over the bureaucracy fails to consider the uncertainty surrounding a legislative committee's policy preferences, but instead focuses solely on policy signals. This view might overstate the efficacy of political control of administrative agencies. This is because greater committee "noise" – that is, more diffuse distribution of committee policy preferences – can hinder its capacity for shaping bureaucratic behavior, because an agency's ability to gauge the true policy signals of the committee becomes more difficult. Although lower noise or uncertainty surrounding committee policy preferences will bring about an absolute gain in the capacity for legislative control over the bureaucracy (ceteris paribus) across policy areas, it will have a differential comparative impact depending on the nature of legislative committees relative to the chamber floor. If one wishes to define democratic responsiveness in terms of clientelism, then homogeneously composed committees consisting of preference outliers will comparatively benefit more in terms of enhanced capacity for legislative control of the bureaucracy than heterogeneous committees that are more indicative of floor preferences. Conversely, the capacity for legislative control of administrative behavior will be comparatively greater for heterogeneous committees relative to homogeneous ones if a broader perspective of democratic responsiveness is held.[5] The next two subsections analyze the concept of "signal" and "noise" and "signal-to-noise ratio" in the context of the capacity of legislative control over an administrative agency.

[5] For different accounts of the heterogeneous versus homogenous legislative committee debate, please see Krehbiel 1990; Shepsle and Weingast 1987; and Hall and Grofman 1990.

TABLE 3.1 *Hypothetical Values of Legislative Committee Policy Signals and Noise*

(Symmetric Conservative and Liberal Policy Signals with Symmetrically Altered Noise Levels)							
Signal (μ)	-40	-40	-40	-40	40	40	40	40
Noise (σ)	0.25	0.50	2.00	10.00	10.00	2.00	0.50	0.25
$\dfrac{\text{Signal}}{\text{Noise}}\left(\dfrac{\mu}{\sigma}\right)$	-160	-80	-20	-4	4	20	80	160
	Clear Conservative Signal		Muted Conservative Signal		Muted Liberal Signal		Clear Liberal Signal	

Viewing Political Influence in Terms of "Signal" and "Noise" Processes

Both signals and noise play a vital role in determining the capacity of a given actor to influence others. As discussed earlier, existing research implicitly treats political signals to bureaucratic agencies as being crystal clear, and hence, are generally viewed as being potent. This might not be a problem for analyzing a unitary actor such as the president, because their policy preferences will be of a singular nature, and thus, investigation of the signal is sufficient.[6] But when examining a political body that consists of members who each have their own individual policy preferences (e.g., a legislative committee), the degree of variance in policy preferences among these individuals is an important measure of uncertainty that affects the effectiveness of this body's transmission of policy preferences in a way that can be acted on by the targeted group (e.g., an administrative agency). Thus, the degree of diffuseness or spread displayed in the legislative committee's policy preference distribution will directly affect its capacity for effective oversight monitoring of administrative agencies.

An illustration will help clarify this thesis. Let us assume that the policy preferences of a legislative committee bounded between -50 (most conservative) and $+50$ (most liberal). Table 3.1 presents a series of hypothetical values of legislative committee signals and noise, and its resulting ratio. These numbers are symmetrical for ease of exposition. In the first four columns, the political signal is -40 ($\mu_{\text{Committee}} = -40$) suggesting that the committee's mean policy preference is rather conservative. However, as the standard deviation surrounding the mean becomes larger, we notice that it dilutes the clarity of that signal. Therefore, a -160 signal to noise ratio ($\mu_{\text{Committee}} \times \sigma_{\text{Committee}} = -40 \div 0.25 = -160$) will make for a clearer conservative policy signal, and hence, enhance legislative control compared to a -4 signal to noise ratio

---

[6] Alternatively, one might posit that policy signals emanating from a unitary actor such as the president may exhibit noise (i.e., a diffuse distribution of policy preferences) if conflicting or varying policy signals are emitted by administration officials.

TABLE 3.2 *The Consequences of the Signal to Noise Ratio for Understanding Legislative Committee Capacity to Induce Agency Responsiveness*

Nature of Signal to Noise Ratio	Substance of Signal	Legislative Committee Capacity for Political Control
$\dfrac{\text{Liberal Signal}}{\text{Low Noise}}$	Clear Liberal Policy Signal	Strong (Liberal Response)
$\dfrac{\text{Liberal Signal}}{\text{High Noise}}$	Muted Liberal Policy Signal	Weak (Liberal Response)
$\dfrac{\text{Moderate Signal}}{\text{Low Noise}}$	Clear Moderate Policy Signal	Strong (Centrist Response)
$\dfrac{\text{Moderate Signal}}{\text{High Noise}}$	Muted Moderate Policy Signal	Weak (Centrist Response)
$\dfrac{\text{Conservative Signal}}{\text{Low Noise}}$	Clear Conservative Policy Signal	Strong (Conservative Response)
$\dfrac{\text{Conservative Signal}}{\text{High Noise}}$	Muted Conservative Policy Signal	Weak (Conservative Response)

$(-40 \div 10 = -4)$. This point is true even though the committee's mean or median policy preference is identical ($\mu_{\text{Committee}} = 40$). Likewise, the last four columns of Table 3.1 also have the same identical political signal of 40 reflecting a liberal legislative committee. The clarity of the signal, however, varies substantially, depending on the degree of volatility surrounding the committee median. The signal's clarity is proportionally reduced as this noise increases.

The basic logic of this illustration supports the main point of this chapter. The extent to which elected officials are capable of shaping administrative behavior is not only conditional on the policy signals or stimuli that they emit but also the degree of clarity by which these signals are transmitted to bureaucratic agencies. If bureaucratic agencies receive mixed signals from a legislative committee that impedes its ability or willingness to adapt to these political preferences, then greater heterogeneity of a legislative committee's policy preferences will necessarily weaken its capacity for effective political control, ceteris paribus.

To illustrate this point within the context of examining the ideological direction of signals emitted from legislative committees to bureaucratic institutions, a categorical typology appears in Table 3.2. This typology assesses each of the following: (1) the policy substantive or ideological nature of the signal to noise ratio, (2) the policy substance underlying the signal itself when considering uncertainty, and (3) legislative committee capacity for political control. The clarity of a given (fixed) signal is a function of its noise. When noise is relatively high (low), policy signals become muted (clear). In turn, the nature of agency responsiveness is predicated not only on the (ideological) direction of the signal but also its clarity. When policy signals are clear in a given ideological direction, legislative committees become more capable of influencing agency behavior in its desired direction. Conversely, muted policy signals will lessen the capability for effective legislative control of the bureaucracy, and thus decrease the likelihood of agency responsiveness.

This basic categorical illustration is a simplification of reality. Nonetheless, this typology implies that in order for legislative committee signals to be conveyed and acted on by administrative agencies, the amount of dispersion in the committee's policy preferences must be relatively low, all else being equal. Otherwise, the agency will either be confused by the political signals that it receives from the legislative committee and/or might play committee members off one another with the intention of obtaining greater agency autonomy (Bryner 1987; Dahl and Lindblom 1953; Hammond and Knott 1996; Wilson 1989).

Next, the effects of changes in committee policy preference distributions on legislative capacity for influencing agency behavior are analyzed. This stylized deductive spatial analysis under conditions of uncertainty will provide generalizeable insights concerning the effect of altering a legislative committee's distribution of policy preferences on its capacity for influencing agency behavior.

LEGISLATIVE COMMITTEE POLICY SIGNALS AND NOISE: A SPATIAL ANALYSIS

Background

The key novel proposition advanced in this chapter is that the distribution of policy preferences on a legislative committee are vital for understanding its capacity to influence bureaucratic behavior. This means that both signals (i.e., location) and noise (i.e., uncertainty) must be jointly considered in such an analysis. In the context of this theoretical story, *signal* refers to the mean or median legislative committee policy preference and *noise* represents the uncertainty associated with the signal captured by the standard deviation of legislative committee policy preferences.

Assume that a legislative oversight committee consists of n individuals and their policy preferences follow a normal probability distribution with a mean equal to μ and a standard deviation equal to σ.[7] Furthermore,

---

[7] The normal distribution is employed as it is a common continuous probability distribution that is consistent with my focus on the continuous treatment of uncertainty. The normal distribution also has the additional advantage of having the mean value equal the median

this preference distribution is based on the unidimensional policy scale assumption commonly employed in existing spatial models of legislative dominance (e.g., Morris and Munger 1998; Weingast and Moran 1983; Woolley 1993). Let μ represent the committee's policy signal, while σ characterizes the noise corresponding to this signal. Furthermore, let us assume that the noise is randomly distributed, and thus the effect of noise is not inclined to bias legislative committee policy signals in a systematic manner.[8] The capacity for effective legislative control over administrative behavior is a function of (1) the distance between the proximity of its signal (i.e., the mean committee member's ideal point) relative to the agency's location, and (2) the amount of uncertainty corresponding to this signal (i.e., standard deviation).

The joint proximity and noise theses are premised on both legislative and agency behavior. Because of the collective action problems systemic to the operation of legislatures, coordinated action within a committee will be made easier if it is closer to the agency's ideal point and also exhibits greater cohesion regarding policy preferences. Thus, the capacity for legislative control over the bureaucracy becomes enhanced when the distance between the committee policy signal and agency location is reduced, and also when the noise surrounding this signal decreases. Administrative behavior also will be consistent with the general thesis concerning signals and noise coming from legislative committees. It has been established that administrative organizations have a difficult time adjusting their behavior to external forces (e.g., Crozier 1964; Cyert and March 1963; Downs 1967; March and Simon 1958; Simon 1997; Stinchcombe 1990). As a result, one might expect that the capacity for legislative control being inversely related to the amount of change necessitated by the agency is consistent with the inertial and adaptive aspects of bureaucratic organizations. This proximity assertion is reasonable because an agency that is closer to the committee's ideal point will require less effort by the latter to control bureaucratic behavior.[9] As noted from the outset of this chapter, the

value, thus not making such distinctions substantively meaningful for the purposes of this analysis.

[8] This simplifying assumption makes the problem and subsequent analysis more tractable. It is reasonable in a rational actor sense in that one would not expect such systematic biases of policy signals to occur if policy-maker reputation matters. Moreover, this assumption is consistent with risk-neutrality insofar that the nature of uncertainty will not bias the responsiveness attributable to the legislative committee policy signal. The relaxation of this assumption and its consequences for legislative capacity for controlling agency behavior is left for future inquiry on this topic.

[9] This argument is especially valid if one assumes that an agency does not behave in a recreant manner. Otherwise, these agencies are subject to heavy oversight monitoring activity by legislative committee(s). There is little evidence to suggest that such behavior is commonplace, because agencies generally operate within a mutually agreed-on zone of acceptable behavior in relation to political superiors consistent with the broad parameters of the agency's policy

argument proposed here is predicated not on whether a legislative committee is willing to exert influence over agencies, but instead its capacity for
such influence. Furthermore, closer proximity between the committee's signal and the agency also will allow for lower transaction costs in altering the
former's behavior, because it requires relatively modest adjustments to be
made by the organization rather than wholesale changes in its operations
and task environment. In sum, the greater the spatial distance the signal
must cover, the less potent it will be in obtaining desired results, ceteris
paribus.

More formally, the capacity for legislative control (LC_{Capacity}) is:

$$LC_{\text{Capacity}} = \alpha(|A - \mu|) + \beta\sigma \qquad \text{where} \quad \alpha, \beta < 0 \qquad (2)$$

where δ represents a positive fixed level of legisaltive capacity, A equals
the agency's location, μ is aggregate policy signal emitted by the legislative
committee, σ is the noise (dispersion) corresponding to the policy signal,
and α, β are corresponding parameters. Put simply, (2) shows that the extent
to which a congressional committee is capable of controlling a bureaucratic
agency is inversely related to the absolute difference between the committee's
signal (μ) vis-à-vis the agency's location (A) and the former's corresponding
standard deviation (σ).[10] Thus, in the limiting case, the maximum amount
of capacity for political control by a legislative committee with respect to an
administrative agency is given by:

$$LC_{\text{Maximum Capacity}} = |A - \mu| = 0, \quad \sigma = 0. \qquad (3)$$

This means that the committee's maximum political control capability occurs when its mean or median policy preference is the same as the agency's
location *and* all committee policy preferences are identical so that no uncertainty is present. Obviously, this condition is a limiting case that is not
observed in empirical practice. What can be done, however, is to analyze
the comparative-static consequences involving changes in the distribution of
a legislative committee's policy preferences under different scenarios. Thus,
the impact of a change in the distribution of committee policy preferences,
in terms of its signal and corresponding noise, on net changes in legislative

mandate (Barnard 1938; Krause 1999; Simon 1997). In the relatively rare instances when
agency behavior is viewed as explicitly recalcitrant to democratic preferences, it is typically
met with swift and stern punishment handed out by legislative overseers (e.g., removal of
agency head within a given presidential administration; drastic budgetary changes; passage
of new enacting legislation).

10 If noise is incorporated into an empirical model, then the magnitude of the Ordinary Least
Squares (OLS) coefficients – including the effects of legislative committee policy signals –
might well be underestimated (especially if the signals are very noisy). If this is a statistical
problem, then it necessitates employing an instrumental variable estimation strategy to arrive
at unbiased estimates of these effects. I thank John Mark Hansen for bringing this point to
my attention.

control capacity can be analyzed. The agency's location is treated as being fixed for simplification purposes. The remainder of this section discusses four distinct scenarios by which the capacity for legislative control over agency behavior can be altered because of changes in the distribution of committee policy preferences. Because a normal distribution is symmetric, all the subsequent comparative-static results presented here hold if the committee distributions and agency location were reversed along the unidimensional policy scale on the X-axis.

Case I: Identical Means, Different Variances – Signal Proximity is Fixed, Noise Augmentation ($|A - \mu_1| = |A - \mu_2|$; $\sigma_2 > \sigma_1$)

What happens to the legislative capacity for shaping agency behavior when the committee's policy signal remains unchanged, but the distribution of policy preferences become more diffuse? The first illustration deals with this particular case. In Figure 3.1, the noise corresponding to the signal rises while the signal itself remains unchanged when the committee's policy preference distribution shifts from C_1 to C_2, where $C_1 \sim (\mu_1, \sigma_1)$ and $C_2 \sim (\mu_2, \sigma_2)$. The Y-axis lists the probability density function (pdf) of legislative committee policy preferences and the X-axis captures the unidimensional ideological policy space. The uncertainty surrounding legislative committee policy preferences will rise in this instance, however, the signal will become neither more or less proximate to the agency. Therefore, the agency should experience greater difficulty in shaping agency behavior, all else being equal. Given a normal pdf, the net loss in capacity with respect to legislative control attributable to an increase in noise from σ_1 to σ_2 is given by the following definite integral consistent with Figure 3.1:

$$
\text{Net Loss}_{\frac{\partial LC_{\text{Capacity}}}{\partial \sigma}} = \int_{\sigma_1[f_1(x_1)]}^{\tau[f_1(x_3)]} \frac{1}{\sigma_1 \sqrt{2\pi}} \exp\left[\frac{(x - \mu_1)^2}{2\sigma_1^2}\right] dx
$$

$$
+ \int_{\tau[f_2(x_3)]}^{\sigma_2[f_2(x_2)]} \frac{1}{\sigma_2 \sqrt{2\pi}} \exp\left[\frac{(x - \mu_2)^2}{2\sigma_2^2}\right] dx
$$

$$
\text{where } \frac{\partial LC_{\text{Capacity}}}{\partial \sigma} < 0. \qquad (4)
$$

The marginal loss in the capacity for political control, as a result of an increase in noise from σ_1 to σ_2 attributable to the committee policy preference signal, is graphically portrayed as the adjacent gray-shaded regions contained in Figure 3.1. Because $\mu_1 = \mu_2$ in this case, there is neither a net gain or loss in capacity regarding legislative control over an agency attributable to the committee policy preference signal by definition. In this case, the marginal change in the signal to noise ratio will decline in value from C_1 to C_2 by the area given by (4).

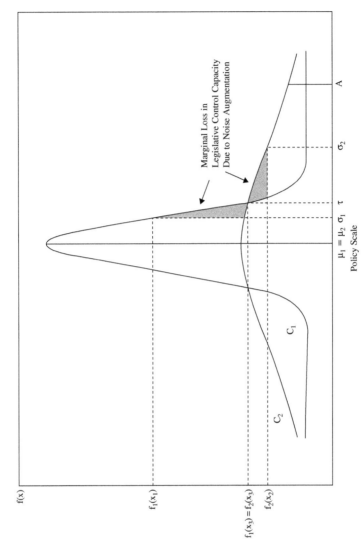

FIGURE 3.1. Fixed Signal Proximity and Noise Augmentation $(A - \mu_1 = A - \mu_2; \sigma_2 > \sigma_1)$

Case II: Different Means, Identical Variances – Greater Signal Proximity, Noise is Fixed ($|A - \mu_1| > |A - \mu_2|$; $\sigma_1 = \sigma_2$)

What are the consequences regarding legislative capacity for control over an agency when its distribution of policy preferences shifts so that uncertainty remains the same but the signal becomes more proximate to the agency's location as one moves from C_1 to C_2? The ability of the legislative committee to influence agency behavior will be enhanced, because its signal becomes more proximate as a result of this distributional shift. Assuming a normal pdf, the net gain in legislative control capacity because of an increase in the proximity of the committee preference policy signal relative to the agency's ideal point from C_1 to C_2: $|A - \mu_1| > |A - \mu_2|$ is given by the following definite integral consistent with Figure 3.2:

$$\text{Net Gain}_{\frac{\partial LC_{\text{Capacity}}}{\partial |A - \mu|}} = \left\{ \int_{\mu_1[f_1(x_2)]}^{\sigma_1[f_1(x_1)]} \frac{1}{\sigma_1\sqrt{2\pi}} \exp\left[\frac{(x - \mu_1)^2}{2\sigma_1^2}\right] dx \right\}$$

$$+ \left\{ \int_{\sigma_1[f_2(x_1)]}^{\mu_2[f_2(x_2)]} \frac{1}{\sigma_2\sqrt{2\pi}} \exp\left[\frac{(x - \mu_2)^2}{2\sigma_2^2}\right] dx \right\}$$

$$\text{where } \frac{\partial LC_{\text{Capacity}}}{\partial |A - \mu|} < 0. \qquad (5)$$

The net gain in capacity for legislative control from the more proximate signal is simply the first brace, which represents the cross-hatched area in distribution C_1, plus the second brace comprising of the similarly marked region from distribution C_2 in Figure 3.2. Therefore, summing these areas provides us with a net gain in legislative capacity to shape administrative behavior as a result of an increase in the proximity of the committee's policy preference signal from μ_1 to μ_2, holding agency location (A) constant. The area of this net gain is portrayed by the dual cross-hatched regions displayed in Figure 3.2. Because $\sigma_1 = \sigma_2$ in this case, there is no change in legislative control capacity due to the committee policy preference noise by definition. In this case, the marginal change in the signal-to-noise ratio will rise in total value from C_1 to C_2 by the area given by (5).

Case III: Different Means, Different Variances – Greater Signal Proximity, Noise Reduction ($|A - \mu_1| > |A - \mu_2|$; $\sigma_2 < \sigma_1$)

The legislative committee's ability to shape administrative behavior will be enhanced as its policy signals become both more proximate to the agency and less noisy consistent with its distribution of policy preferences shifting from C_1 to C_2. Assuming a normal pdf, the net gain involving legislative control capacity attributable to a more proximate change in the signal

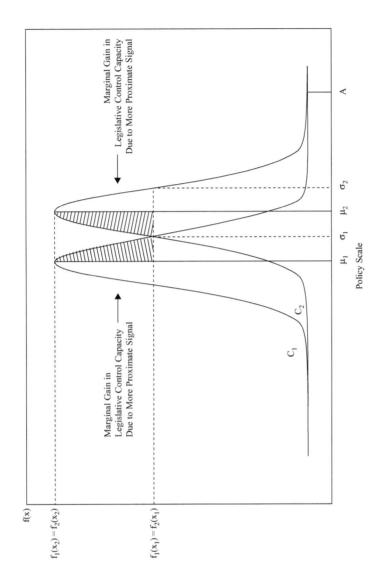

FIGURE 3.2. Greater Signal Proximity and Fixed Level of Noise ($A - \mu_1 > A - \mu_2$; $\sigma_1 = \sigma_2$)

from μ_1 to μ_2 is given by the following definite integral consistent with Figure 3.3:

$$\text{Net Gain}_{\frac{\partial LC_{\text{Capacity}}}{\partial |A - \mu|}} = \int_{\delta[f_2(x_2)]}^{\mu_2[f_2(x_3)]} \frac{1}{\sigma_2 \sqrt{2\pi}} \exp\left[\frac{(x - \mu_2)^2}{2\sigma_2^2}\right] dx$$

$$\text{where } \frac{\partial LC_{\text{Capacity}}}{\partial |A - \mu|} < 0. \tag{6}$$

The net gain in legislative control capacity from the more proximate signal is simply the definite integral expression that encompasses the cross-hatched area in distribution C_2. This area represents the net gain in capacity for legislative control as a result of an increase in the proximity of the committee's policy preference signal from μ_1 to μ_2, holding agency location (A) constant.

A similar corresponding net gain also arises from noise reduction in the distribution of legislative committee policy preferences from σ_1 to σ_2 based on movement from distributions C_1 to C_2 reflected in the gray-shaded regions in Figure 3.3. The definite integral consistent with this area is:

$$\text{Net Gain}_{\frac{\partial LC_{\text{Capacity}}}{\partial \sigma}} = \int_{\delta[f_2(x_1)]}^{\sigma_2[f_2(x_2)]} \frac{1}{\sigma_2 \sqrt{2\pi}} \exp\left[\frac{(x - \mu_2)^2}{2\sigma_2^2}\right] dx$$

$$+ \int_{\sigma_1[f_2(x_1)]}^{\delta[f_2(x_2)]} \frac{1}{\sigma_2 \sqrt{2\pi}} \exp\left[\frac{(x - \mu_2)^2}{2\sigma_2^2}\right] dx$$

$$\text{where } \frac{\partial LC_{\text{Capacity}}}{\partial \sigma} < 0. \tag{7}$$

The marginal gain in the capacity for political control, as a result of legislative committee noise reduction from σ_1 to σ_2, is attributable to decreased uncertainty surrounding the legislative committee's policy preference signal. The total effect of a marginal change in the signal-to-noise ratio on a rise in legislative capacity for controlling administrative behavior is due to both noise reduction and a more proximate signal that is given by the sum of the areas consisting of (6) and (7).

Case IV: Different Means, Different Variances – Greater Signal Proximity, Noise Augmentation ($|A - \mu_1| > |A - \mu_2|$; $\sigma_2 > \sigma_1$)

Assuming a normal probability distribution, the net gain in for legislative control over an agency because of a (more proximate) change in the signal

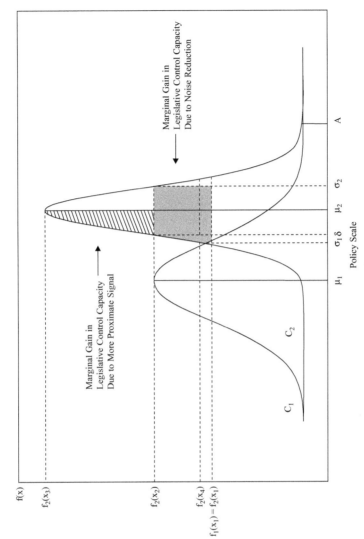

FIGURE 3.3. Greater Signal Proximity and Noise Reduction $(A - \mu_1 > A - \mu_2; \sigma_2 < \sigma_1)$

91

from μ_1 to μ_2 is given by the following definite integral consistent with Figure 3.4:

$$\text{Net Gain}_{\frac{\partial LC_{\text{Capacity}}}{\partial |A-\mu|}} = \int_{\mu_1[f_1(x_2)]}^{\delta_1[f_1(x_3)]} \frac{1}{\sigma_1\sqrt{2\pi}} \exp\left[\frac{(x-\mu_1)^2}{2\sigma_1^2}\right] dx$$

$$\text{where } \frac{\partial LC_{\text{Capacity}}}{\partial |A-\mu|} < 0. \tag{8}$$

The net gain from in enhanced legislative control capacity from a more proximate signal is represented by (8), and is graphically portrayed by the gray-shaded region in distribution C_1 in Figure 3.4. This area simply represents the rise in legislative control capacity as a result of an increase in the proximity of the committee's policy preference signal from μ_1 to μ_2, holding the agency's ideal point, A, constant.

The corresponding net loss in capacity due to an increase in legislative committee noise from σ_1 to σ_2 based on movement from distribution C_1 to C_2 is given by the definite integral consistent with this area portrayed in Figure 3.4:

$$\text{Net Loss}_{\frac{\partial LC_{\text{Capacity}}}{\partial \sigma}} = \int_{\delta_2[f_2(x_1)]}^{\sigma_2[f_2(x_2)]} \frac{1}{\sigma_2\sqrt{2\pi}} \exp\left[\frac{(x-\mu_2)^2}{2\sigma_2^2}\right] dx$$

$$+ \int_{\phi[f_2(x_2)]}^{\delta_2[f_2(x_1)]} \frac{1}{\sigma_2\sqrt{2\pi}} \exp\left[\frac{(x-\mu_2)^2}{2\sigma_2^2}\right] dx$$

$$+ \int_{\sigma_1[f_1(x_1)]}^{\tau[f_1(x_2)]} \frac{1}{\sigma_1\sqrt{2\pi}} \exp\left[\frac{(x-\mu_1)^2}{2\sigma_1^2}\right] dx$$

$$\text{where } \frac{\partial LC_{\text{Capacity}}}{\partial \sigma} < 0. \tag{9}$$

This net loss in legislative control capacity resulting from more diffuse committee policy preferences from σ_1 to σ_2 reflects increased uncertainty surrounding its policy signal. This area is graphically portrayed in Figure 3.4 as the cross-hatched region. In this case, the capacity for legislative influence over an agency rises when the distribution moves from C_1 to C_2 as long as the net gain from having a more proximate signal given by the total cross-hatched area (8) is *greater* than the noise increase reflected in the total shaded area denoted by (9). Conversely, the effect of a marginal change in the signal-to-noise ratio from C_1 to C_2 will result in a decline in legislative capacity in shaping administrative behavior, because the net gain from having a more proximate signal given by the cross-hatched area given by (8) is *less* than the rise in noise reflected in the shaded area denoted by (9). If the net gain from having a more proximate signal given by the area (8) is *equal* to the noise increase captured in the area denoted by (9), then the marginal impact of a

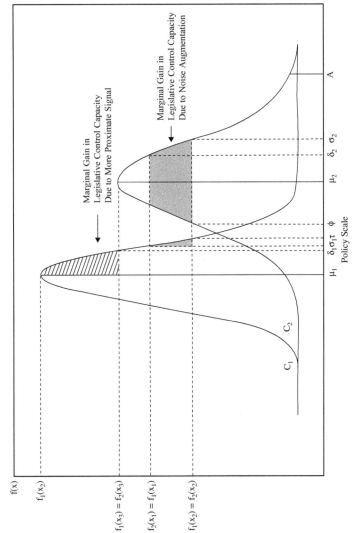

FIGURE 3.4. Greater Signal Proximity and Noise Augmentation ($A - \mu_1 > A - \mu_2$; $\sigma_2 > \sigma_1$)

Within the figure:

f(x)

$f_1(x_2)$

$f_1(x_3) = f_2(x_3)$

$f_2(x_1) = f_1(x_1)$

$f_1(x_2) = f_2(x_2)$

Marginal Gain in Legislative Control Capacity Due to More Proximate Signal

Marginal Gain in Legislative Control Capacity Due to Noise Augmentation

C_1

C_2

μ_1 $\delta_1 \sigma_1 \tau$ ϕ μ_2 δ_2 σ_2 A

Policy Scale

change in the signal-to-noise ratio on legislative capacity for influence agency behavior will become zero as the committee's policy preference distribution shifts from C_1 to C_2.

Summary

Changes in the distribution of policy preferences on a legislative committee can have direct consequences for its capability to influence agency behavior. This does not only refer to the central tendency of this distribution (i.e., signal) as is commonly analyzed but also the amount of dispersion contained in the legislative committee. The four illustrations show the comparative-static conditions by which political control for a legislative oversight committee becomes either easier or more difficult. All else being equal, a reduction in noise from a legislative committee's policy signal results in a decline in their capability of shaping agency behavior consistent with its own preferences. This is because not only is it cognitively easier for an agency to process such information and adjust accordingly but also more difficult to shirk by playing members off of one another. A closer (distant) policy signal, based on the legislative committee's mean or median, enhances (diminishes) its adeptness at obtaining desired agency behavior, ceteris paribus. This is due to less effort being expended by both legislators and agencies to behave in tandem when their respective policy preferences more closely mirror one another, all else being equal. Simply, policy signals that are more proximate to the agency and contain less noise or uncertainty are more likely to be effective in seeking to obtain agency responsiveness to legislative preferences. Because the proximity of committee policy signals relative to the agency and level of noise each exert a countervailing impact on the efficacy of legislative control, both the first (μ) and second moments (σ) of a legislative committee's distribution of policy preferences must be considered when analyzing its capacity for successful monitoring of administrative behavior.

IMPLICATIONS

Scholars studying problems of principal agency involving political-bureaucratic relationships have subsumed that legislative committees send unfettered policy signals to administrative agencies. Whether or not bureaucratic agencies are responsive to a legislative committee is based on this fundamental assumption. Much of the theoretical analysis and statistical evidence over the past two decades indicates that oversight committees are effective at monitoring agency behavior. The insights gleaned from this perspective provide limited information on this topic because it fails to consider variations in the clarity of the policy signal being emitted from the legislative oversight committee. This chapter has made an initial attempt to investigate the consequences of varying policy signals and noise on legislative-bureaucratic relationships consistent with the common "top-down" principal-agent paradigm.

The goal of this chapter is a simple one – not all policy signals coming out of legislative committees are alike and, hence, should not be viewed as such. This is true with respect to the signal itself as well as its subsequent impact on the group for which it is intended. This is because the noise surrounding such policy signals reflects the degree of uncertainty contained therein. Based on the present investigation, one should expect legislative control of the bureaucracy to be the most vibrant when the legislative committee's policy signal is both close relative to the agency's location and also contains little noise or uncertainty, all else being equal. Those instances in which the committee signal is distant from the agency and contains considerable noise should translate into a weakened capacity for garnering bureaucratic responsiveness, ceteris paribus. In all likelihood the omission of noise or uncertainty as a meaningful component of explaining agency-political relationships likely overstates the capacity of elected officials to mold administrative behavior toward its own preferences.

The topic of signaling influence under uncertainty has important ramifications for understanding issues of responsiveness in a representative democracy. Thus, the political responsiveness of administrative agencies to legislatures might vary depending on the nature of the signal and noise associated with the distribution of committee policy preferences. Specifically, democratic accountability of administrative agencies by legislative committees is conditioned to the extent by which the latter has cohesive policy preferences that enable it to engage in effective collective action, and is also sufficiently proximate for agencies to adapt accordingly. In situations in which high policy disagreement is present among legislators and it is also distant from the agency's ideal point to begin with, bureaucratic organizations will be able to exercise greater autonomy from oversight monitoring activity. As a result, policy behavior is least subject to this form of democratic control in policy environments that tend to be conflictual and isolated from the agency's view of its policy mandate. For instance, this might mean that an agency engaged in distributive policy (e.g., agriculture policy) is more naturally ripe for legislative control compared to if they implemented a redistributive policy (e.g., tax policy). This is because committee preferences in the former case tend to be more homogenous and closely correspond to those of the implementing agency in question (e.g., House Agriculture Committee and U.S. Department of Agriculture), while they are more heterogeneous and out of sync with the agency (e.g., House Tax Committee and Internal Revenue Service) in the latter case.

The purpose of this chapter has been to show that the degree to which a legislative committee can shape administrative behavior is a function of its capacity for such control efforts reflected by the distribution of its policy preferences. Students of institutional politics focusing on issues of legislative control over the bureaucracy must consider seriously the precise nature of policy signals emitted by legislative committees and its subsequent impact on agency behavior.

References

Albright, Thomas L., and Harold P. Roth. 1992. "The Measurement of Quality Costs: An Alternative Paradigm." *Accounting Horizons* 6:15–27.

Barnard, Chester I. 1938. *The Functions of the Executive*. Cambridge, MA: Harvard University Press.

Black, Duncan. 1958. *The Theory of Committees and Elections*. London: Cambridge University Press.

Bryner, Gary C. 1987. *Bureaucratic Discretion: Law and Policy in Federal Regulatory Agencies*. New York: Pergamon Press.

Crozier, Michel. 1964. *The Bureaucratic Phenomenon*. Chicago: University of Chicago Press.

Cyert, Richard M., and James G. March. 1963. *A Behavioral Theory of the Firm*. Englewood Cliffs, NJ: Prentice Hall.

Dahl, Robert A., and Charles E. Lindblom. 1953. *Politics, Economics, and Welfare*. New York: Harper and Row.

Dodd, Lawrence C., and Richard L. Schott. 1979. *Congress and the Administrative State*. New York: John Wiley and Sons.

Downs, Anthony. 1957. *An Economic Theory of Democracy*. New York: Harper and Row.

Downs, Anthony. 1967. *Inside Bureaucracy*. Boston, MA: Little, Brown.

Faith, Roger L., Donald R. Leavens, and Robert D. Tollison. 1982. "Antitrust Pork Barrel." *Journal of Law and Economics* 15:329–42.

Fenno, Richard F., Jr. 1973. *Congressmen in Committees*. Boston, MA: Little, Brown, and Company.

Grier, Kevin. 1991. "Congressional Influence on U.S. Monetary Policy: An Empirical Test." *Journal of Monetary Economics* 28:201–20.

Hall, Richard L., and Bernard Grofman. 1990. "The Committee Assignment Process and the Conditional Nature of Committee Bias." *American Political Science Review* 84:1149–66.

Hammond, Thomas H., and Jack H. Knott. 1996. "Who Controls the Bureaucracy?: Presidential Power, Congressional Dominance, Legal Constraints, and Bureaucratic Autonomy in a Model of Multi-Institutional Policymaking." *Journal of Law, Economics, and Organization* 12:119–66.

Krause, George A. 1996. "The Institutional Dynamics of Policy Administration: Bureaucratic Influence over Securities Regulation." *American Journal of Political Science* 40:1083–121.

Krause, George A. 1999. *A Two-Way Street: The Institutional Dynamics of the Modern Administrative State*. Pittsburgh, PA: University of Pittsburgh Press.

Krehbiel, Keith. 1990. "Are Congressional Committees Composed of Preference Outliers?" *American Political Science Review* 84:149–63.

March, James G., and Herbert A. Simon. 1958. *Organizations*. New York: Free Press.

McCubbins, Matthew D., Roger G. Noll, and Barry R. Weingast. 1987. "Administrative Procedures as Instruments of Political Control." *Journal of Law, Economics, and Organization* 3:243–77.

McCubbins, Matthew D., Roger G. Noll, and Barry R. Weingast. 1989. "Structure and Process as Solutions to the Politicians Principal-Agency Problem." *Virginia Law Review* 75:431–82.

Moe, Terry M. 1985. "Control and Feedback in Economic Regulation: The Case of the NLRB." *American Political Science Review* 79:1094–116.

Moe, Terry M. 1987. "An Assessment of the Positive Theory of 'Congressional Dominance'." *Legislative Studies Quarterly* 12:475–520.

Morris, Irwin, and Michael Munger. 1998. "First Branch, or Root? The Congress, the President, and the Federal Reserve." *Public Choice* 96(3/4):363–80.

Niskanen, William A. 1971. *Bureaucracy and Representative Government*. Chicago: Aldine-Atherton.

Ogul, Morris. 1976. *Congress Oversees the Bureaucracy*. Pittsburgh, PA: University of Pittsburgh Press.

Scher, Seymour. 1963. "Conditions for Legislative Control." *Journal of Politics* 25: 526–51.

Scholz, John T., Jim Twombly, and Barbara Headrick. 1991. "Home Style Political Controls Over Federal Bureaucracy: OSHA Enforcement at the County Level." *American Political Science Review* 85:829–51.

Shepsle, Kenneth, and Barry Weingast. 1987. "The Institutional Foundations of Committee Power." *American Political Science Review* 81:85–104.

Simon, Herbert A. 1997. *Administrative Behavior*. 4th ed. New York: Macmillan.

Stinchcombe, Arthur L. 1990. *Information and Organizations*. Berkeley: University of California Press.

Taguchi, Genichi, Subir Chowdhury, and Shin Taguchi. 1999. *Robust Engineering: Learn How to Boost Quality While Reducing Costs and Time to Market*. New York: McGraw-Hill.

Taguchi, Genichi, and Don Clausing. 1990. "Robust Quality: Reducing Defects Through Quality Loss Functions." *Harvard Business Review* 68: 65–72.

Taguchi, Genichi, and Seiso Konishi. eds. 1986. "Taguchi Methods: Signal-To-Noise Ratio for Quality Evaluation." *Quality Engineering Series, Vol 3*. Dearborn, MI: American Supplier Institute.

Tunner, Joseph. 1990. "Is an Out-of-spec Product Really Out of Spec?" *Quality Progress* 23:57–9.

Weingast, Barry R., and Mark J. Moran. 1982. "The Myth of Runaway Bureaucracy: The Case of the FTC." *Regulation* 6:33–8.

Weingast, Barry R., and Mark J. Moran. 1983. "Bureaucratic Discretion or Congressional Control: Regulatory Policymaking by the Federal Trade Commission." *Journal of Political Economy* 91:765–80.

Wilson, James Q. 1980. *The Politics of Regulation*. New York: Free Press.

Wilson, James Q. 1989. *Bureaucracy: What Government Agencies Do and Why They Do It*. New York: Basic Books.

Wood, B. Dan, and Richard Waterman. 1994. *Bureaucratic Dynamics: The Role of a Bureaucracy in a Democracy*. Boulder, CO: Westview Press.

Woolley, John T. 1993. "Conflict among Regulators and the Hypothesis of Congressional Dominance." *Journal of Politics* 55:92–114.

4

Bureaucracy and Uncertainty

Laurence J. O'Toole, Jr.
Kenneth J. Meier

Bureaucracy, unique among the major political institutions, is designed to deal with uncertainty as a matter of course.[1] Standard operating procedures (SOPs), incremental decision making, operational criteria of consistency, permanent files, and the reliance on rules are all bureaucratic efforts to reduce uncertainty. Indeed, bureaucracy often has been recognized as an institutional island of stability in the stormy seas of political change. As France transformed its regime from one republic to another in wrenching shifts over the years, the Gallic bureaucracy continued to perform its functions virtually without interruption. Max Weber observed that bureaus tend strongly toward stability and indefinite perpetuation. "Once it is fully established,"

---

[1] By uncertainty, we mean situations in which decision makers face influences that are unanticipated and potentially destabilizing. This notion, then, includes much more than is encompassed in the narrow decision-theoretic concept. For the latter, uncertainty references circumstances in which a decision maker can identify all possible options and all the consequences that could possibly flow from these, but not which consequences will follow from each alternative. We expand this concept in two ways for our treatment. First, we also include what decision theorists would call "risk": full knowledge of all alternatives and possible consequences, plus probabilistic knowledge of which are more likely than others, for a given choice. And, second, we also include situations in which decision makers confront the need to make choices without knowing the full set of alternatives possible or the complete range of possible consequences. Our concept, therefore, is closer to the common-sense notion of uncertainty. As Burden suggests in Chapter 1 of this book, furthermore, the extent of uncertainty is a matter of degree, not a simple dichotomy.

This chapter is part of an ongoing research effort on the role of public management in complex policy settings. We have benefitted from the helpful comments of Stuart Bretschneider, Amy Kneedler Donahue, H. George Frederickson, Carolyn Heinrich, Patricia Ingraham, Laurence E. Lynn, Jr., H. Brinton Milward, and Hal G. Rainey on various aspects of this research program. Needless to say, this chapter is the responsibility of the authors only.

he observed, "bureaucracy is among those social structures which are the hardest to destroy" (Weber 1946, 228).[2]

Despite these advantages in institutional design, nonetheless, bureaucracies face as a matter of course three major types of uncertainty – policy, resource, and programmatic – with this last type in turn consisting of three primary subtypes – causal uncertainty, implementation uncertainty, and target uncertainty.

Policy uncertainty involves imprecision and sometimes inconsistency in the specification of policy goals. Goals may be uncertain because of the multiple principals problem (that is, bureaucracy must respond to Congress, the president, courts, etc.), the inability of political principals to agree on goals before adopting a policy, or the potential for long-term coalitional drift. Policy uncertainty is accentuated by the short tenure in office of the president's political appointees, those high-level officials charged with providing day-to-day direction for federal agencies: about twenty months on average. Goals also can accumulate over time, with new statutes and directives approved under successive political principals, so that even if individual goals are precise, sets of them accruing like so many barnacles on the hull of the ship of state may conflict. A given bureaucracy then must deal with an excess of "discretion" that really reflects a need to make a choice among incompatible objectives. For example, should the Department of Energy seek cheaper fossil fuels or develop more stable and sustainable forms of energy? Policy uncertainty coupled with the pattern of annual financial appropriations used in Washington generates uncertainty about resources – that is, about whether or not the bureaucracy will be allocated sufficient resources to attain the policy goals specified.

Although not all bureaucratic agencies are equally exposed to the appropriations cycle, most tap it for at least a substantial part of their resources.[3] Even when bureaucratic units receive sufficient funding over time, the resources may not be committed at the outset, or they may be offered in unpredictable quantities from one year to the next, so that agencies must try

---

[2] Bureaucracies seek certainty for two reasons. First, it facilitates performance – that is, the attainment of values. Bureaucracy can support a range of important values, including fairness, reliability, competence, and efficiency. Each of these is advantaged to the extent that disruption and uncertainty are minimized, so it is no surprise that the bureaucratic design is well adapted to managing and routinizing the disruptive potential of uncertainty.

Second, bureaucracies seek certainty for political reasons. Because bureaucracy has a competitive advantage over other political institutions in dealing with uncertainty, the presence of uncertainty has implications for bureaucratic interactions with other political institutions. By creating certainty for itself and relative uncertainty for others, bureaucracy gains political power. The implications of this fact are beyond the scope of this chapter, but are directly relevant to any discussion that relates uncertainty to the interaction among political institutions.

[3] Exceptions include the Federal Reserve Board and most of the federal credit programs.

to accomplish their tasks in a feast-or-famine resource environment. Money, what is more, is not the only resource that bureaucracy must budget. In the U.S. national government, for instance, and in many other ones as well, agency positions (jobs) and funds are budgeted separately, so that a bureau might find itself with sufficient financial resources but insufficient personnel; and the rules of the game do not allow the former to be simply converted into the latter. Agencies can try to cope with this last-mentioned uncertainty threat either by employing temporary staff or by contracting out work to private companies, a practice that has grown greatly in recent years (Light 1999).

Although policy and resource uncertainty affect all political institutions, programmatic uncertainty is primarily a bureaucratic issue. Programmatic uncertainty involves the question of whether or not the bureaucracy can execute an effective program of policy action.

Programmatic uncertainty is exacerbated by both political and resource uncertainty but by itself can be an additional challenge to bureaucracies. Three types of programmatic uncertainty can be important. Uncertainty attributable to *causal theory* (Mazmanian and Sabatier 1990) means that decision makers simply do not know enough (about the actions of others, the consequences of these, or even the consequences of their own choices) to select program actions or elements that they can be sure will lead to desired outcomes. Everyone favors effective public education, for instance, but many different kinds of curricula and teaching approaches are used because even the best education specialists cannot say for certain just how to craft the educational process to be sure that children learn. Other examples are plentiful. Will abstinence-only sex education actually reduce teen pregnancy? Will technical assistance to farmers about nonpoint-source agricultural runoff improve water quality in the nation's rivers and streams? Will boot camps for first-time offenders really reduce recidivism and lower crime rates?

An additional kind of programmatic uncertainty is *implementation uncertainty* – that is, uncertainty associated with the challenge of assembling predictable and cooperative action among implementers themselves. This issue is at the heart of public management – coordinating people and other resources to carry out policies. It requires dealing with this challenge within the bureaucracy and often between the bureaucratic unit and other agencies, other governments, and nongovernmental organizations that may play a part in executing the program (nonprofit agencies or businesses under contract).

A third contributor to programmatic uncertainty is *target*, or demand, *uncertainty*.[4] How many children will show up on the first day of a school

---

[4] Policy scholars use the term "targets" or "target population" to designate individuals whose behavior the program seeks to change.

year?[5] And how many of these will need instruction in English as a second language? Teachers need to be hired, classrooms readied, and curricula planned in advance, but demand is inevitably somewhat uncertain.[6]

This chapter addresses these issues within the context of an existing model of bureaucratic activities. The institutional advantages of bureaucracy allow it to overcome some types of uncertainty (programmatic) better than others (policy), although strategies for dealing with all forms can be found. Attempts to reduce uncertainty have predictable consequences; and these in turn have ramifications, some of which other political institutions must consider.

THE NATURE OF BUREAUCRACY

Bureaucracies are institutions designed in part to reduce uncertainty. They seek to create order out of chaos by classifying and sorting inputs (clientele, resources, etc.), defining job duties, and specifying procedures that will be used to implement policy. They are instrumentally rational organizations – that is, they are typically focused on connecting means with ends efficiently (Simon 1947) – and their structure is characterized by jobs linked to each other in superior-subordinate relationships. The existence of written records and the preference for consistency (or precedent) makes bureaucracy a relatively predictable organization (Weber 1946). And, although bureaucrats' uncertainty about their own preferences can be real, this kind of institutional setting encourages stable and predictable preferences. The near-permanence of the settings in which bureaucrats make discretionary choices gives credence to an old maxim of bureaucratic politics known as Miles' Law: where one stands depends on where one sits.

These design factors of bureaucracy coupled with incremental decision processes generally guarantee that bureaucratic organizations will change only slowly. Indeed, change imposes costs on bureaucratic units and can reduce efficiency, at least in the short run. This means that bureaucracies are autoregressive systems; the best predictor of what a bureaucracy will do this year is what the organization did last year.

Collectively the main structural factors that enhance the stability and predictability of bureaucracies are termed "hierarchy," in the shorthand to be used in this chapter. In contrast to other political institutions, all bureaucracies can be considered hierarchical. Among bureaucracies, however, the degree of hierarchy varies from those that are highly predictable formal organizations (e.g., military organizations) to those that are more decentralized, collegial, and informal (e.g., universities).

---

[5] Some districts face even greater uncertainty. At the start of the 2000–1 school year, the Houston Independent School District had 176,000 students registered. Enrollments continued to increase until mid-November, when they peaked at 210,000.

[6] With the national teachers' shortage an additional source of uncertainty in recent years is whether or not teachers will be available, particularly in fields of math and science.

This hierarchical variation can be by bureaucratic design. A well-known truism about bureaucratic management is that hierarchical organizations fare best in relatively stable environments (for a classic statement, see Thompson 1967). This permits the unit to separate tasks into their component parts, specialize, and put together a production process that copes with the problems. In so doing, as Simon (1965) has argued, hierarchies offer an "architecture of complexity" that can cope with modest amounts of programmatic uncertainty within limited parts of the organization, while still being differentiated enough to insulate the rest of the structure from the potentially disturbing influence. In contrast, in rapidly changing environments the preferred organizational structure is less hierarchical and less patterned, so that individual parts of the organization can respond to the variation in environmental demands without restructuring the entire organization (see Zaltman, Duncan, and Holbek 1973).

Individual bureau chiefs and other managers can reinforce or soften the hierarchical nature of an organization. Participatory leaders can turn a hierarchy into an more collegial organization by adopting one of several such management styles. Similarly, nonhierarchical organizations can be run "by the book" and in this way become more hierarchical.

The hierarchical variation also can be part of policy design, that is, established by other political institutions when they adopt a policy. Many policies (e.g., mental health, family planning) are designed to be implemented not by single bureaucracies but by complex networks composed of several agencies, often at different levels (national, state, local) of government. These networks frequently incorporate private-sector actors and are different from traditional hierarchies in that the authority to compel performance is lacking – that is, networks must induce cooperation from the relevant participants rather than command it (Hall and O'Toole 2000).

A THEORETICAL MODEL

To assess how bureaucracies deal with uncertainty, we begin with O'Toole and Meier's (1999) general model of managing programs and organizations.[7] The model takes the following form:

$$O_t = \beta_1(H + M_1)O_{t-1} + \beta_2(X_t/H)(M_3/M_4) + \varepsilon_t$$

where

O is some measure of output,
H is a measure of hierarchy normalized to range from 0 to 1,

---

[7] This chapter is part of a larger research agenda on the role of governance in public programs. We have retained a common set of terms to permit readers to see how the various papers relate to each other.

M denotes management, which can be divided into three parts

M_1 management's contribution to organizational stability through additions to hierarchy/structure,

M_3 management's efforts to exploit environmental changes,

M_4 management's effort to buffer environmental shocks,

X is a vector of environmental forces,

ε is an error term,

the t and t-1 subscripts denote time periods, and

β_1 and β_2 are estimable parameters.

The first term on the right side is considered the internal portion; the second term is the environmental segment. Policy and resource uncertainty comes primarily although not exclusively from the environment and the political actors that reside there. Programmatic uncertainty arises in both the internal and external portions of the model.

The "internal" aspect of the model explicitly incorporates the autoregressive and incremental nature of organizations by including a lagged output measure on the right hand side of the equation. The model incorporates structural variation, because hierarchy can be considered one end of a continuum with more fluid networks on the opposite pole. As the hierarchy variable H moves toward zero, the model estimates how management affects programs in networklike settings.

The nature of this model and some of its components can be useful for seeing how bureaucracy deals with the various kinds of uncertainty identified earlier. (For an initial test of some key components of this model in one policy setting, see Meier and O'Toole 2001, 2002, forthcoming; O'Toole and Meier forthcoming.) In general, a simple perusal of the model's logic shows that both the internal and the environmental portion of the model involve the influence of structure (H) and also management (the several Ms). In the following two sections, we focus successively on internal and environmental factors that can generate uncertainty. In each case, we analyze how structural and managerial responses can mitigate the impact of uncertainty in its various forms.

INTERNAL OPERATIONS AND THE CHALLENGE OF UNCERTAINTY

Consider the first term on the right side of the equation. This expression says that bureaucracies are stable; they tend to do the same things – or at least deliver the same level of performance – from one time period to the next. Some factors work to reinforce this tendency. One is the structural stability of the setting (hierarchy, or H), while the other is the efforts of managers within the agency who devote attention and energy to keeping operations going efficiently and effectively (M_1). Both have to do primarily with programmatic uncertainty, particularly that portion arising from causal theory and implementation.

Implementation Uncertainty

As suggested earlier, stable hierarchical structures can reduce uncertainty among bureaucratic actors. One reason has to do with what stable hierarchy can do for internal production. Clear lines of authority ensure that all bureaucratic decision makers know the rules of the game whereby conflicts get resolved within an agency. Furthermore, the hierarchy and the routines associated with it can direct information and decision-making criteria to the desks where such data are needed, thus simplifying complexity for otherwise overburdened bureaucrats.

This structural impact is not due merely to the efforts of top managers to give direction to their subordinates, a set of influences implied in the M_1 part of the first term. The structure (H) itself exerts an influence. Information does not simply flow from the top downward; a great deal of it travels in the opposite direction. Hierarchical bureaucratic structures filter and remove complex information as it travels upward toward superiors. At each successively higher level, administrators receive the inputs of many subordinates and would be overwhelmed with complexity – and, thus, uncertainty – if subordinates did not remove most of the raw data and pass along only a portion, including information about uncertain and nonroutine actions that cannot be resolved at the level below (Downs 1967). As this process continues up the line, it enables successive rounds of decision makers to focus their attention on a portion of the complexity, thus gradually reducing uncertainty to manageable levels.

Tullock (1965) called this process "uncertainty absorption," thus emphasizing its key role in how bureaucracy addresses this challenge. When it works well, uncertainty absorption can be a big help. But there are many possibilities for informational filtering to remove the "wrong" information and treat as routine and relatively unimportant key data about changing circumstances or new opportunities. The U.S. military, for instance, possessed vast amounts of information about hostile Japanese intentions toward the Pacific fleet, in places like Pearl Harbor, Hawaii, immediately prior to the attack on December 7, 1941. But the bureaucracy self-filtered it out before reports reached the top (Wohlstetter 1962). The Challenger disaster presided over by the National Aeronautics and Space Administration (NASA) resulted from several causes, many having to do with what happened to information immediately prior to the launch decision. For instance, engineers in the contracted firm Morton Thiokol and in NASA sought to brief their superiors about the relationship between launch temperature and hardware tolerances, but they did not focus attention clearly on the key relationship, which was obscured in a mass of irrelevant graphics and data (Tufte 1997, 38–52). Also, political pressures to launch on a regular schedule discouraged NASA managers from signaling upward the uncertain prospects for launch success that were widely recognized at lower levels (Romzek and Dubnick 1987).

In short, although bureaucratic structure generally absorbs uncertainty through filtering information flows upward, there is no guarantee of consistent success. Improperly conducted, uncertainty absorption can ultimately cause uncertainties to affect the unit severely and negatively (see Hammond and Thomas 1989). Filtering information is one of several forms of uncertainty removal that we call buffering. Buffering in more general terms is discussed later in this chapter, since it often focuses on the environment.

What other features of bureaucracy affect uncertainty? The files or records of an agency serve as a repository of precedent, so that when new issues arise, they are handled through the rationale applied to earlier cases. The unique factors that inevitably arise in new situations, therefore, are seen through the lens of earlier decisions, producing more stability and certainty than would otherwise exist.[8]

Once standard operating processes are in place within a bureau and once these are supported by the regulations and detailed understandings developed within the structure, altering current practices becomes costly. Not only do new understandings have to be developed, negotiated, and communicated widely; these also have to be learned by all relevant parties, and new modes of coordination must be honed. All of these steps take time and other resources. Bureaucrats are acutely aware of the advantages that stable hierarchy provides in minimizing coordination costs and maintaining efficient output (Williamson 1975). So bureaucracy protects its processes and procedures even when it might seem sensible to make alterations in light of new circumstances. Sometimes this stability gets taken to extreme form, and agencies (and their staff) can become attached to means over ends (Merton 1940). For example, armies usually prepare to fight the last war, not the next one. The trick is to balance the closedness and certainty of stable hierarchy with the need for some alteration in response to new circumstances.

As the first term of the model implies, the less hierarchically stable an administrative unit or program is, the less the structure itself reinforces the ongoing processes and routines from one time period to the next. Some programs, in particular, are spread across multiple bureaucratic units, in and out of government, and in these more networked circumstances, the SOPs and jargon and common understandings typically do *not* provide as much reinforcement for the operational status quo. Networks are more open to change and uncertainty internally, therefore, in addition to being more open to certain kinds of environmental influences as well (see the second term in the model). Efforts to estimate the value of parameters in such networks,

---

[8] Knowledge that the courts might be asked to review some of these decisions later, and that courts treat precedent as an important principle, reinforces this bureaucratic tendency.

therefore, can be expected to yield larger standard errors than in stable hierarchies; this result reflects uncertainty on the part of analysts and also actors in the network setting (see Burden's comments in the introductory chapter to this book; also O'Toole and Meier 1999, 521).

As the first term of the model indicates, in addition to structural influences that can work to maintain stable practices into the future, the internal management of public agencies also influences how programmatic uncertainty is controlled. The M_1 term in the model references the whole set of steps that managers can take to keep agency productivity going and to reduce entropy (the loss in orderliness over time in a fairly stable system).

Public management involves a complex set of practices, and this chapter provides only a general sketch (for a more complete treatment see Rainey 1997). To make matters more complicated, good public managers recognize that sometimes the introduction of a certain amount of purposeful uncertainty can also be helpful, by testing new ways of doing things or rethinking the logic of production and performance.

Management can help internally by serving as a coordination point, as well as through such system-maintenance efforts as motivating and rewarding bureaucratic workers, and crafting an atmosphere of sufficient certainty so that everyone knows what is expected and how they should use their energies (Barnard 1938). Good managers enhance internal stability and certainty by building trust. Managers – and units they create expressly for such purposes – can monitor performance and identify bottlenecks in the production of a complex set of goods and services.[9] The same can be said for other system-maintenance functions, such as performance monitoring and performance appraisal. Managers also help to resolve differences between subordinate units in ways that preserve the benefits of current operations where possible.

Furthermore, through a whole array of subtle administrative efforts, managers can help shape and render predictable the actions of disparate bureaucrats in widely separated field offices over extended periods. As Herbert Kaufman documented in a classic study of the U.S. Forest Service, such standard approaches as visits from headquarters, rotation of subordinates among multiple field offices, the development of standard reporting forms and policy guidance manuals, and influence by an agency over its own recruitment and socialization efforts all can work to control the uncertainty that can enter implementation (Kaufman 1960). Advanced information technology creates new opportunities to routinize far-flung operations, as well.

---

[9] The reader should note that internal bureaucratic means of control follow the same patterns as attempts by external political institutions to control the bureaucracy. The difference is that bureaucratic means and monitoring always exist and are regularly used.

Causal Theory Uncertainty

All these efforts are aimed primarily at managing what we have called implementation uncertainty. Public managers in the bureaucracy can assist as well with both causal theory uncertainty and demand/target uncertainty. When bureaucracies are tasked with doing things about which little is known, even steady implementation can result in unpredictable output. Public managers can support continued operations under these circumstances by generating systematic information on cause-effect links in the policy sphere of interest. Such actions are limited, however, because bureaucracies are not pure laboratories and can rarely afford the luxury of controlled basic testing. The larger political world demands quick action even in an uncertain world. So public managers help to battle uncertainty by finding ways of acquiring and using information that can increase knowledge while still devoting effort to practical performance.

Managers, for instance, can establish offices of policy analysis within the agency. These subunits typically explore program options and perform studies to see what can be expected from program interventions in the real world. Cadres of such specialists can provide assistance in reducing the uncertainties associated with causal theory (for coverage of the roles of policy analysts, see Wildavsky 1979).

Managers in the bureaucracy also aim at uncertainty reduction by trying to develop information about what is actually going on as a result of their agency's actions. Program evaluation, for instance, is a process aimed at determining just what impact a program has on the outcomes of interest. Much program evaluation is conducted outside of the implementing agencies, including by other parts of government, like the U.S. General Accounting Office. But implementing agencies frequently conduct their own evaluations to clarify causal theory, with the aim of improving the match between policy intentions and actions.[10]

Beyond such investigations, agencies sometimes try out policy ideas on a relatively small scale before committing time, huge finances, and entire careers to new courses of action. Pilot programs are sometimes initiated precisely to find out whether a policy idea works in practice. For instance, do income maintenance efforts reduce people's ambition to work, and does constructing public housing improve living conditions for the bulk of a city's residents? Pilot programs managed by the bureaucracy can be valuable sources of information to combat uncertainty from causal theory. At the same time, there is often pressure to expand pilot programs too quickly, or to too many sites, because the political system is often impatient with a deliberate pace on pressing policy issues.

---

[10] The classic case of an internal evaluation was the Pentagon Papers, which were designed to be a critical look at Defense Department actions during the Vietnam War.

For that reason, administrators often rely on the experiences developed in other jurisdictions (for instance, experiments in welfare reform in other states) rather than their own pilot projects.[11] The nature of the federal system, with many different subnational governments possessing substantial independent authority in many areas of policy, helps to inform bureaucrats and additional decision makers in other jurisdictions and thus can reduce causal theory uncertainty, particularly in bureaucratic units whose external monitoring of such developments is fed into the internal operations for review.

Oftentimes, as well, other substantive specialists with knowledge of causal issues in particular policy sectors inform the bureaucracy from the outside. As Hugh Heclo observed, "issue networks" of experts (academic as well as those employed in think tanks) as well as partisans sometimes become active in the environments of agencies and seek to inform bureaucrats and other policy actors about the latest knowledge developments in the field – or, sometimes, of their own pet theories and preferred modes of action (Heclo 1978; see also Kingdon 1995). Although these channels reflect the potential for influence from the environment, administrators have discretion over the degree to which they invite and encourage such contributions to the internal deliberations about policies and programs.

The overall issue of how to deal with uncertainty arising from causal theory is particularly tendentious because, although it is a predilection of experts to delay action until "all the facts are in," for many kinds of policy initiatives government must take action before such matters are clarified. Environmental policy, to take one prominent example, often involves making judgments about the right course of action far in advance of the most important consequences (as with global climate change) and while experts continue to debate the scientific merits (and interested parties continue to debate the tradeoffs). Here, uncertainty management may mean developing processes of learning and consensus building, rather than merely waiting for science and designing processes to implement it (for a theoretical and comparative analysis of such efforts in environmental policy, see Arentsen, Bressers, and O'Toole 2000).

Target Uncertainty

We have sketched many of the structural and managerial factors that can influence two of the three types of programmatic uncertainty typically encountered in the bureaucracy, implementation, and causal theory. Demand or target uncertainty also is important.

---

[11] Virtually all state agencies have a network that communicates information to similar agencies in other states.

Demands or expressed needs for agency action come from clients, aggrieved parties, and interested groups. For some agencies, the workload is remarkably steady, or at least predictable, in part because the uncertainty stemming from the target population is low (e.g., social security retirement programs). By contrast, many bureaucratic units are much more subject to the vicissitudes of target needs or demands. Disaster agencies cannot know in advance which years will be calm and which turbulent. A wide variety of service agencies, from police departments to child abuse units to public hospitals, are expected to assist all who request help and do so quickly and effectively. In some settings, demand uncertainty can overwhelm the best-laid plans of managers. Because the nature of many of these tasks requires that detailed information be used to make decisions on the part of frontline workers, an agency's programming of routines is of minimal help. Lipsky (1980) has argued that in such "street-level bureaucracies" the immediate needs and demands drive out managerial planning and rational action. In these situations, frontline workers may develop coping strategies to survive – such as queuing or rationing cases to deal with the easiest or the most urgent first, or stereotyping members of the target groups on the basis of superficial information to help them size up complicated situations quickly and aid their decision making.[12] To the extent that these patterns are found, we can interpret them as relatively maladaptive internal bureaucratic reactions to essentially uncontrollable uncertainty.

DEALING WITH UNCERTAINTY FROM THE ENVIRONMENT

This point serves as another reminder, if one is needed, that the bureaucracy's environment generates much of the uncertainty for agencies. The environment and the uncertainty it offers is not totally threatening; opportunities as well as difficulties are proffered by outside forces and events. The discussion earlier references resource and policy uncertainty, and both aspects are included in the "X" term of our model. X refers to a matrix of environmental forces; some can be exploited by bureaucracy, whereas others threaten continued performance.

The model's environmental term includes these forces as a set of influences. They may be mediated by an agency's management, which can work to exploit environmental opportunities (seeking to use a favorable opportunity for budget improvement, for instance) and limit constraints or potential problems (such as challenges from a hostile legislative committee or an antagonistic interest group). The ratio of M_3 to M_4 can be considered a measure of the uncertainty-taking (versus -avoiding) stance of a bureau's management (see the chapter by Krause in this book). It depends both on the strategy

---

[12] A current controversial case of stereotyping is the use of race as a criterion to stop motorists or airport passengers.

and personality of managers as well as on the array of resource and policy uncertainties in the environment.

Skillful bureaucratic managers adjust their strategies and tactics to manage potentially disruptive uncertainty from outside while using opportunities to alter the status quo to assist performance (and perhaps longer-term support). A huge literature on bureaucratic politics treats these issues in great depth (Golden 2000; Meier 2000; Rourke 1984).

Agency managers can work to build budgetary support for their programs in the larger political world (Fenno 1964). Continuing and stable financial resources are of great value, and given the competition for scarce funding and the system's penchant for incremental decision making, only a few can be successful on a regular basis. Management sometimes exploits (and orchestrates) pressure from interest groups, clients, political principals, and others to leverage the budget (see Wildavsky 1984). For example, the U.S. Department of Agriculture created an interest group, the Farm Bureau, and used the Farm Bureau's demands to seek larger budgets from Congress.

Policy uncertainty, too, is a major preoccupation of top management in the bureaucracy. One might think that agencies would wait until the political actors decide what to do and then march efficiently in the prescribed direction. But, in practice, policy uncertainty is a more prolonged, sometimes nearly intractable, condition.[13]

Political uncertainty is exacerbated by the plethora of political principals, particularly in a separation-of-powers system such as the United States, who have different preferences and seek to point the bureaucracy in different directions. The president may have one priority, houses of Congress have others – particularly when they are in the hands of the opposition – and often disagree with each other in any event; and oversight committees in the legislature may or may not reflect the preferences of the overall chamber. Meanwhile, the judiciary may have weighed in with a set of constraints and concerns that further circumscribe the bureaucracy's policy space – although additional court action can unpredictably change things again. The result may resemble a situation in which the bureaucracy does not lack for policy direction but suffers from an excess of policy guidance. As a consequence, the bureaucracy is thrust into discretionary action – acting in some direction even while the political principals are in disagreement, and hoping the result produces sufficient agreement from policy makers to continue support into the future (for a classic statement, see Long 1949).

Political principals are not the only sources of policy uncertainty in the environment. Other stakeholders, including interest groups, are likely to seek influence over what the agency is doing; the interactions of agencies with

---

[13] Because bureaucracy usually participates in the policy discussions with other political institutions (see Krause 1997), they are sometimes able to learn about political institutions' intentions that do not appear in the final legislation or other policy pronouncement.

such other actors in the environment can resemble games of incomplete and imperfect information, as Burden sketches in the introductory chapter to this book. Bureaucratic managers do not simply respond to these potential sources of policy uncertainty. Administrators look to build reliable coalitions with important interests and legislative committees (Meier 2000). On occasion, the results are so stable that analysts have dubbed such patterns "triple alliances" or "iron triangles." In corporatist political systems such as Austria or Sweden, interests organized into peak associations explicitly bargain with bureaus as collaborative equals, and the resulting decisions commit all parties to support and execute any agreements reached. In the United States, this style of uncertainty management is rare, but here bureaus sometimes seek to shape the very interest-group forces that surround them – for instance, by helping to institutionalize support and minimize organized opposition (Maass 1951) – and also by involving stakeholders in some decision making related to the agency's programs, thereby reducing uncertainty and external threats. This last strategy is known by the familiar term of "cooptation," a process that has acquired a negative connotation but may be a sensible approach to a complex and potentially destabilizing bureaucratic environment (the seminal study is Selznick 1949).

Management and the Environment

Administrators simply cannot focus on performance and internal management alone. Caring about performance and management thrusts responsible administrators into active attention to their political environment, a potent source of policy uncertainty. Administrators must work their complicated environment to build sufficiently able coalitions to stabilize policy and manage policy-related uncertainty. And this process may be a continual rather than a sporadic effort.

Agency managers vary in how proactively they work to shape the policy directions to which they are then subject. Some of this variation is explained by the task and the technology involved in the agency's mandate – health bureaucracies, for instance, produce clearly measurable results through the use of expertise that is widely respected, even if not widely understood – and managers of health agencies typically have more influence in shaping policy than managers of, for instance, welfare bureaucracy (Wilson 1989). Part of the variation has to do with the energy and skill of managers themselves as they work outward in their networked environment. In any case, policy uncertainty can be expected to be an important aspect of the challenges arising for bureaucracy.

Structure and the Environment

The structure of bureaucracy, not just its management, also plays a role in handling uncertainty arising from environmental forces. Note that structure appears in the second term of the model as well as the first. In part, this double appearance reflects a mathematical statement of the point with which this chapter opened: bureaucracy is uniquely designed to deal with uncertainty. Its structure facilitates the continual challenge of addressing and reducing the impact of uncertainty, while also permitting the exploitation of outside forces under some conditions. The 1/H term in the model's environmental portion indicates that stable, hierarchical structure can be considered a source of protection that reduces the impact of uncertainties emanating from the environment. (The H term in the first part of the model also indicates that such bureaucratic structure stabilizes internal production and the reproduction of current practices into the future.)

Bureaucratic structure as well as management can buffer the environment. By buffering we mean smoothing out or protecting from outside forces that can influence program performance. Buffering can be caused or facilitated by managerial actions, structural features of the bureaucratic setting, or both.

Managerial Strategy

First, note that not all managerial efforts to deal with the environment constitute buffering. Sometimes managers take advantage of environmental factors to help support what the agency is doing.

Second, not all exploitative moves by managers (M_3 in our model) involve the expansion of uncertainty. Some may amount to a manager's taking advantage of outside forces to protect current operations, thus reducing uncertainty. When certain perturbations threaten to disrupt a steady flow of needed resources or when policy actors in the environment pose a threat to the agency as it goes about its business, a manager might reach out to seek additional funds, find alternative sources of human resources, or activate supportive political principals, all with the objective of stabilizing the setting. In short, exploitation of the environment can be supportive or even defensive, and need not be inevitably risky. Indeed, doing nothing in an uncertain or hostile environment may be the riskiest course a manager can pursue (see Kaufman 1991). As an example, in response to a sunset law that could have eliminated the Consumer Product Safety Commission (CPSC) in 1978, the CPSC mobilized its political supporters to gain reauthorization (Meier 1985). Earlier, the separation-of-powers design was discussed as an institutional arrangement that virtually guarantees continual production of policy uncertainty in the bureaucratic environment. We also should note that multiple principals additionally offer opportunities for managers to activate supporters selectively, as needed, to reintroduce some equilibrium (McCubbins, Noll, and Weingast 1990).

Third, both managers and program structures have the capacity to buffer bureaus from some sources of uncertainty in their environments, often in the service of stable and effective program performance. If management opts to buffer, several forms are available.

One type of buffering might be thought of as a barricade: a "wall" of some height that stops all external forces (all Xs) smaller than a certain size from penetrating the agency and its programs. Here, the potentially disturbing forces are effectively separated from internal operations, provided the forces are not so large they overwhelm the buffer. Buffering of this kind might be especially useful when a bureau is situated in a situation in which significant amounts of destabilizing background forces ("noise") appear on a regular basis, but rarely are these of such magnitude that they become substantial. The erecting of structural barriers, in particular, can protect an agency while also allowing those inside to stay alert to the potential for large shocks. In general, structure can provide some of this kind of protection. Agencies also can employ personnel to work at the boundary between the bureau and its environment (e.g., Congressional or public affairs liaison, etc.) to deflect potentially disruptive influences, while also passing along signals from particularly persistent outside actors or on subjects that are especially salient.

Another kind of buffer can be thought of as a filter: of the full set of outside forces, some are allowed to penetrate into internal operations, while others are stopped. Here the distinction is not primarily in terms of amplitude but, rather, subject matter or issue. Agencies, for instance, may want to deal with attacks that aim to undermine the core mission of the unit, while ignoring disputes about procedural fairness of day-to-day operations. Clearly, as Sabatier and Jenkins-Smith (1993) have argued, program advocates operate with cognitive maps in which some issues are more central and more deeply held. Agencies might design buffers to draw their attention only for some of these more important challenges.

Both structure and management can assist in such filtering. Subunits can be designed so that certain issues are tracked regularly within an agency. This is a structural bias toward issue-specific filtering. (Some Xs have easy entrance, others none at all; the Centers for Disease Control and Prevention, for example, closely monitors some diseases but not others.) Managers also can instruct their subordinates to treat signals on certain topics as matters of high priority (e.g., adverse drug reactions in the Food and Drug Administration). The information systems of some agencies are elaborately differentiated to distinguish high- from low-priority signals. Of course, such systems can work poorly, and the study of bureaucracy is littered with examples of filters, including information systems, that functioned to screen out very relevant signals about key sources of uncertainty.

A variant is a filter that, in effect, can be turned on or off. During some periods (for example, while the statute legitimating a bureau's programs is up for reauthorization), the agency opens its boundaries to many outside signals. The U.S. Department of Agriculture, for example, sponsors a series of public conferences in the years prior to reauthorization of major farm bills to generate new ideas and assessments of current policy. Here, the filter has a temporal dimension. Again, the purpose is to let some signals or shocks through and buffer against others.

Still another form that a buffer might take is as a dampener: external shocks have impact, but the amplitude is reduced by some amount. The buffer absorbs some of the energy from the external disturbance, so as to manage the diminished force that remains. Bureaucratic jargon, categories, and paperwork help to dampen the huge range of variation in external influences, thus converting them into a few categories to which the bureaucracy has developed reasonably adaptive responses. Layers in a bureaucratic system can have a dampening impact as well, even if the layering is not explicitly hierarchical.

One additional way that structure can lessen environmental perturbations is possible when public programs are administered via a network of two or more organizations, or parts of organizations. Network structures can decrease certain kinds of uncertainty while possibly increasing others. The first term of our model suggests that it is tougher to continue stable output from a networked arrangement, since the multiple ways that hierarchy can order social action and resolve conflict are diminished. (Individual units within the network may be quite hierarchical and stable; the issue has to do with the operations among the nodes rather than within them.) Over time, networks also can be settings for stable and predictable activity; but as a class of structural forms, they coordinate less than does a pure stable hierarchy.

Still, when shocks from the environment do enter a network, the looser coupling there provides a structural buffer that can compartmentalize the perturbations from outside. The point here is similar to the "architecture of complexity" discussion earlier.

In addition, the *ways* that nodes in a network are linked with each other can be of critical significance for impacts on uncertainty. Sometimes multiple units are involved in the implementation of policy, but they are not connected in collaboration; rather they face overlapping jurisdictions and competition within a policy sector. Here, uncertainty can increase for individual bureaucratic units, while the result for the overall system is increased reliability – more bureaucratic actors competing with more rivals – increases the odds that *someone* will address the problem and clients will be served. (For an important study of these relationships, see Bendor 1985.) Exposing bureaus to uncertainty can be a way of reducing uncertainty for clients or other stakeholders. Uncertainty for whom?, then, can be an important question.

CONCLUSION

Bureaucracies, we have seen, are institutions designed to deal with uncertainty, often in the interests of stable, equitable, and predictable public action. They are the part of the political system that has the strongest claim to protection from disrupting influences. Still, bureaucratic performance, particularly in democratically accountable political settings, is typically subject to a variety of channels that can funnel and even catalyze uncertainty.

Some kinds of uncertainty have to do with the tasks of performance. These include programmatic uncertainty related to causal theory, implementation, and targets. Others are more clearly derived from external stimuli related to policy or resources needed for production. Our model offers a helpful way of thinking about both the sources of uncertainty and the multiple ways that bureaus have available to respond to it. The key variables in general are structure and public management, although – as we have seen – each of these encompasses many dimensions and tradeoffs.

Bureaucracy typically aims for uncertainty reduction and possesses impressive features that can insulate standard procedures and performance from perturbing influences. But the struggle is constant, and bureaus are often buffeted much more than bureaucrats expect, or would prefer. Still, this conclusion is not necessarily a sign of overall system failure. Effective and efficient performance demands substantial uncertainty reduction. Yet, open, accountable, and responsive government requires the "inconvenience" of shocks and changes to the established programs and ways of doing business. While sometimes inconvenient and often uncomfortable, a balance between these two is a reasonable overall objective.

References

Arentsen, Maarten, Hans Bressers, and Laurence J. O'Toole, Jr. 2000. "Institutional and Policy Responses to Uncertainty in Environmental Policy." *Policy Studies Journal* 28, 3:597–611.

Barnard, Chester I. 1938. *The Functions of the Executive.* Cambridge, MA: Belknap Press of Harvard University.

Bendor, Jonathan B. 1985. *Parallel Systems: Redundancy in Government.* Berkeley: University of California Press.

Downs, Anthony. 1967. *Inside Bureaucracy.* Boston, MA: Little, Brown.

Fenno, Richard. 1964. *The Power of the Purse.* Boston, MA: Little, Brown.

Golden, Marissa Martino. 2000. *What Motivates Bureaucrats?* New York: Columbia University Press.

Hall, Thad E., and Laurence J. O'Toole, Jr. 2000. "Structures for Policy Implementation: An Analysis of National Legislation, 1965–66 and 1993–94." *Administration and Society* 31, 6:667–86.

Hammond, Thomas H., and Paul A. Thomas. 1989. "The Impossibility of a Neutral Hierarchy." *Journal of Law, Economics, and Organization* 5:155–84.

Heclo, Hugh. 1978. "Issue Networks and the Executive Establishment." In Anthony King, ed., *The New American Political System.* Washington, DC: American Enterprise Institute: 87–124.

Kaufman, Herbert. 1960. *The Forest Ranger.* Baltimore, MD: The Johns Hopkins University Press.

Kaufman, Herbert. 1991. *Time, Chance and Organizations*. 2nd ed. Washington: Brookings.

Kingdon, John W. 1995. *Agendas, Alternatives, and Public Policies*. 2nd edition. New York: HarperCollins.

Krause, George. 1997. *A Two Way Street*. Pittsburgh, PA: University of Pittsburgh Press.

Light, Paul C. 1999. *The True Size of Government*. Washington, DC: Brookings.

Lipsky, Michael. 1980. *Street-Level Bureaucracy: Dilemmas of the Individual in Public Services*. New York: Russell Sage.

Long, Norton E. 1949. "Power and Administration." *Public Administration Review* 2:257–64.

Maass, Arthur. 1951. *Muddy Waters: The Army Corps of Engineers and the Nation's Waters*. Cambridge, MA: Harvard University Press.

Mazmanian, Daniel A., and Paul A. Sabatier. 1990. *Implementation and Public Policy: With a New Postscript*. Latham, MD: University Press of America.

McCubbins, Mathew D., Roger G. Noll, and Barry R. Weingast. 1990. "Structure and Process, Politics and Policy: Administrative Arrangements and the Political Control Over Agencies." *Virginia Law Review* 75:431–82.

Meier, Kenneth J. 1985. *Regulation*. New York: St. Martin's Press.

Meier, Kenneth J. 2000. *Politics and the Bureaucracy* 3rd ed. Ft. Worth, TX: Harcourt Brace.

Meier, Kenneth J. and Laurence J. O'Toole, Jr. 2001. "Managerial Strategies and Behavior in Networks: A Model with Evidence from U.S. Public Education." *Journal of Public Administration Research and Theory* 11:271–95.

Meier, Kenneth J. and Laurence J. O'Toole, Jr. 2002. "Public Management and Organizational Performance: The Effect of Managerial Quality." *Journal of Policy Analysis and Management* 21, 4:629–43.

Meier, Kenneth J., and Laurence J. O'Toole, Jr. Forthcoming. "Public Management and Organizational Performance: The Impact of Managerial Networking." *Public Administration Review*.

Merton, Robert K. 1940. "Bureaucratic Structure and Personality." *Social Forces* 17:560–8.

O'Toole, Laurence J., Jr., and Kenneth J. Meier. 1999. "Modeling the Impact of Public Management: Implications of Structural Context." *Journal of Public Administration Research and Theory* 9, 4:505–26.

O'Toole, Laurence J., Jr., and Kenneth J. Meier. Forthcoming. "*Plus ça Change:* Public Management, Personnel Stability, and Organizational Performance." *Journal of Public Administration Research and Theory*.

Rainey, Hal G. 1997. *Understanding and Managing Government Organizations* 2nd ed. San Francisco: Jossey-Bass.

Romzek, Barbara S., and Melvin J. Dubnick. 1987. "Accountability in the Public Sector: Lessons from the Challenger Tragedy." *Public Administration Review* 47, 3:227–38.

Rourke, Francis E. 1984. *Bureaucracy, Politics and Public Policy* 3rd ed. Boston, MA: Little-Brown.

Sabatier, Paul A., and Hank C. Jenkins-Smith, eds. 1993. *Policy Change and Learning: An Advocacy Coalition Approach*. Boulder, CO: Westview.

Selznick, Philip. 1949. *TVA and the Grass Roots*. Berkeley: University of California Press.

Simon, Herbert A. 1947. *Administrative Behavior*. New York: Free Press.

Simon, Herbert A. 1965. "The Architecture of Complexity." *General Systems Yearbook* 10, reprinted from *Proceedings of the American Philosophical Society* 106 (1962).

Thompson, James D. 1967. *Organizations in Action*. New York: McGraw-Hill.

Tufte, Edward R. 1997. *Visual Explanations: Images and Quantities, Evidence and Narrative*. Cheshire, CT: Graphics Press.

Tullock, Gordon. 1965. *The Politics of Bureaucracy*. Washington, DC: Public Affairs Press.

Weber, Max. 1946. *From Max Weber: Essays in Sociology*. Translated and edited by H. H. Gerth and C. Wright Mills. New York: Oxford University Press.

Wildavsky, Aaron. 1979. *Speaking Truth to Power: The Art and Craft of Policy Analysis*. Boston, MA: Little, Brown.

Wildavsky, Aaron. 1984. *The Politics of the Budgetary Process*. 4th ed. Boston, MA: Little, Brown.

Williamson, Oliver. 1975. *Markets and Hierarchies*. New York: Free Press.

Wilson, James Q. 1989. *Bureaucracy*. New York: Basic Books.

Wohlstetter, Roberta. 1962. *Pearl Harbor: Warning and Decision*. Stanford, CA: Stanford University Press.

Zaltman, Gerald, Robert Duncan, and Jonny Holbek. 1973. *Innovations and Organizations*. New York: Wiley.

5

Uncertainty and Political Debate

How the Dimensionality of Political Issues Gets Reduced in the Legislative Process

Bryan D. Jones
Jeffery Talbert
Matthew Potoski

James March (1994) has repeatedly argued that uncertainty in decision making is far more fundamental than is implied by the standard models of choice based on probability theory. It influences every aspect of the decision-making process, and is not satisfactorily captured by the risk and uncertainty models commonly used in decision science, Bayesian or otherwise. Why not? Why are students of public policy so dissatisfied with traditional subjective expected utility models of choice? One explanation is that uncertainty in politics involves both individual-level uncertainty and collective choice uncertainty. Individual-level uncertainty involves how a single decision maker comes to a decision in a complex choice situation. Collective choice uncertainty affects how individual utility calculations are combined to yield an outcome in a decision-making body.

We argue here that even individual level expected utility approaches are unsatisfactory for the study of politics and public policy. The major reason is that uncertainty in the traditional approaches is applied solely to the alternative set. A decision maker is expected to calculate the risk or uncertainty associated with the pursuit of an alternative strategy that affects a goal. A situation in which a decision maker has multiple goals greatly expands the difficulty of calculations, but does not change the basic formulation of the problem, so long as the decision maker can somehow reduce the several dimensions to a direct benefit calculation.

Uncertainty, however, affects the alternatives we consider in choice (the traditional model), the attributes we use to evaluate the choice, and the institutional context of the decisions (Jones 1996, 2001). Decision makers struggle with three fundamental types of uncertainty: how to characterize a problem (here termed the *design* problem, or attribute uncertainty), how to assess the effects of an alternative based on that characterization (alternative uncertainty), and in collective decision contexts, how actors' preferences interact with institutions to aggregate individual decisions into collective choices (collective decision uncertainty).

When confronting decisions, we are often uncertain about how to characterize both the relevant attributes (what are the relevant criteria for deciding what is best?) and the relevant alternatives (how do the available options stack up along the different attributes?). What are the relevant attributes for choosing among political candidates? Should we evaluate their ideology? Policy positions? Should we hold them accountable for the performance of the economy? Once we have settled on a set of attributes, we still need to identify the different alternatives and how they compare. Which candidate's policy positions best match my own? Who did the most to improve the economy?

Finally, this chapter considers a third type of uncertainty that occurs when actors engage in collective decision making. Such uncertainty occurs as actors evaluate alternatives along multiple dimensions and focus on different attributes. In such cases, a single actor may not know how other actors' behaviors (whether strategic or not) interact with the rules of the decision context to produce collective choices. Multiple evaluative attributes, because they allow the possibility of decision cycling, can make it difficult for a member of a collective decision-making body to predict the effect of his or her vote on the outcome (Potoski 2001).

In this chapter, we present a dynamic theory of uncertainty that shows how attribute, alternative and collective decision uncertainty vary across decision contexts. We demonstrate how decision processes and procedures reduce uncertainty by collapsing the attribute structure of choices from multiple evaluative dimensions down to a single dimensional choice. This dynamic occurs at both the individual (for example, when a voter selects a candidate) and institutional levels (for example, when the U.S. House of Representatives processes bill proposals into laws). Thus, we assert not only that alternatives, attributes, and collective decision making are essential for understanding uncertainty but also that understanding uncertainty is vital for understanding politics and political outcomes.

DECISIONAL UNCERTAINTY AND PROCESS TRACING

We make three key claims. The first is that *all individual choices must be made in one-dimensional spaces.*[1] The number of dimensions refers to the

---

[1] A dimension can be viewed as a "standard of measurement for relevant variable properties of alternatives" (Riker 1986, 143). Dimensions classify alternatives and choices depicted in spatial arrangements. In the classic unidimensional liberal-conservative model, a single axis represents individual choices along a continuum so that voters favor proposals lying closer to their ideal state of affairs. Policy proposals can also have multiple evaluative dimensions that individually, or in concert, form the basis for legislators' policy decisions. Consider some simple examples of agendas of varying dimensional structures in a legislative arena.

number of attributes people use when making specific decisions. No matter how many attributes may characterize a choice, and no matter how the alternatives facing a decision maker are ordered on the multiple dimensions, a single decision maker must reduce the comparisons among the alternatives to a single dimension, termed the choice dimension.[2] This should be utterly uncontroversial; it is in fact an empirical claim that all models of decision making adopt explicitly or implicitly. Rational choice implies quite simply that a decision maker can choose the best among a set of alternatives that he or she has reduced to a single dimension, termed *utility*. Psychological models of decision making similarly assume such a reduction. *Lexicographic choice* means that a decision maker attends only to the most salient of the attributes characterizing the choice alternatives. *Elimination by aspects* suggests that a decision maker uses a lexicographic strategy, moving to a second dimension only if two or more alternatives tie on the first attribute (Tversky 1972). *Satisficing* implies that decision makers attend to aspiration levels for multiple goals, or decision-making attributes, and are able to adjust choice according to the disjuncture between the aspiration level and performance (Simon 1996). All these theories assume a final, single dimensional choice, although they disagree over what that dimension is.

In virtually any choice situation in politics, a decision maker must collapse complex, multifaceted choice situations into a single dimension. Because in most circumstances there exists considerable uncertainty about just how to combine the various facets or attributes of a choice situation into a single choice dimension, how the initial space is collapsed is infused with uncertainty. In a multiattribute choice situation, the weights used to combine the attributes into a single dimensional choice space are affected with uncertainty (Jones 1996). We term this *attribute-uncertainty*. Our second claim is that *theories of individual choice must incorporate attribute-*

A one-dimensional (liberal-conservative) issue context contains consistent coalitions on each side of all policy proposals, with the coalitions changing only as moderate legislators vote with either the conservative or liberal coalitions, depending on how a particular proposal favors either side. A multidimensional issue contains multiple patterns of coalitions that vary depending on which dimensions are most salient for each issue. In a multidimensional issue context, economic issues may pit a coalition of legislators favoring redistributing wealth against a coalition that favors laissez-faire economic policies. A different pattern surrounds social issues such as abortion that arise in the same issue context, pitting social conservatives (some of whom may favor laissez-faire economics while others favor economic redistribution) against a coalition of social liberals (whose members also may contain both economic liberals and economic conservatives). In the multidimensional issue context, legislators with similar preferences along the same dimension should vote together on issues along that dimension, while they should be dispersed for issues along other dimensions (see Talbert and Potoski 2002).

[2] A "dimension" might not be quantified; we require only that it allow a decision maker to compare alternatives, which does not seem possible in the absence of some single standard of comparison.

uncertainty as well as alternative uncertainty to model decision making properly.

These two claims imply that a dynamic process must exist that reduces a complex, multiattribute choice situation to a single choice dimension. Psychologists use process tracing to follow how single individuals come to a choice. It is similarly possible to use process tracing to follow how policy proposals mutate in moving toward a policy choice, with the important caveat that the process involves multiple individuals in various institutional roles. In this paper, we propose an approach that allows the observation of this process quantitatively. If we study the life of a proposal in a legislative assembly, we should be able to trace this process from complex initial formulation to single-dimensional choice.

Our final claim is that *decision uncertainty also depends on the institutional context in which the decision takes place.* The rules governing how the individual decisions of group members are aggregated into a collective choice can affect the level of uncertainty confronting the group members. In our empirical example, we show how the rules of the House reduce this uncertainty in collective decision uncertainty by transforming the complex, multidimensional structure of the set of bill proposals into a simpler, unidimensional set of legislation.

For the purposes of this study, we may divide the legislative process into two stages. The first we term the *policy debate stage*, in which legislative proposals are introduced, packaged, and debated. The second is the *policy choice stage*, in which final decisions on proposals are made. In the policy debate stage of the process, a new issue or problem first comes within the purview of the members of a decision-making body. In Congress, this can be reflected by bill introductions or by committee hearings. For example, Jones (1994, 149–54) shows in an analysis of keywords used by the Congressional Information Service that the policy topics that served as the focus of Congressional committee hearings from 1925 through 1990 were characterized by from two to four major dimensions of evaluation. During the same period, Poole and Rosenthal (1997) indicate that one or sometimes two dimensions characterize Congressional roll call voting.[3]

In this chapter, we extend this logic to a more systematic approach to tracing policy choices. We investigate these agenda dynamics by comparing the dimensional structures of legislators' bill cosponsoring and floor voting activities during the 103rd and 104th Congresses. We show that at the policy debate stage the policy proposals are judged along multiple evaluative

---

[3] Dimensioning approaches all rely on the statistical leverage offered by multiple observations on the same stimulus object. Hence, a high-dimensional solution cannot be viewed as evidence against the claim made above that decision makers must reduce a complex choice situation to a single dimension to make a choice. This is a major reason that the claim, while empirical, is extremely difficult to test.

dimensions. At the *choice stage* on the legislative floor, the issue agenda reveals a low dimensional structure. The analyses show that bill cosponsoring contains at least three and as many as five distinct dimensions. Floor voting takes place in a far lower dimensional space.

ATTRIBUTE-BASED INFORMATION PROCESSING

Much decision making involves not comparing alternatives but comparing the attributes that characterize those alternatives. Attribute-based information processing starts with the assumption that policy alternatives (or other objects of choice, such as political candidates in an election) are located in a multiattribute space. Simply put, alternatives have multiple consequences. (For a full analysis of attribute-based information processing, see Jones 1996.) How these attributes are traded off against one another and subsequently combined into a choice dimension clearly involves uncertainty, but political scientists, economists, and many decision scientists have conveniently ignored this source of uncertainty in most studies of choice.

It is worth briefly reexamining the classical model of consumer choice from economics. That model for two goods or services is presented in Figure 5.1. The model incorporates tradeoffs between goods, and these tradeoffs are nonlinear functions of the amount of the goods involved: the assumption of declining marginal utility implies such nonlinear tradeoffs. It is now clear, however, that the model treats goods as some sort of "Gestalt," instead of approaching them as bundles of attributes (Jones 2001, 41–2). Furthermore, the model involves no uncertainty, and to our knowledge no expected utility models of choice have incorporated such uncertainty. Rather, these models have concentrated exclusively on alternative uncertainty to the exclusion of attribute uncertainty. So the "goods" in consumer choice theory, adopted as "issues" in the spatial theory of political choice, incorporate

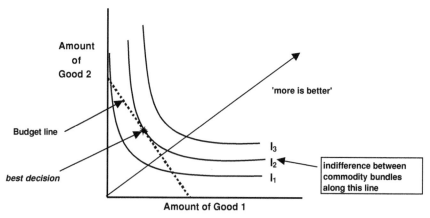

FIGURE 5.1. Consumer Choice Theory

TABLE 5.1 *The Decision Matrix*

		Attributes			Benefits (Weighted Net Benefits Rule)
		D_1	D_2	$D_3 \ldots D_m$	
	A_1	b_{11}	b_{12}	$b_{13} \ldots b_{1m}$	$\sum\limits_{k=1}^{m} w_k b_{1k} = B_1$
	A_2	b_{21}	b_{22}	$b_{23} \ldots b_{2m}$	$\sum\limits_{k=1}^{m} w_k b_{2k} = B_2$
Alternatives	A_3	b_{31}	b_{32}	$b_{33} \ldots b_{3m}$	$\sum\limits_{k=1}^{m} w_k b_{3k} = B_3$
	.	.	.	. .	.
	.	.	.	. .	.
	.	.	.	. .	.
	A_j	b_{j1}	b_{j2}	$b_{j3} \ldots b_{jm}$	$\sum\limits_{k=1}^{m} w_k b_{jk} = B_j$

neither an attribute-based approach to choice nor do they offer any room for uncertainty beyond that associated with alternatives. Surely this is an unsatisfactory state of affairs.

Let us turn to an approach that is capable of addressing attribute uncertainty. Table 5.1 presents the basic decision matrix, in which a set of alternatives is related to a set of attributes. The alternatives can be thought of as "yea" or "nay" on a roll-call vote (then j would $= 2$); the attributes might be legislator ideology, party position, constituent preference, policy impact, or other consequences of the action. Note that the tradeoffs implied in the matrix are linear; we do not try to address the issue of nonlinear tradeoffs implied by declining marginal utility. This is a tradeoff itself that is well worth making, as we illustrate later.

To decide what action to take, a fully rational decision maker would (1) decide the attributes necessary to characterize the problem; (2) decide on the relevant alternative set; (3) add weights to each of the relevant attributes; (4) take a weighted sum of each of the alternatives across the attributes; and (5) select the alternative that receives the highest score. This last process would simply involve comparing the Bs. (In the spatial model of choice that most political scientists are familiar with, the Bs would be (inverse) distances from the ideal point of the decision maker on a line.)

Heuristic decision making involves a decision maker taking short cuts on this highly demanding process. For example, satisficing avoids weighting and summing by setting "aspiration levels" on each attribute; that is, the decision maker makes sure that an alternative is "good enough" on each attribute. Lexicographic decision making picks the attribute that is most important, and chooses the best alternative on that dimension; further study of attributes is eliminated. Whatever the strategy used for reducing a complex space will reduce uncertainty.

If the attribute space is only a single dimension, then rational choice is much simplified. Weighting and summing preferences across dimensions is unnecessary. Uncertainty in one-dimensional circumstances may be directly assessed by the variance of the alternative on the (single) attribute. The higher the variance, the more uncertain is the decision maker about the impact of the policy. Note, also, that in the multiattribute situation the actual choice is nevertheless made in a single dimension – the weighted net benefits dimension – rather than in the complex attribute-alternative space. *Choices are invariably made in one-dimensional spaces. As a consequence, how a complex, multiattribute decision space is collapsed into a single-dimension choice space is a critical aspect of democratic decision making.*

Just as heuristics can shape individual decisions, institutions can shape uncertainty in collective decision making. Legislatures can structure institutions to reduce uncertainty in collective decisions. When policies are technically complex, legislatures can delegate policy responsibility to experts in committees (Krehbiel 1991) or bureaucracies (Bawn 1995; Epstein and O'Halloran 1999). Although delegation can reduce some uncertainty, it does not eliminate all uncertainty inherent in collective decisions, particularly where policy proposals are judged along multiple evaluative dimensions. In such circumstances, as we discuss below, the inherent instability of majority decisions leaves boundedly rational decision makers uncertain about how their individual decision will influence collective outcomes.

FROM THE PROBLEM OR DEBATE SPACE TO THE CHOICE SPACE

Decision making in the policymaking process has elements in common with decision making in general, because of key aspects of the cognitive architecture of humans (Jones 2001). It also has a unique component, because of the institutional structure within which political decision making takes place. The institutional context can structure how decisions are made and the type of uncertainty actors confront when different rules shape how individual decisions are aggregated into collective outcomes. In a general sense, we examine in this chapter how these two elements interact in the legislative process.

In the language of cognitive psychology, the problem space is the symbolic reconstruction of the problem facing the individual. It is an "in the head" reconstruction of the task that faces the decision maker. The design problem is how an individual fits a problem space (how he or she understands a problem) to the actual problem that he or she faces (Simon 1977). The path-breaking problem-solving studies of Allen Newell and Herbert Simon (1972;

Simon 1996) fixed the problem by prespecifying it, and then examined the process of problem solving against this objective background. For example, they studied crypt-arithmetic, in which subjects are asked to manipulate letters that stand for numbers and for which there exists a single solution. This allowed the study of problem-solving strategies against a fixed task environment with attention directed by experimenters, thereby controlling much of the inputs that would occur in real-world decision making. Problem-solving experimenters used a process tracing methodology to examine (and model with computers) the methods used by subjects. A major finding of these studies was the reliance on heuristic decision making, cognitive short cuts that often mislead the problem-solver, and a great deal of trial-and-error in search for solutions.

In political debate, of course, there is often no agreed-on problem definition. The policy solution employed is contingent on the definition of the problem, and much political debate concerns how to characterize a complex policy issue (Rochefort and Cobb 1994). Moreover, problem solutions involve not just what might work to solve a policy challenge, but also involve ways to solve other political challenges – constituency preferences, interest group inputs, legal and constitutional constraints. As a consequence of such political complexity, search processes in politics involve two kinds of very distinct processes. One is a search for new alternatives to solve a problem, at least solve it given our current understanding of the problem. Traditional policy analysis is directed at this kind of search and evaluation of the discovered alternatives.

The other procedure involves a "search" for the proper attributes that characterize the alternatives. We do not normally think of this process as a search, and often refer to the discovery of a new attribute as the "recognition of relevance." Suddenly we see that the problem we are addressing can be viewed in a completely different light. The mathematical analogue of this phenomenon is adding a new dimension or attribute to the problem space.[4] The problem we address may have exactly the same alternative set, but the shift in dimensionality means that the existing alternatives are reevaluated.

Information is often organized relative to attributes, but in many situations the relevant attributes are either not so clear or the set of relevant attributes is open – that is, new attributes may be brought in to the structure of the choice situation. In the complex or fluid situations that often characterize politics, the limited cognitive capacity of humans to process information generally causes a collapse of the complex structure of political reality into a more limited (that is, lower dimensional) decisional space. The decision maker generally attends to fewer dimensions than the situation, objectively, requires (Jones 1994; Margolis 1987; Steinbrunner 1974), and may,

---

[4] The adding of a new dimension in a choice situation is mathematically equivalent to a shift in the weight of that dimension from zero to some positive value.

for example, force issues into a low-dimensional ideological space (Hinich and Munger 1994).

Uncertainty problems are exacerbated in collective decision making, particularly for choices with many alternatives and multiple evaluative attributes. One primary source of problems is cycling. In collective decision making on issues with multiple evaluative dimensions, any majority decision can be overturned by a countermajority. In such contexts, individuals can be uncertain about what the ultimate majority decision will be. Strategic behavior further exacerbates this uncertainty. Consider the case of killer amendments, amendments proposed to destroy rather than improve a bill (Wilkerson 1999). A legislator deciding whether to support a killer amendment would need to know not only her own preferences across all alternatives and attributes (properly weighted by the net benefit rule as in Table 1), but also the preferences of the other legislators (and whether they will behave strategically). Moreover, different institutional arrangements such as rules governing agenda control, amendments and so on, can affect how uncertainty for both individuals making decisions and how individual decisions are aggregated to collective outcomes. In such situations, picking the decision strategy that will best maximize the outcome requires knowing other actors' preferences, decision strategies, and how they interact with the rules governing the decision context.

To better understand collective uncertainty as opposed to individual uncertainty, consider for example the case of buying a car. For an individual, the task boils down to identifying the relevant attributes (gas mileage, size, safety, etc.), the relevant alternative set (the makes and models of the cars and their options), the importance of the attributes (e.g., gas mileage vs. safety), taking the weighted sum of these attributes and selecting the car with the highest score. However, consider the case in which a group is making a choice about what car it should buy. How will group preferences be aggregated? Will the members first vote on the relative importance of the attributes? (e.g., whether to pursue a safe, but gas guzzling vehicle?). Or, will the group rank order their preferences from a list of cars (e.g., first preference for the Honda Prelude, second preference for the Ford Fiesta, etc.). Depending on the rules for aggregating group preferences into collective decisions, the preferences and weights across the various attributes, and the decisions of the other members of the group, a member may engage in a variety of strategies for getting the group decision closest to her desired outcome. For example, one member may attempt a logroll by supporting another member's proposal (perhaps that the car purchased have a sun roof) in exchange for the member's support for her own proposal (to buy a car with front wheel drive).

Majority decision cycling, logrolling, and other strategic behaviors make it difficult to predict the outcome of collective decision making using members' preferences alone, particularly when the group members face both attribute and alternative uncertainty about their own choices and those of other members of the group. Thus, collective decision uncertainty is heightened even further as options are assessed along multiple evaluative dimensions, even though for individuals the final decision is reduced through computation or heuristic to a single dimensional choice.

For reasons of heuristic coping with complex choice situations and the problematic nature of collective choice, the structure of the low-dimensional attribute space within which choices are made will almost never completely correspond to objective, high-dimensional political reality. Fitting a problem-space to a multifaceted reality invariably involves distortion. We need not (indeed, the authors of this chapter do not) assume a relativistic reality. All we need to recognize is that decisions must be made in lower dimensional spaces than the reality on which we operate.

TYPES OF UNCERTAINTY

In light of the above discussion, we may distinguish between four distinct concepts, all relating to the notion of uncertainty. They are:

AMBIVALENCE: Ambivalence occurs when people are aware of the attributes that structure a choice but are conflicted about how to balance or tradeoff the attributes. Ambivalence occurs only when a problem is well understood; that is, a design for the problem has been specified.

ALTERNATIVE UNCERTAINTY: This type of uncertainty occurs when people are unsure of the consequences of an act, when consequences are defined along a single dimension. Alternative uncertainty may be assessed by the variance of the decision consequences (Gilligan and Krehbiel, 1990, 546). This is the traditional understanding of uncertainty.

ATTRIBUTE UNCERTAINTY: This type of uncertainty occurs when decision makers are unsure of the decision design. That is, they are unsure of just what attributes are relevant to the choice, and they are uncertain about what weights to apply to these attributes when evaluating the value of the alternatives that are being actively considered. This form of uncertainty is more complex to measure, but is associated with the variance of the b coefficients in Table 5.1 (see Jones 1996).

COLLECTIVE DECISION UNCERTAINTY: This type of uncertainty can occur when groups make majority decisions across multiple evaluative dimensions. In such contexts where majority cycles and strategic behavior are possible, individual decision makers may not know how their choices will affect collective outcomes. Such uncertainty can exist even under perfect information, although imperfect information can certainly exacerbate it.

A key contention here is that reduction in dimensionality reduces uncertainty. This is not an obvious implication of the argument presented here, however. If a set of alternatives are embedded in a high-dimensional space, and the symbolic space used by participants in the policy debate matches the true task environment, then uncertainty (in some objective sense) would be low. A mismatch would theoretically increase uncertainty. *Uncertainty, however, is not simply an objective entity, any more than utility is. Uncertainty has an important subjective component.* Experienced or subjective uncertainty is almost certainly associated with high-dimensional problem spaces. Human information-processing, which is basically a serial process, dictates extreme difficulties in handling complex, multifaceted stimuli in which tradeoffs among goals are involved (Jones 1994, 2001). Most of us feel more uncertain when faced by a confusing, multiattribute problem than when we face a low-dimensional, fully specified choice structure.

This suggests separating *bias* in the fit of a design to a problem from *uncertainty* (Jones 1996). Bias could be theoretically measured by the degree of fit between the design employed by a decision maker and the actual dimensionality needed to structure a choice. This is likely to be impossible in practice; but let us note that many of the debates about whether political choice is one-dimensional or multifaceted is addressed at the bias implied in using single-dimensional models to study political choice.

Subjective attribute-based uncertainty is almost certainly attenuated with a reduction in the dimensionality of the problem or debate space within which policies are considered. This is only one source of uncertainty, the other being alternative-based uncertainty, which is associated with the precision with which a policy is located on a dimension. Collapsing a dimensional choice space has the consequence of reducing one source of uncertainty, but it will not reduce alternative uncertainty.

Finally, we reemphasize that human decision making is premised on *subjective*, not objective, uncertainty. People make decisions based on their estimates of utility *and* on their estimates of uncertainty. The connection between objective and subjective uncertainty is an issue for empirical study.

SEARCH

How do complex spaces get simplified in politics? In problem-solving studies, much trial-and-error occurs as people try one method of solving the problem, work it through, and then discard it to try another. This is the traditional idea of search – alternative by alternative. But in real-world decision making, trial-and-error search procedures also affect the construction of a design space. What attributes are critical for understanding a problem, and what weights are these attributes to be given in evaluating the outcome?

Much political debate involves arguments concerning the relevant attributes that characterize a decision design. Is a tax cut proposal a choice about whether to spend money on public proposals or to return money to taxpayers, on the one hand, or is it about macroeconomic effects, on the other? Actually, in this case as in many others, there are many other potentially relevant attributes. What do constituents want? What public programs are in need of funding? What is the effect on the debt (and hence the long-run viability of government programs)? Why not address the payroll tax rather than income tax rates? How should any reduction in tax rates be phased in?

Lots of attributes are potentially relevant to a tax cut proposal, or any other complex policy proposal. Often political debate is predictable and not productive, but just as often the exploration of attributes underlying a choice is instructive and dynamic. If there existed complete certainty about the set of attributes that characterizes a policy proposal, there would be little need for (or opportunity for) political debate.

Once a design space is established, a decision-maker can evaluate and compare the relative benefits of each alternative (the extent of the tax cut, from none to $X). Strictly speaking, these calculations cannot be done until the design is established. In practice, in political debates, the two processes are often conflated.

WINNOWING POLICY DIMENSIONALITY

In the policy-making process, institutional arrangements act to limit the consideration of high-dimensional spaces. In effect, the actions of institutions winnow high-dimensional debate spaces into manageable choice spaces. How does this happen? We direct our attention to the U.S. legislative process.

Theories of public policy describe a process in which ideas first become issues on the legislative arena through bill introductions, pass through committees, and reach the floor for final decision. Each legislative session, thousands of bills are introduced, yet only a select fraction progress through the entire legislative process to become public laws. At any stage in the process in which an individual legislator must make a choice, the complex debate space, consisting of multiple attributes, must be somehow collapsed into a single-dimensional choice space. Thus, by the time issues are decided on the legislative floor, legislators' decisions exhibit a unidimensional structure, with virtually all bills (and legislators) aligned along a liberal-conservative continuum. Scholars have posited a variety of institutional explanations for how this winnowing occurs; explanations include gatekeeping committees (Shepsle and Weingast 1981, 1987), parties (Aldrich 1995; Cox and McCubbins 1993; Rohde 1991) or some combination of institutions (Maltzman 1997).

In this chapter, we do not identify the precise process underlying the dimensional reduction, although a few candidates stand out. The legislative process may select only those bills that align legislators along a single dimension. Conversely, logrolling and vote trading across dimensions may realign multidimensional coalitions along a single dimension. Each of these explanations have an important dynamic in common: the legislative agenda as revealed through roll call voting on the floor will appear to be low-dimensional, even if the underlying issue agenda before the floor is multi-dimensional, because of structure induced equilibrium arrangements such as institutionalized vote trading and logrolling (whether through committees or parties). In either case, the lower dimensional structure of floor voting greatly simplifies legislators' decision process. Without complex, multidimensional voting, there is little room for the various strategies that complicate collective decision making.

The most conspicuous point at which all or most legislators must make explicit choices is the floor voting stage. By this point, legislative institutions have collapsed a complex, multidimensional issue agenda down to a unidimensional set of decisions. Once the one-dimensional choice space is constructed, then for the rational legislator the task is to maximize utility, which in the spatial model is assumed to be choosing the policy that is the shortest distance between the legislator's ideal point on the choice dimension.

The collapsing of a complex decision space into a simple choice space is depicted in Figure 5.2. Two alternatives are characterized by three attributes in the debate space. But through a winnowing process, this complex debate space is winnowed into a single-dimensional choice space, perhaps liberal to conservative ideology (Hinich and Munger 1994). However the winnowing takes place, judgment in the choice space is straightforward; our hypothetical

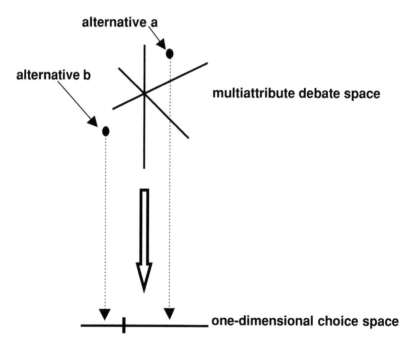

FIGURE 5.2. A Complex Debate Space is Winnowed into a One-Dimensional Choice Space

legislator votes for alternative b (as it is the closest to his or her ideal point in the choice space).

It is of course possible that different legislators harbor different single-dimensional choice spaces. The existing literature strongly suggests that there exists a low-dimensional choice space at the floor voting stage (and perhaps a one-dimensional alignment) (Poole and Rosenthal 1997). So, analytically, the process of winnowing occurs for all individuals asked to make a choice, but in reality the process of shedding dimensionality from the debate space occurs collectively and institutionally.

The collapsing of a high-dimensional debate space into a single-dimensional choice space has the consequence of reducing both attribute uncertainty and collective decision uncertainty (by definition). But uncertainty is only part of the issue of choice; the other involves bias. If the debate space is collapsed in a manner that leads to a misrepresentation of the original problem that the proposed legislation was designed to address, then *bias* has been introduced. Whether the collapsed space has resulted in bias depends on how the space has been reduced. If the net benefits rule is used, then the collapsed choice space is just a direct simplification of the complex problem space. If, by contrast, heuristic shortcuts are used, then the existence of bias is an empirical question. The institutional aggregation of individual decisions into collective choice also may restructure the content of individual choices.

EMPIRICAL ANALYSIS

Our goal is to test whether the dimensional structure of issues is reduced during the legislative process, which we argue would be associated with a reduction of subjective uncertainty. Few methods are available to produce the ideal test of the dimensional structure of issues. Most involve taking static snapshots of the dimensional structure at successive points through time. The literature has usually taken one of two paths: a detailed case study approach for a few selected issues, or an aggregated scaling approach for all issues. The case study approach offers the most compelling evidence, yet critics raise important questions as to the generalizability of the findings. The aggregate scaling exercises answer the generalizability question, but are subject to interpretation difficulty. Because we are modeling how uncertainty is reduced through the legislative process, we feel the comprehensive approach offers the best method to explore the dimensional structure of all issues at two distinct points in the policy process.

To model the dimensional structure of political issues, we analyze legislators' floor votes and bill cosponsoring during the 103rd and 104th Congresses. Bill cosponsoring provides a first opportunity for members to reveal issue preferences on bills before they reach the floor for final vote. Analyzing these decisions can allow comparisons of the dimensional structure of the decision space (legislative floor, where uncertainty is low) and the debate space (bill cosponsoring, where uncertainty is high). Of the few systematically observable actions of members prior to formal committee action, sponsoring and cosponsoring legislation offer the best indicators of member behavior (Schiller 1995).

For each Congress, we recorded whether each member cosponsored each proposed bill (scored one, else zero), as reported by the *Legislate* information service. There were 6,632 and 4,900 sponsored bills in the 103rd and 104th Congresses, respectively. Of those sponsored bills, our dataset includes the 3,303 bills in the 103rd Congress that had at least one cosponsor, and 3,152 bills in the 104th Congress that had at least one cosponsor. The average number of cosponsors per bill was 16 in the 103rd Congress and 14 in the 104th. Finally, we obtained roll call voting data from Poole and Rosenthal's data warehouse. For each recorded floor vote, each legislator's "yes" vote is scored one and "no" votes scored zero. There were 1,094 roll call votes in the 103rd congress and 1,321 roll call votes in the 104th.

To test for the dimensional structure of issues through the legislative process, we apply Poole and Rosenthal's (1997) nominal three-step estimation (NOMINATE) procedure to floor votes and bill cosponsoring data for the 103rd and 104th Congresses. Poole and Rosenthal's NOMINATE is available on their website along with detailed instructions for preparing the datasets for analysis, and for interpreting the output. We organized the cosponsoring information according to NOMINATE format and computed the dimensions for each Congress. The task for the floor voting was somewhat simpler, since the data is readily available in the proper format. We computed the floor dimensions using the same methods.

NOMINATE is a statistical technique similar to factor analysis that has proven effective for identifying the dimensional structure of binary choice data (Poole and Rosenthal 1997). NOMINATE applies a logit specification to binary data in order to compute dimension scores that gauge each legislator's position along multiple spatial dimensions, thus measuring the number of evaluative dimensions legislators use when making bill cosponsoring decisions and roll call voting decisions.

As in all dimensioning techniques, there is no formal statistical test for identifying the number of dimensions in NOMINATE. Interpretation is based on several components, usually with multiple sources of comparative information. We follow Poole and Rosenthal's (1997) criteria and use the Aggregate Proportional Reduction in Error (APRE). In the analysis below, each significant dimension improves the fit of the model (reduces the error as indicated by a high APRE). Thus, our test compares the APRE for cosponsoring with the APRE for floor voting.

One problem using scaling methodology concerns how many dimensions we can expect the method to extract from roll call and cosponsoring data. NOMINATE has come under critique for underestimating the number of roll call dimensions (Heckman and Snyder 1997; Koford 1991), although if these charges are valid, they apply both to our roll call and cosponsoring NOMINATE analyses. In other words, if NOMINATE underestimates the number of roll call dimensions, it also underestimates the number of bill cosponsoring dimensions. It is also the case that ideology or party identification can constrain the dimensionality of the cosponsorship estimates of the debate space. Using cosponsorships to estimate the debate space is conservative; it is likely to yield fewer dimensions than a hypothetically pure measure of the debate space would yield.

Results

APRE is that amount that an additional dimension improves the statistical fit of the model (reduces the number of errors). Figure 5.3 compares the APRE increases for each additional dimension in NOMINATE analyses of roll call votes and bill cosponsoring for the 103rd and 104th Congresses. Following Poole and Rosenthal's (1997) relatively informal standards, we look for the number of dimensions that increase the APRE by more than 2 percent,

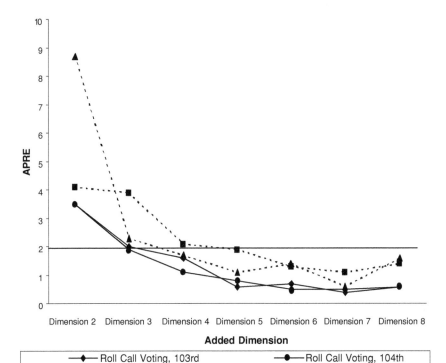

FIGURE 5.3. Changes in APRE with Added Dimensions in Roll Call and Cosponsoring, House of Representatives (103rd and 104th Congresses)

which indicates the point beyond which adding additional dimensions fails to improve the fit of the model. Figure 5.3 shows the remaining relevant information.

Figure 5.3 indicates that in both Congresses bill cosponsoring (dashed lines) contain more dimensions than roll call voting (solid line). The APRE increases for the 103rd Congress bill cosponsoring exceeds both the 2 percent threshold and the roll call APRE increases through the fourth dimension. The 104th Congress shows a similar, though less pronounced, pattern. The APRE increases for bill cosponsoring clearly exceeds the 2 percent threshold for three dimensions, suggesting that the prefloor issue debates are divided along multiple dimensions. In both Congresses, the roll call APRE increase exceeds 2 percent only for the second dimension, suggesting a lower dimensional decision structure than the structure of prefloor legislative issues.

Thus APRE results for the 103rd and 104th Congresses suggest that there are three to four dimensions in bill cosponsoring and one dimension in the floor voting. A distinct collapsing of the initial debate space seems to have occurred. (Extended analysis of the dimensional and issue-content of the dimensions can be found in Talbert and Potoski 2002.)

All in all, dimensional analyses of legislators' cosponsoring and floor voting decisions suggest that the decision context facing legislators varies dramatically at different stages of the legislative process. At the problem or debate phase, where policy proposals are introduced and debated, the agenda is quite complicated as legislators look to package their proposals along favorable dimensions. In this context, legislators' uncertainty is high. At the individual level, multiple evaluative dimensions complicate legislators' assessments of the relevant attributes of policy proposals. At the collective level, issues and proposals in the debate phase are ripe for the serial shifts (Jones 1994), logrolling, and issue manipulation that characterize legislative strategy. After passing through the legislative machinery – through the committee hearings and review, party caucuses, and so on – the dimensional structure of these bills has been substantially simplified. Roll call voting is essentially unidimensional, and thus legislators' uncertainty is much lower for floor voting than for decisions made prior to the floor.

CONCLUSIONS

In this chapter, we argue that uncertainty in policy debates has several sources. One is associated with variability in how participants character-ize a problem; we associate this characterization with the dimensionality of the matrix relating alternatives to the attributes that underlie the alternatives. A second, more familiar, source is variability on the location of a policy on the attributes. Both of these components enter the decision-making process through their subjective manifestations. That is, people make decisions not on objective uncertainty, but of their estimates of uncertainty, in a manner analogous to subjective utility. A final source of uncertainty occurs when institutions aggregate individual decisions into collective outcomes. Majority cycling and strategic behavior undermine individual legislators' ability to anticipate how their decisions will influence the collective choice.

Using measures of the dimensionality of legislative choices, we show that the space characterizing the introduction of bills in Congress is of higher dimensionality than in the roll call voting stage. We cannot be sure that the collapsing of this space is associated with the reduction of subjective uncertainty, but the finding is instructive. In any case, we observe that the dimensionality of the space within which policy proposals are introduced and presumably debated is more complex, in terms of the attributes needed to characterize the space, than the space within which final policy choices are made.

References

Aldrich, John H. 1995. *Why Parties? The Origin and Transformation of Political Parties in America.* Chicago: The University of Chicago Press.

Bawn, Kathleen. 1995. "Political Control versus Expertise: Congressional Choices about Administrative Procedures." *American Political Science Review* 89: 62–73.

Cox, Gary W., and Mathew D. McCubbins. 1993. *Legislative Leviathan: Party Government in the House.* Berkeley: University of California Press.

Epstein, David, and Sharyn O'Halloran. 1999. *Delegating Powers: A Transaction Cost Politics Approach to Policy Making under Separate Powers.* New York: Cambridge University Press.

Gilligan, Thomas, and Keith Krehbiel. 1989. "Asymmetric Information and Legislative Rules with a Heterogeneous Committee." *American Journal of Political Science* 33:459–90.

Gilligan, Thomas, and Keith Krehbiel. 1990. "Organization of Information is a Rational Legislative." *American Journal of Political Science* 34:531–64.

Heckman, James J., and James M. Snyder. 1997. "Linear Probability Models of the Demand for Attributes with and Empirical Application to Estimating the Preferences of Legislators." *RAND Journal of Economics* 28:S142–S189.

Hinich, Melvin, and Michael Munger. 1994. *Ideology and the Theory of Political Choice.* Ann Arbor: The University of Michigan Press.

Jones, Bryan D. 1994. *Reconceiving Decision-Making in Democratic Politics.* Chicago: The University of Chicago Press.

Jones, Bryan D. 1996. *Attributes, Alternatives, and the Flow of Ideas: Information Processing in Politics.* Seattle: Center for American Politics and Public Policy, University of Washington.

Jones, Bryan D. 2001. *Politics and the Architecture of Choice.* Chicago: The University of Chicago Press.

Koford, Kenneth. 1991. "Dimensions in Congressional Voting." *The American Political Science Review* 83:949–62.

Krehbiel, Keith. 1991. *Information and Legislative Organization.* Ann Arbor: The University of Michigan Press.

Maltzman, Forrest. 1997. *Competing Principals.* Ann Arbor, MI: University of Michigan Press.

March, James A. 1994. *A Primer on Decision-Making.* New York: Free Press.

Margolis, Howard. 1987. *Patterns, Thinking and Cognition.* Chicago: The University of Chicago Press.

Newell, Allen, and Herbert A. Simon. 1972. *Human Problem Solving.* Englewood Cliffs, NJ: Prentice Hall.

Poole, Keith, and Howard Rosenthal. 1997. *Congress: A Political-Economic History of Roll Call Voting.* New York: Oxford University Press.

Potoski, Matthew. 2001. "Implementation, Uncertainty, and the Policy Sciences." *Policy Currents* 11:2–5.

Potoski, Matthew and Jeffery Talbert. 2000. "The Dimensional Structure of Policy Outputs: Distributive Policy and Roll Call Voting." *Political Research Quarterly* 53:695–710.

Rochefort, David, and Roger Cobb, ed. 1994. *The Politics of Problem Definition.* Lawrence: University Press of Kansas.

Riker, William H. 1986. *The Art of Political Manipulation.* New Haven, CT: Yale University Press.

Rohde, David W. 1991. *Parties and Leaders in the Postreform House.* Chicago: The University of Chicago Press.

Schiller, Wendy J. 1995. "Senators as Political Entrepreneurs: Using Bill Sponsorship to Shape Legislative Agendas." *American Journal of Political Science* 39:186–203.

Shepsle, Kenneth A., and Barry Weingast. 1981. "Structure-Induced Equilibrium and Legislative Choice." *Public Choice* 37:503–29.

Shepsle, Kenneth A., and Barry Weingast. 1987. "Why are Congressional Committees Powerful?" *American Political Science Review* 81:929–45.

Simon, Herbert A. 1977. *Models of Discovery.* Boston, MA: D. Reidel.

Simon, Herbert A. 1996. *The Sciences of the Artificial.* 3rd ed. Cambridge, MA: MIT Press.

Steinbrunner, John D. 1974. *The Cybernetic Theory of Decision: New Dimensions of Political Analysis.* Princeton, NJ: Princeton University Press.

Talbert, Jeffery and Matthew Potoski. 2002. "Transforming Issue Debates into Policy Decisions." *Journal of Politics* 64:864–91.

Tversky, Amos. 1972. "Elimination by Aspects: A Theory of Choice." *Psychological Review* 79:281–99.

Wilkerson, John D. 1999. "'Killer' Amendments in Congress." *American Political Science Review* 93:535–52.

PART 2

CITIZEN AND ELECTORAL POLITICS

6

Declining Uncertainty: Presidents, Public Opinion, and Polls

John G. Geer
Prateek Goorha

The purpose of our chapter is to encourage scholars to think differently about the concept of *uncertainty*. We know that decisions of all sorts are confronted by the lack of perfect information. This obstacle is a permanent feature of decision making. It is, of course, sometimes important theoretically to assume that perfect information exists. For instance, the analytic usefulness of the theory of perfect competition is beyond doubt, and rests in part on the assumption of full information. However, that approach reflects an effort to improve our understanding of decision making by considering it in a pristine setting. The real world is far different, making it critical that we pay close attention to the impact of uncertainty on the behavior of key actors or institutions. Of course, the very purpose of this edited volume is to advance the understanding of this subject within the context of American politics.

We hope to advance this goal by taking a slightly unorthodox look at the topic. Many of the chapters in this book address how uncertainty poses a stumbling block for good (or at least efficient) decision making. That perspective is, of course, not only reasonable, but also important, especially as we puzzle over the workings of American politics. Rather than seeking to sort out the role of uncertainty in political decision making, however, we want to offer a different line of thought: that while uncertainty exists and will surely always exist, changes in the amount of information available to decision makers varies over time, making uncertainty a *dynamic*, time dependent concept. So, although we may be "uncertain" about the political landscape, we may in some cases be *less* uncertain than in the past. The rise of the "information age" suggests (implicitly) that the level of uncertainty is not likely to be constant across time. If this is true, any shift in the amount of accurate information will have important implications for decision making.

We thank Ben Radcliff and Geoff Layman for helpful comments on an earlier draft. We also want to express our appreciation to Barry Burden for his support and advice about this project. Without his patience and efforts, this chapter would never have been written.

To make this argument, this chapter has four parts.[1] First, we clarify briefly how we think about uncertainty, drawing explicit attention to different *levels* of it. Second, we talk about the rise of public opinion polls as a good example of this potential change in uncertainty and how the polls have lessened uncertainty about presidents' knowledge of public opinion. Third, we consider how declining uncertainty about public opinion may have altered the behavior of presidents over the last seventy-five years, which, in turn, suggests a potential rethinking of the institution of the presidency and the actors who occupy that office. In the last (and fourth) section we shall conclude with some general observations about the need to think of uncertainty in an ever-changing historical context. Our goal here is to introduce a new perspective in the study of the presidency and to encourage scholars to think differently about uncertainty.

CONCEPTUAL UNDERPINNINGS

The typical decision is to assume either a situation of "certainty" or "uncertainty." This dichotomy is quite crude, covering up some potentially important differences. While certainty concerns one identifiable (and unrealistic) category, the latter, in common parlance, involves a vast range of possibilities. Burden (2003, 6), in the introduction to this book, makes this exact point, noting that uncertainty should be thought of as an "amount or a degree rather than as a quality that is merely present or absent." Following Burden's lead, it makes sense to realize that different decision-making contexts should have differing amounts of information and hence, differing amounts of uncertainty. Here we note that even within the same context, the level of information possessed can be vastly different among the relevant actors. These are two distinct types of information asymmetries. This point is obvious, yet it is usually underappreciated.

For decision theorists, whether they study business management or political economics, a given event or situation is characterized by uncertainty *ex ante* if a known or readily estimable probability schedule cannot be ascribed to it. According to this definition of uncertainty, however, it is important for us to acknowledge the difference between risk and uncertainty, for in the former it *is* possible to ascribe a probability schedule to the outcomes.[2] It should be clear then that uncertainty is usually a less desirable state of affairs than is risk, because uncertainty does not allow for any measurement of it, whereas risk can be measured, albeit with error. This provides us with a more interesting foundation for debate on "uncertainty" than does a dichotomous

---

[1] Many of these parts build on and extend Geer's (1996) *From Tea Leaves to Opinion Polls*.

[2] The treatment of uncertainty and risk in such a manner is not novel and is at least as old as the seminal contribution on uncertainty made by Knight (1921). See Arrow (1951) for a shorter and more formal summary.

view of uncertainty, in which an event is certain if we know which action leads to what outcome and uncertain if we do not. An infinite number of combinations and gradations are possible if we allow risk to be a sliding scale and certainty and uncertainty the endpoints.[3]

In an effort to illustrate our general argument, let us consider the recent changes in information that involve purchasing a car. Twenty years ago, car buyers did not have a lot of information about the actual cost of the car and the price of upgrades, such as air conditioning or a sun roof. Now nearly all that information is available via the Internet and other sources, in part because of increased competition. The end result of this has been a transformation in the car business. First, dealers no longer receive as big a profit on new automobiles, because buyers' uncertainty has lessened dramatically, forcing dealers to compete for the business of more informed buyers. Hence, the public pays less for cars than they would under the old information regime. Second, the haggling that often was associated with new car purchases has diminished in light of this decrease in uncertainty to the point where some automobile manufacturers (e.g., Saturn) just have a set price for a vehicle and have done away with bargaining. Third, car dealers now have turned to service and used cars as the important ways to turn a profit and urge buyers instead to purchases extended warranties (playing on their uncertainty about the car's long-term reliability).[4]

We are hardly the first to argue that uncertainty involves a range of possible values, varying, in effect, between 0 and 1 where 0 stands in for certain outcomes and 1 for fully uncertain outcomes.[5] We also are not the first to note that there have been changes in the amount of uncertainty across different decision-making contexts. However, we want to draw attention to changes in uncertainty *within* a given decision-making context. That is, if there are shifts in the kinds of information available, we should see a concomitant change in the behavior of relevant actors. These shifts can fall along at least two dimensions.

---

[3] To frame this distinction in more familiar terms for political scientists, we can imagine a continuum mapping the distribution of voters' preferences as estimated by politicians. If we assume that the median voter's position is the point of interest for support-seeking politicians, the condition of complete information would be akin to drawing a perpendicular line through the median voter's preferences. There would be no doubt where the voters' opinions and attitudes lie for rational politicians. A risky outcome, by contrast, is one that faces a situation of higher variance *and* higher bias in estimating the median voter's preferred outcome. A completely uncertain outcome is one where no probabilistic estimate exists for the median voter's position. Because this technical definition of uncertainty is of little interest for this chapter, we will merge this notion of risk within the conceptual category of uncertainty.

[4] This of course is not surprising, because the premise of Akerlof's (1970) seminal piece on uncertainty was indeed the market for "lemons" where measurement costs are higher than in the new car market due to information asymmetry.

[5] Our view does differ a bit from Burden's. We are folding his scale presented in the introductory chapter, using a continuum of uncertainties rather than a continuum of probabilities.

The first is historical or temporal: decision makers at one point in time might behave systematically different than decision makers at another point. Consider the conduct of the recent war on terrorism. The American military was awash in information about troop strength of the Taliban, the locations of these forces, and their capabilities. That context affected greatly the decisions made by the American high command. By contrast, consider the situation facing the many generals of the U.S. Civil War. They confronted a situation with high levels of uncertainty. They were not sure where or how many troops the opposition possessed. The uncertainty led to numerous mistakes and misjudgments on the battlefield. Would Lee have fought at Gettysburg if Stewart had provided the critical information he needed about the disposition of Union troops?[6]

The other dimension of this argument falls under the general rubric of comparative politics. If we seek to study the behavior of voters, for example, it would be important as we develop a general theory to realize that different contexts will have varying levels of information available to voters. Numerous factors, depending on how we specify our model, would dictate the context. The level of literacy might be one relevant variable. The extent of a vibrant free press also would be important, as would the degree to which the government collects and releases data about the state of the nation, providing grist for the mills of the public and of elites. So as we develop theories about political actors of all types, we need to be sensitive to the different "information" environments they face as they make their decisions. For the purposes of this book, concerning American politics, we shall set aside the study of comparative politics and aim our fire at this historical angle.[7]

THE RISE OF POLLS AND THE DECLINE OF UNCERTAINTY

We shall argue below that the rise of polls represents a significant change in the amount of uncertainty politicians face about the state of public opinion (see Geer 1996).[8] Polls do not, of course, represent anything close to "perfect" information.[9] But because they represent a sufficient departure

---

[6] It is also worth noting that the *speed* with which information now reaches decision makers is much faster than in the past. This change warrants attention as well and helps contribute to this decline of uncertainty. We make a few brief references to this issue in our chapter, but it is not our focus.

[7] One could quibble with the distinction we make between the historical and comparative dimension, as both can be thought of as falling under the broad umbrella of "context." Although true, we make this distinction because political science is defined by subfields and we simply want to work within those intellectual traditions.

[8] Ferejohn and Noll (1978) also offer an important perspective on the role of uncertainty in the study of politicians and view polls as one way politicians can lessen their uncertainty. Their argument is different than ours, but it is a valuable contribution in this general area.

[9] One need only scan the vast amount of research on public opinion to come across frequent warnings about the errors embedded in the results of survey research (Brehm 1993;

from the politics prior to the 1930s and 1940s, we can usefully think of politicians falling within two different eras of information: prepoll (i.e., poorly informed) and postpoll (i.e., well informed).[10]

This historical perspective is critical to understanding our basic argument. For example, Robert Eisinger (2000) titled his book on presidential polling *The Illusion of Certainty*. That title highlights a view of polls and their importance that differs markedly from our argument. Although polls do not provide absolute certainty, it is the comparison between the quality of information about public opinion provided by polls to what was available prior to polls that defines our argument. That even though certainty about public opinion remains an illusion, declining uncertainty is, nevertheless, a reality. In the same spirit as Eisinger, Larry Jacobs and Robert Shapiro (2000) argue that politicians do not pander to public opinion. Again, it is true that politicians do not blindly follow polls. They are, as Jacobs and Shapiro point out, too smart for that kind of knee-jerk reaction. However, it is quite likely that politicians now "pander" *more* to public opinion than before because of the rise of polls and the resulting increase in accurate information that is now available to politicians.[11] Hence, under the logic of our argument, the title of Jacobs and Shapiro's book might read "Politicians Now Pander More."

Polls and Declining Uncertainty[12]

Have polls changed the level of uncertainty? Our answer is a resounding yes. Surveys, despite their flaws, represent a significant improvement in the

Crespi 1988; Erikson and Tedin 2000; Mueller 1994; Page and Shapiro 1992; Stimson 1991; Zaller 1992).

[10] The pre-poll era, as defined here, only concerns that period from the extension of mass suffrage in the 1820s to the advent of polls. The situation was probably much different prior to the 1800s, when electorates were very small and voting was public. In the eighteenth century, there were so few voters in legislative districts (often less than two hundred; Kelley 1983), politicians could learn *firsthand* of their constituents' preferences. For an interesting and informative historical account of measuring public opinion, see Herbst (1993). While the development of polls serves as the turning point in the quality of information available to politicians, the break is not quite so clean as we are suggesting. The history of the public opinion poll itself is an interesting one. At first, pollsters used flawed theories of sampling (Converse 1987; Crespi 1988) and paid little attention initially to the effects of question-wording (Kahneman and Tversky 1984). Thus, early polls contained lots of errors, as best symbolized by the famous 1948 misprediction of Thomas Dewey's victory over Harry Truman. But over the last fifty years, much progress has been made on these fronts (Brehm 1993; Converse 1987; Moore 1992; Schuman and Presser 1981).

[11] We would quibble, by the way, with the term "pander." It is quite possible that politicians who pander are also being more democratic, that is, responding to the wishes of the public. One person's "pander" may be another person's "responsiveness." This debate does not fit in the context of this chapter, but we still wanted to signal our reservations with the normative implications of the term pander.

[12] This section comes largely from Geer (1996); see that book for even more discussion of polls, information, and uncertainty.

quality of information available to politicians. At one level this point is obvious, as few would argue that polls do not represent at least a modest increase in the quality of information available about public opinion. But the amount of increase becomes clearer when we recall explicitly the kinds of information available prior to polls. In so doing, we get a better sense of how polling data led to an important shift in politicians' ability to read public opinion.

When prepoll politicians wanted to get a handle on public opinion, they could turn to a wide variety of sources for such information. Among the more common ones were the results of previous elections, attendance at political rallies, content of newspapers, letters from constituents, personal conversations with supporters, views of political allies, and the claims of relevant interest groups (see Bryce 1921; Converse and Pierce 1986; Eisinger 2000, 2001; Exline 1922; Ginsberg 1986; Herbst 1993; Mendelsohn and Crespi 1970; Smith 1939).

These sources of information have two basic flaws. First, politicians had to infer the electorate's opinions from *indirect* indicators. So rather than getting readings from a cross-section of citizens, politicians had to weave various bits and pieces of information into some general notion of what the public actually desired. Eric Foner (1988, 315), for instance, reports that the Democratic gains in the 1867 local elections convinced Republican "moderates that issues like disenfranchisement, black voting in the North and impeachment must be avoided at all costs." McPherson (1988, 688) finds that Republicans interpreted the GOP gains in the 1863 elections "as signs of a transformation of public opinion toward emancipation." But, of course, the connection between the proportion of votes cast for a particular party in any election and the public's thinking on specific issues is tenuous at best (Dahl 1990; Kelley 1983).

Grover Cleveland, by contrast, used newspapers as a guide to sorting out the public's views on the possible repeal of the Sherman Silver Purchase Act (Glad 1964, 80). William McKinley also was interested in tracking opinion during his presidency, especially in regard to the Spanish-American conflict. To make these judgments, McKinley relied not only on newspapers but also "consulted men throughout the country" (Hilderbrand 1981, 12). Hoover went a step further, by systematically content analyzing newspapers to create "a confidential quantifiable measurement" of public sentiment (Eisinger 2000, 23).

Such sources, while they had merit, did not directly tap the views of average citizens. Instead, these indicators were a product usually of elite opinion that was treated, by assumption, as true reflection of the broader public's thinking.

The second, and perhaps more important, problem was that these sources of information were often wrong. Russell Neuman (1986, 3), for instance, comments that prior to scientific surveys the "voice of the people was the voice of those who chose to speak out – those who voted, wrote letters to editors, went to public meetings, wrote to legislators, or hired professional lobbyists to represent their interests in the corridors of power." Ginsberg (1986) stresses a similar theme, observing that at the time those who cared most about an issue shaped public opinion. But, as we know, the engaged differ systematically from the less engaged (Zaller 1992), thereby yielding a biased account of public opinion. This bias could be quite large because the "engaged," as suggested above, tend to hold their preferences more intensely, leading them to speak in such loud tones that political leaders could easily hear and hence be influenced by them more easily.

Just consider for a moment that if the major source of information about public opinion for today's officeholders came from interest groups. What would presidents think the state of the public opinion would be on issues like abortion or environmental protection? The reading would be dramatically different, leading to presidents to think of these issues in different ways. Or assume that Clinton had ignored the polls of Mark Penn and instead relied heavily on the editorial page of *The Washington Post* as a guide to the public's thinking. Such a change would surely put a different cast on what the "public" was thinking on such matters as affirmative action and welfare reform.

James Bryce (1921, 155) provides an insightful testimony about the difficulty of assessing the public mood, prior to the advent of polls:

How is the drift of Public Opinion to be ascertained? That is the problem which most occupies and perplexes politicians. They usually go for light to the press, but the press, though an indispensable, is not a safe guide, since the circulation of a journal does not necessarily measure the prevalence of the views it advocates.... Neither are public meetings a sure index, for in populous centres almost any energetic group can fill a large hall with its adherents.... Stray elections...are much relied on, yet the result is often due rather to local circumstances than to a general movement of political feeling.

Bryce (1921, 156), then, recommended that the best "index" for a politician was to go into local neighborhoods and talk with people so as to assess their "attitudes and proclivities." Whether Bryce's reasoning was sound or not is open to dispute. But the point is that politicians of that era had only rough guesses about public opinion.

The development of survey research recast the information available to politicians. Public officials no longer have to tease out the views of the public from indirect measures. They now have the means on a large and systematic scale to follow Bryce's recommendation of talking with constituents. This more direct indicator supplies politicians with a much better view of their constituents' opinions. So, for example, rather than trying to sift through newspapers to get a handle on the public's thinking, as Lincoln or Cleveland did, Bill Clinton knew, according to one poll, that "voters preferred devoting the surplus to Social Security over a tax cut by 82 percent to 16 percent" (Harris 2000, A2).

Thus, polls not only provide a direct link between politicians and citizens, but they also supply an *explicit* estimate of opinion for *specific* issues. Because surveys might ask whether respondents favor prescription drug coverage for seniors or whether they support a tax increase on the rich, the information they provide speaks directly to particular issues. Before polls, information, as mentioned above, often had only a loose relationship to the issue in question. Of course, some information was tied to particular issues, such as the tone of newspaper editorials that tackled a subject directly. But still such a connection was not as clean as that generated by polls. The proportions generated by polls provide information in a form that fits the thinking of vote conscious politicians.

Another difference in character of information provided by polls is a less biased reading of the opinions of the *mass* electorate. By tapping the views of a representative sample of the citizenry, surveys eliminate the bias favoring the engaged over the less engaged.[13] Thus, politicians have a much more accurate reading of what the average citizen thinks about political matters.

A third, and usually underappreciated, change that the rise of polls initiated is a decline in the prospects for rationalization. With the uncertainty of the measures available prior to surveys, predispositions of politicians surely influenced their interpretation of the "data." If, for example, a politician supported increasing tariffs, there was probably *some* information about public opinion that could be considered consistent with that view. Polls in contrast provide less room for such interpretations, since a finding that 75 percent of the public disagrees with your position is hard to explain away. In fact, because politicians from both sides of the aisle view surveys as accurate gauges of public opinion, polls have become a quasi-institution in American politics.

Despite all these advantages, any one poll can be misleading, as can any one question in a series of polls. The way samples are drawn and the framing of questions make a big difference in the results. But with the proliferation of polls (and questions) among both candidates and the news media (Lavrakas and Traugott 2000), the multiple indicators provide a sound

---

[13] Ginsberg (1986) makes a spirited attack on the normative implications that arise from the advent of polls. He finds it troublesome that polls have led to a "pacification" of opinion by sidestepping the views of activists and interest groups that used to define "public opinion" in a more active way. His argument has much appeal, but it hinges on the idea that the less engaged and less informed should have a smaller voice on issues than the more engaged, vocal segments of society. There is certainly reason to fear manipulation of the less engaged by elites, but it is unclear why the more engaged elements of the electorate should carry more weight. On the surface at least, such an argument runs counter to the notion "one person, one vote."

overall assessment of the direction and intensity of public opinion. For example, when different polls converge on a similar finding, there should be more confidence about what the public thinks. In contrast, if disagreement about public sentiment exists among different polls, politicians should view opinion as more unsettled – important information in itself.

The accuracy of polls seems pretty clear (Erikson and Tedin 2000; Warren 2001). A good test of that claim involves their ability to predict the outcome of elections. Consider, for example, the state polls conducted about three weeks prior to the 1992 presidential election. According to *Hotline*, those polls predicted the winner of the state 88 percent of the time, even in the special circumstance of a three-candidate race.[14] Among the six cases in which there was an "error," the actual proportions reported in the polls were within the statistical margin of error. So one could argue that state polls had an *unblemished* record in 1992. In addition, the mean difference in the predicted Clinton vote and his actual vote was just three percentage points. Even in the highly contested and controversial presidential election of 2000, preelection polls did pretty well. On the day prior to the election, the Zogby poll forecasted the outcomes of all fifty states in the presidential battle. They did not make an error. They viewed a number of states as "too close to call," and all of them were – including the now famous case of Florida. But in no case did a Bush state fall to Gore or visa versa.[15]

Largely because polls can provide accurate information, politicians now trust their results. At first, politicians were generally skeptical about the accuracy of polls (Herbst 1993; Jacobs 1993). But, as time has passed, and as the older generation of politicians has faded from the scene, more and more (younger) politicians have accepted polls as reliable and valid indicators of opinion. The current generation of politicians grew up with polls, and they not only trust them, but also they know how to take advantage of them.

Bill Clinton perhaps best embodies this trend, bringing the use of polls to a new level in the White House (Harris 2001). Clinton's pollster Mark Penn played a critical role in the Clinton presidency, using polls to identify those issues that would draw the public's support and to identify those issues that might prove to be landmines for the president. George W. Bush appears not to be as avid a consumer of polls as Clinton, but polls still have worked their way into policy decisions surrounding the Afghan war (DeYoung and Milbank 2001).[16]

---

[14] These data are from The American Political Network, which compiled the various polls available for the fifty states at periodic intervals during the 1992 campaign. Geer secured these data with the kind help of Doug Mills.

[15] See <http://www.zogby.com> for details.

[16] Besides accuracy, there is another informational edge gained by politicians who use polls to judge opinion. Surveys (and other technological changes) allow for quicker feedback and hence quicker reactions to shifts in opinion. Thus, even if an initial error is made in judging opinion, it can be corrected swiftly. Hence, mistakes in the era of polls are short term in

The Changing Concept of Public Opinion

Polls have had another effect on public opinion. Namely, survey research has led to a reconceptualization of "public opinion" itself. Prior to polls, politicians and political observers thought of public opinion as something surrounded by uncertainty (see Geer 1996). But with the advent and proliferation of polls, observers began to think of "public opinion" differently. In particular, the rise of polls helped to forge an aura of scientific precision when assessing the public's attitudes.[17] As early as 1948, Blumer (1948, 554) contended that "by virtue of its sampling procedure, current public opinion polling is forced to regard public opinion as an aggregate of equally weighted opinions of disparate individuals." Bogart (1972, 15) writes that polls give the "form and the appearance of measured precision to what was formerly visceral in origin and nebulous in shape." More recently, Herbst (1993) has noted this conceptual shift, and like others, raised normative concerns about it. But whether it is for good or bad, we now think of the concept differently than just seventy-five years ago.

The proportions generated by polls help to forge this scientific-based conception. Prior to surveys, politicians surely never thought, for instance, that 56 percent of the public favored a particular position on an issue. Instead, their guesses probably led them to judgments about whether most of the people or a few of the people favored a particular position. As a result, public opinion in the era of polls was no longer a "glorified kind of fortune telling" (Gallup and Rae 1940); it had become something concrete and tangible. For instance, changes in the Gallup Poll approval rating of presidents are treated as a real change in the public's judgment of the chief executive (Brehm 1993; Brody 1991; see later, too).

After the introduction of public opinion polls, the increased precision with which politicians could now measure opinion lessened the conceptual ambiguities. Philip Converse (1987, S13) notes, for instance that "what the firm establishment of a public opinion polling industry has done is to homogenize the definition and to stabilize it for the foreseeable future." Converse (1987, S14) then goes on to state "public opinion is what opinion polls try

---

nature, which minimizes their potential impact. In contrast, the feedback loop was much longer during the prepoll era. Politicians lacked the quick access to information provided by surveys, as well as accurate readings showing any sudden shifts in opinion. Thus, when mistakes were made, they were not corrected quickly because no one detected that they were "mistakes."

[17] The scientific aspect of polls was actually the product of two technological changes: the advent of sampling and measurement theory (Price 1992). Sampling theory allowed pollsters to get a representative segment of the electorate to participate, thereby greatly lessening the biases of previous indicators. Measurement theory was also important, because scales were developed that allowed researchers to ask questions that provided a valid and reliable indicator of the public's views on particular issues. These dual developments gave credibility to the idea of a "scientific" sample survey.

to measure or what they measure with modest error."[18] Perhaps Key (1961, 536) put it best when he observed that:

In an earlier day public opinion seemed to be pictured as a mysterious vapor that emanated from the undifferentiated citizenry and in some way or another enveloped the apparatus of government to bring it into conformity with the public will. These weird conceptions... passed out of style as the technique of the sample survey permitted the determination, with some accuracy, of opinions within the population.

As a result, the conceptual shift underlying the term "public opinion" reinforces the claim the there is less uncertainty in estimating the views of citizens. It is important to note that this change is one of perception. That is, the accuracy of polls has led to a rethinking of the concept itself. This development makes the increase in the quality of information even more real to political actors as they make their decisions.

HOW DECLINING UNCERTAINTY AFFECTS PRESIDENTIAL BEHAVIOR

In a democracy, public opinion matters. It matters for many reasons. Among them is the simple fact that politicians' livelihood depends on understanding the state of public opinion. If any office-seeking (or office-holding) politician knows what the public wants, that information provides the basis to shape and mold the policies to pursue and actions to undertake. The incentives surrounding democratic government force politicians to pay close attention to the opinions and views of voters. To do otherwise risks a brief political career.

It is therefore not a surprise that presidents have made extensive use of polls. FDR was the first to use survey research (Steele 1974). But it was a new method that did not yet have widespread acceptance and hence was used only in a piecemeal fashion. Truman and Eisenhower exemplified that pattern, making only sporadic use of polls (Eisinger 2000). But with the election of John Kennedy, polls became much more important to presidents and to White House operations (Jacobs 1993; Jacobs and Shapiro 2000). LBJ continued the trend. He studied surveys, paying close attention, for example, to his standing in the Gallup Poll. Nixon even authorized competing polls to get additional readings on public opinion (Jacobs and Shapiro 1995). Carter and Reagan further advanced the use of polls, with Reagan holding frequent meetings with his pollster, Richard Wirthlin (Hinckley 1992). And, as noted earlier, Clinton took the use of polls to new levels when governing

---

[18] Note that Converse is being careful about recognizing explicitly that surveys contain errors. This care reflects an attempt to counteract more simplistic definitions, which suggest "public opinion consists of people's reactions to definitely worded statements and questions under interview conditions" (Warner 1939, 377).

(Harris 2001). Dick Morris (1997) certainly supports this claim, writing extensively about Clinton's use of Penn's polls.[19]

This reliance on polls lessens presidents' uncertainty about public opinion, which, in turn, affects their behavior.[20] In what follows, we will suggest possible changes that may have resulted from the use of polls. These changes include not only shifts in the behavior of individual presidents but also shifts in the institutional foundations of the presidency itself.

Presidential Popularity

Because polls have proven to be accurate indicators of public opinion, these readings have gained legitimacy in the eyes of most political actors. For example, after the tragedies of 9–11, Bush became an extremely popular president. There were many indications of that popularity, but the main one was his stratospheric ratings in the Gallup Poll (and other media-based surveys). The Democrats were surely tired of hearing about the popularity of Bush, but they could do little about it. The Gallup Poll provides an *independent* and hence *legitimate* read on Bush's (or any president's) standing with the public. Disgruntled, partisan actors cannot credibly challenge such findings. But without the cloak of polls, Bush (or any "popular" president) might be an easier target for attack. There would be disagreement on the extent of the popularity, providing an opening for partisan attacks.

The power of polls in providing a voice for the views of the public in the corridors of government is clear. Consider the Lewinsky scandal and Clinton's impeachment. Nearly all the talking heads in Washington and key figures on both sides of the aisles were ready to get rid of Clinton for his involvement with Lewinsky and his attempt to cover up the relationship. Yet, despite the outpouring of negative coverage, Clinton remained popular (Kagay 1999; Zaller 1998). In fact, much to the amazement of many pundits, Clinton's popularity ratings *increased*. This surge gave Clinton one card to play in this drawn-out scandal. The people, despite his many flaws, still felt he was doing a good job and they did not want him removed from office. This gave him what one might call his "get out of jail free card."

Imagine the situation without polls. What would have happened? Obviously, we are only speculating. But prior to polls, politicians from both parties would have made varying claims about public opinion. There were many conservative groups that were very unhappy with Clinton. Their unhappiness could have been used as a sign of what the "public" wanted. Other groups, such as African Americans, could have come to the president's

---

[19] See also Warren (2001) for an account of the frequent use of polls by politicians other than presidents.

[20] Geer (1996) has sought to tease out the many implications for the behavior of politicians that flow from the information gained represented by polls. For more details on that argument, see Chapters 2 through 6.

defense. But there would have been disagreement and Clinton would not have had his ace in the hole. To illustrate our point further, consider instead the battle over the League of Nations some eighty years earlier. Both Wilson and Lodge claimed public opinion was on their side. But there was no independent, unbiased reading of the electorate's views. Hence, this battle was carried on at the elite levels, with little direct input from the public. A Gallup Poll would have changed that debate in significant ways. If the public had supported the treaty and strongly endorsed Wilson's leadership, the twenty-eighth president's hand would have been greatly strengthened. If the data told a different story, Lodge would have been in an even stronger position.

It makes sense that popular presidents have more clout in Washington than less popular ones (Kernell 1993). But the problem was that prior to polls there was no unbiased, agreed-on indicator of popularity. That "uncertain" situation allowed politicians to offer their own interpretations of the president's actual standing with the electorate. But the development of survey research changed that by providing the president with a scientific indicator of the public's thinking. John Brehm (1993) aptly notes that presidential approval is very much the political equivalent of the "Dow Jones index."

Presidential Leadership

The decline of uncertainty also has implications for how and whether presidents engage in leadership.[21] One model of behavior would be that presidents are driven solely by polls. If a poll says the public wants x, they advocate x. That is, of course, a highly simplified version of the impact of polls on the actions of presidents. The reality is that the impact is far more subtle, but still consequential.

First, polls provide information on the *two* key dimensions of public opinion: the *salience* of an issue and the *position* the public takes on it. Both pieces of information are critical to sorting out how politicians might behave.

If presidents are interested in maximizing their public support (a reasonable goal, see Kernell 1993; Geer 1996), then they will tend to follow public opinion on *highly* salient issues. Now prior to polls, politicians had the same set of incentives. However, they lacked the information to be able to follow opinion with much consistency. That is not the case anymore. Now this is not to say that presidents, in the era of good information, always follow the results of polling data when staking out positions on highly salient issues. They might just have personal convictions that keep them from doing so. They also might have a past record on this issue that serves as a kind of

---

[21] Even though we are talking about presidential leadership, remember that the effects of polls extend to all political leaders (see Geer 1996).

anchor. In addition, institutional barriers may prevent such action. But the point is that presidents will be *more likely* to follow public opinion with accurate readings of citizens' views for highly salient issues than poorly informed chief executives. Hence, with the introduction of polls, there should be a *decline* in leadership on the pressing issues facing the public (see Geer 1996).[22]

When one considers the universe of issues, the far more common type of issue is one of *low salience*. This kind of issue offers different opportunities to modern, well-informed presidents. First, a low salience issue provides presidents a *chance* for leadership, because they could rally the public to their side. It is far easier for presidents to convince to public to adopt a new position on an issue than to get them to change their mind on an existing one. This type of leadership is important and with the information from polls it should be *more* common today than in the era prior to surveys. Hence, the decline of uncertainty has *mixed* effects on the frequency of leadership.

But there is more to the story. Presidents need to be judicious in selecting issues to rally the public. It is a costly undertaking and cannot be done with great frequency. And, given the large number of low salient issues, many may be left untouched. But, even those "ignored" issues can prove valuable to well-informed presidents. For example, an issue with little salience to the broader public, but one of great importance to an interest group or potential set of contributors, could be helpful to any president. By keeping the issue under the radar screens of the broader public but still taking action on the matter, presidents may be able to build support among key constituencies.

The cumulative result of these kinds of behaviors leads presidents to moderate on highly salient issues, but potentially polarize on some low salience issues, if it advances the interest of some important set of activists or financial contributors. Such constituencies are likely to hold more extreme views of issues than average citizens, since, on average, people with strongly held views will tend to be more ideological than the less engaged. This fuels the potential polarization.

As a result, the information from polls predicts in the aggregate an *increase* in polarization of American politics, where presidents now more confident of the public's thinking can use some small issues to pay off key groups of supporters. Scholars often have talked about the increase in polarization in American politics, but the causal mechanism behind this change has not involved the impact of information on decision making (e.g., Carmines and Stimson 1989; Hetherington 2001; King 1997). We offer a new theoretical angle to this important development.

---

[22] This decline may be a source of concern, but if one has any faith in the judgments of the public, this development may in fact advance democratic outcomes.

Institutional Change in the Presidency

A further implication of the decline in uncertainty should be a bolder president who is willing to stake out more positions on issues with greater confidence than before. In other words, we have what Greenstein (1978) calls the "modern" president, Tulis (1987) the "rhetorical" president, or Kernell (1993) the "public" president. The usual argument behind these changes include the deep national crisis stemming from the Great Depression (Greenstein 1978), Wilson's effort to redefine the presidency (Tulis 1987), the decline of parties (Gamm and Smith 1998), or the need for presidents to go over the heads of Congress to rally support (Kernell 1993). All of these ideas have merit. But the decline of uncertainty, which was forged by the development of the public opinion poll, may also be part of the story.

When presidents "go public," it would help for them to know what the citizenry wants. That information would give them a guidepost to what issues will play well and what issues will not. Prior to polls, presidents did take their case to the public from time to time (and even during the nineteenth century; see Lararcy 1998). But with nebulous information about public opinion, they would be more hesitant to go over the heads of Congress and appeal directly to voters. They would be reluctant to risk their reputations, because if a hostile public rebuffs them, that outcome undermines presidential prestige. And, as Neustadt (1990) has long reminded us, much of presidential power is informal and tied to perception of power. "Rebuked" presidents suffer a decline in clout due to diminished credibility. Hence, poorly informed presidents would not be less inclined to stake out large numbers of positions for fear of weakening their hand further.

But with the information from polls, presidents have a much better sense of the issues that are popular with the public and those that are not. They could use that information to identify those issues on which to "go public." It makes sense that support-maximizing presidents would be more willing to rally the public, if they have reason to believe it will work. This argument provides an additional hypothesis to explain the long discussed institutional change that has altered the workings of the presidency during the twentieth century. The rise of good information is not an argument meant to supplant these other explanations. It is meant to be complementary. Given that the institutional change that has unfolded in the presidency over the last one hundred years is extensive, the causes of it are surely many. Our goal here is simply add another variable into the mix. And, given the institutional presence of polls in the White House (Eisinger 2001; Jacobs and Shapiro 2000), it is important to tease out these theoretical implications.

Presidential Character

We have assumed so far that presidents want to maximize their public support. While that goal remains at the core of our argument, we now want to acknowledge that politicians who seek the presidency do more than just play to the "median voter"; they also are concerned with advancing their own policy objectives. By relaxing this assumption about politicians maximizing popularity, we are able to offer insights into the relative of success of different *types* of presidents.

Suppose that there are two types of presidential contenders – "popularity maximizers" (those interested solely in public support), and "policy maximizers" (those interested in adopting policies as close as possible to their own preferred outcome). Assume further that the public is able to determine with reasonable accuracy the views of presidents (and potential presidents) on matters of public policy. If so, those actors driven solely by maximizing public support will have a built in advantage over chief executives with policy interests in an era of good information. The former will be able to forge greater levels of popularity, which will, in turn, lead to more success at the polling booth. Hence, over time we should see presidents increasingly being "popularity maximizers," as the policy oriented actors are weeded out of the political game.

By contrast, these forces worked differently in the prepoll era. The lack good information made it harder for popularity maximizing presidents to succeed. By not knowing with much precision where the public stood, they made more mistakes and were in fact not able to maximize their popularity as effectively as in the era of polls. Therefore, policy-oriented presidents would have a greater likelihood of success. They would not always beat the popularity maximizer in elections, but they are *more* likely to succeed in that era. The public would not only give them credit for their commitment to their views, but their opinions occasionally would be aligned with the median voter.

Our argument, in short, is that the ratio of popularity maximizers to policy maximizers will change. Specifically, we should see a trend toward more popularity maximizers among the pool of successful candidates in the era of good information. That means, on average, we should see a shift in the kinds of people who will occupy the presidency. There has been a chorus of complaints that presidents tend not to be real leaders but, rather, followers of public opinion (e.g., Will 1995). Our argument provides a theoretical explanation for this observed change in presidential character.

Implications of Increasing Information Asymmetry

While presidents have much more information about public opinion, the citizenry, too, has far more information available to them about presidents than one hundred years ago. The rise of the mass media has provided an important vehicle to inform the public on a range of topics. Even though both set of actors are better informed, we believe there is a potential increase in "information asymmetry" that warrants attention. For us, information asymmetry denotes the gap between the level and quality of information for each set of actors.[23] Asymmetry exists when one side has better or more information than the other. This increase in asymmetry has potentially important implications for the presidency, in particular, democratic governance, in general.

It is fair to say that elites usually have more information than the mass public. That claim is backed up with decades of empirical research (e.g., Delli Carpini and Keeter 1997; Zaller 1992). What is less appreciated, however, is that this gap need not be stable over time (see Geer 1996). As we have claimed in this chapter, there has been an upsurge in information about public opinion over the last seventy-five years. Yet it is politicians that have an incentive to make the most use of that additional information. Presidents want to absorb all the data about public opinion, since their jobs ride on knowing what the citizenry wants. Voters, by contrast, do not have the same set of incentives. Downs (1957) reminds us that the electorate in fact has reason to be ignorant. That is not true for politicians. So that elites will benefit disproportionately from the information age – not because they are trying to keep citizens from learning about politics and presidents, but because it is more in the interest of elites to know what is going on.

Yet democratic government requires a fair exchange of information between the people and their leaders. As J. R. Pole (1983, 89) notes, "it would be virtually impossible to construct a theory of democracy which did not include" a *two-way* flow of information. Polls alter that flow, potentially generating a growing gap in the exchange of information that could become very troubling. When that danger point might arise is unclear. Perhaps we have already reached it. We do not know. But increasingly we will be entering uncharted waters at rapid speeds. And we do need to ensure that we find ways for *all* relevant decision makers to make use of good information as they make respective choices. In this way, we can ensure that democratic societies gain the benefits from the availability of that information. We do know, however, that the growing imbalance of information between what the public knows and public officials know could lead to additional opportunities for presidents to behave in a strategic manner – some of which could undermine public interest.[24] Remember that well-informed presidents will be better able to practice leadership (as described earlier), but they also will

---

[23] The application of information asymmetry to the principal-agent model has provided us with numerous important contributions, most in the field of the so-called New Institutional Economics (see Moe 1984 for an excellent review).

[24] This conclusion might be questioned by some readers, because an immediate application of the Coase theorem would suggest that the public would obtain relevant knowledge – given the costs of accumulating it have decreased over the years – whenever the costs of not doing so outweigh the benefit that would hence accrue (Coase 1960). Therefore, given all else the same, we can expect that this gap that we are predicting will increase only at a decreasing rate.

have more opportunities to use issues to advance their standing with interest groups and/or financial contributors. It is these latter sets of behaviors that could pose problems for society.

CONCLUDING THOUGHTS

Uncertainty is a fact of life. As Burden observes in the Introduction, it is like death and taxes: something we can always count on as fixtures in our day-to-day existence. But while uncertainty is a constant, the amount of it is not. We have discussed a case in which it is reasonable to conclude that uncertainty has declined and that, in turn, this decline has had important implications for politics. Presidents, armed with polls, will be more likely to follow opinion on issues of great importance to the public than in the past, will be more able to lead opinion on low salience issues than before, and adopt more polarized positions on "ignored" low salience issues than in the past. This argument is valuable in and of itself, because public opinion matters in a democracy and better information about it is surely to have many influences (see Bartels 1996; Geer 1996; Lohmann 1998).

Our example of presidents and polls is not likely to be the exception – in fact, it might be the rule. We are in the midst of the information age. Developments in telecommunications and computer technology, for instance, have provided important changes both in the quality of information and the speed with which it comes to our attention. It took days for many northerners to learn of Abraham Lincoln's assassination in 1865, but today we learn about events around the world as they have unfolded in the streets. Because of all these changes, it is now common to talk about being awash in information. And with the spread of the Internet and other kinds of technology, this trend is only going to continue.

Scholars, of course, have begun to think and to write about the many implications that this surge in information has for society, in general, and for politics, in particular (Beniger 1986; Cherny 2000; Dizard 1989; Ferejohn and Kuklinski 1990; Graber 1988; Kamarck and Nye 2002; Lukes 1989; Neuman 1991; Ricci 1993; 1996). But, because this transformation is recent, we still lack a good grasp of its ramifications. One of the implications, however, is that uncertainty in general may be on the decline. That decline, as we have so often stressed, becomes especially clear when we think of the issue within an historical setting. One need only imagine the uncertainty Andrew Jackson faced as he battled over the U.S. Bank, as compared to the kind of information Bill Clinton had when deciding what to do with the newfound federal budget surplus.

We should note that a rise in the level of available information does not, in all contexts, ensure a decrease in uncertainty. Burden makes reference to the fact that sometimes more information can create more uncertainty. For example, if you suddenly learn about a disease that could affect your health (e.g., AIDS), that increase in knowledge could conceivably lead to greater uncertainty about your future and doubts about what kinds of behavior you should engage in. This kind of scenario is different from the one we address in this chapter. We observe not only that there is now more and better information about public opinion than in the past, but the concept itself has changed. Politicians are now more likely to think of "public opinion" as measurable and precise. This conceptual change reinforces our claim that there is declining uncertainty. If this surge in information had caused politicians to view public opinion as more nebulous and less well measured, then the problem Burden discusses could indeed be a concern. It is certainly true that knowledge of AIDS led many people to feel more uncertain about their health and about healthy sexual practices. But in our case, the gain in information led to a corresponding rise in confidence about the accuracy with which public opinion is measured.

Finally, it is worthwhile to step back and note that in political analysis of institutions, the rules of the game often are formed on the basis of the level and quality of information relevant rational actors possess (e.g., Cruise O Brien and Helleiner 1980; Milgrom and Roberts 1986; also Altfeld and Miller 1984). A change in information should cause changes in the rules of the game. This is a general claim. Our specific claim involves the presidency, the most visible institution in American politics. We have argued that the rise of polls has led to a reduction of uncertainty about public opinion, which, in turn, had forged changes in the public behavior of presidents if not the very characteristics of the candidates themselves. It is for these kinds of reasons that the study of uncertainty remains central to the study of American politics. We are acutely aware that this argument only scratches the surface of the potential impact of information on presidential behavior. The institutional ties presidents build with Congress, political parties, and the mass media also warrant attention. It is our hope that this argument, although incomplete, stimulates further discussion about the implications of the underappreciated, dynamic nature of uncertainty and how these changes play across the American political landscape.

References

Akerlof, George A. 1970. "The Market for 'Lemons': Quality Uncertainty and the Market Mechanism." *Quarterly Journal of Economics* 84:488–500.

Arrow, Kenneth. 1951. "Alternative Approaches to the Theory of Choice in Risk-Taking Situations." *Econometrica* 19:404–37.

Altfeld, Michael F., and Gary J. Miller. 1984. "Sources of Bureaucratic Influence: Expertise and Agenda Control." *Journal of Conflict Resolution* 28:701–30.

Bartels, Larry M. 1996. "Uninformed Votes: Information Effects in Presidential Elections." *American Journal of Political Science* 40:194–230.

Beniger, James. 1986. *The Control Revolution: Technological and Economic Origins of the Information Society.* Cambridge, MA: Harvard University Press.

Blumer, Herbert. 1948. "Public Opinion and Public Opinion Polling." *American Sociological Review* 13:542–54.

Bogart, Leo. 1972. *Silent Politics: Polls and the Awareness of Public Opinion.* New York: Wiley Interscience.

Brody, Richard A. 1991. *Assessing the President.* Stanford: Stanford University Press.

Brehm, John. 1993. *The Phantom Respondents.* Ann Arbor: University of Michigan Press.

Bryce, James. 1921. *Modern Democracies.* New York: Macmillan.

Carmines, Edward G., and James A. Stimson. 1989. *Issue Evolution.* Princeton, NJ: Princeton University Press.

Cherny, Andrei. 2000. *The Next Deal.* New York: Basic Books.

Coase, Ronald. 1960. "The Problem of Social Cost." *Journal of Law and Economics* 3:1–44.

Converse, Phillip E. 1987. "Changing Conceptions of Public Opinion in the Political Process." *Public Opinion Quarterly* 51:12–24.

Crespi, Irving. 1988. *Public Opinion, Polls, and Democracy.* San Francisco: Westview Publishing.

Cruise O Brien, Rita, and G. K. Helleiner. 1980. "The Political Economy of Information in a Changing International Economic Order." *International Organization* 34:445–70.

Dahl, Robert A. 1990. "Myth of the Presidential Mandate." *Political Science Quarterly* 105:355–73.

DeYoung, Karen, and Dana Millbank. 2001. "Military Plans Informed by Polls." *Washington Post*, October 19, A19.

Delli Carpini, Michael X., and Scott Keeter. 1997. *What Americans Know about Politics and Why it Matters.* New Haven, CT: Yale University Press.

Dizard, Wilson P. 1989. *The Coming Information Age.* New York: Longman.

Downs, Anthony. 1957. *An Economic Theory of Democracy.* New York: Harper and Row.

Eisinger, Robert M. 2000. "Gauging Public Opinion in the Hoover White House." *Presidential Studies Quarterly* 30:643–61.

Eisinger, Robert M. 2001. *The Illusion of Certainty.* Unpublished book manuscript.

Erikson, Robert S., and Kent L. Tedin. 2000. *American Public Opinion.* 6th ed. New York: Longman.

Ferejohn, John A., and Roger G. Noll. 1978. "Uncertainty and the Formal Theory of Political Campaigns." *American Political Science Review* 72:492–505.

Ferejohn, John A., and James H. Kuklinski, ed. 1990. *Information and Democratic Processes.* Urbana: University of Illinois Press.

Foner, Eric. 1988. *Reconstruction: America's Unfinished Revolution, 1863–77.* New York: Harper and Row.

Gallup, George, and Saul Rae. 1940. *Pulse of Democracy.* New York: Simon and Schuster.

Gamm, Gerald, and Renee Smith. 1998. "Presidents, Parties, and the Public: Evolving Patterns of Interaction, 1877–1929." In *Speaking to the People*, ed. Richard J. Ellis. Amherst: University of Massachussetts Press.

Geer, John G. 1996. *From Tea Leaves to Opinion Polls.* New York: Columbia University Press.

Ginsberg, Benjamin. 1986. *The Captive Public.* New York: Basic Books.

Glad, Paul W. 1964. *McKinley, Bryan, and the People*. Philadelphia: Lippincott.

Graber, Doris. 1988. *Processing the News: How People Tame the Information Tide.* 2nd ed. White Plains, NY: Longman.

Greenstein, Fred I. 1978. "The Rise of the Modern Presidency." In *The New American Political System*, ed. Anthony King. Washington, DC: AEI.

Harris, John F. 2000. "Policy and Politics by the Numbers." *Washington Post*, December 31, A1.

Harris, John F. 2001. "Clintonesque Balancing of Issues, Polls." *Washington Post*, June 24, A1.

Hetherington, Marc J. 2001. "Resurgent Mass Partisanship: The Role of Elite Polarization." *American Political Science Review* 95:619–31.

Herbst, Susan. 1993. *Numbered Voices*. Chicago: University of Chicago Press.

Hilderbrand, Robert. 1981. *Power and the People: Executive Management of Public Opinion in Foreign Affairs*. Chapel Hill: University of North Carolina Press.

Hinckley, Ronald H. 1992. *People, Polls, and Policy Making*. New York: Lexington Books.

Jacobs, Lawrence R. 1993. *The Health of Nations*. Ithaca, NY: Cornell University Press.

Jacobs, Lawrence R., and Robert Y. Shapiro. 1995. "The Rise of Presidential Polling: The Nixon White House in Historical Perspective." *Public Opinion Quarterly* 59:163–95.

Jacobs, Lawrence R., and Robert Y. Shapiro. 2000. *Politicians Don't Pander*. Chicago: University of Chicago Press.

Kagay, Michael. 1999. "Public Opinion and Polling During Presidential Scandal and Impeachment." *Public Opinion Quarterly* 63:449–63.

Kahneman, Daniel, and Amos Tversky. 1984. "Choices, Values, and Frames." *American Psychologist* 39:341–50.

Kamarck, Elaine, and Joseph S. Nye. 2002. *Governance.com*. Washington, DC: Brookings.

Kelley, Stanley, Jr. 1983. *Interpreting Elections*. Princeton, NJ: Princeton University Press.

Kernell, Samuel. 1993. *Going Public: New Strategies of Presidential Leadership*. Washington, DC: CQ Press.

Key, V. O. 1961. *Public Opinion and American Democracy*. New York: Alfred Knopf.

King, David C. 1997. "The Polarization of American Parties and Mistrust of Government." In *Why People Don't Trust Government*, ed. Joseph S. Nye, Phillip Zelikow, and David C. King. Cambridge, MA: Harvard University Press.

Knight, Frank. 1921. *Risk, Uncertainty, and Profit*. New York: Houghton Mifflin.

Lararcy, Mel. 1998. "The Presidential Newspaper: The Forgotten Way of Going Public." In *Speaking to the People*, ed. Richard J. Ellis. Amherst: University of Massachussetts Press.

Lavrakas, Paul J., and Michael Traugott. 2000. *Elections Polls, News Media, and Democracy*. Chatham, NJ: Chatham House.

Lohmann, Suzanne. 1998. "An Information Rationale for the Power of Special Interests." *American Political Science Review* 92:809–27.

Lukes, Timothy W. 1989. *Screens of Power: Ideology, Dominance, and Resistance in an Information Society*. Urbana: University of Illinois Press.

McPherson, James M. 1988. *Battle Cry for Freedom*. New York: Oxford University Press.

Milgrom, Paul, and John Roberts. 1986. "Relying on the Information of Interested Parties." *RAND Journal of Economics* 17:18–32.

Moe, Terry M. 1984. "The New Economics of Organization." *American Journal of Political Science* 28:739–77.

Moore, David W. 1992. *The Super Pollsters*. New York: Four Walls Eight Windows.

Morris, Dick. 1997. *Behind the Oval Office*. New York: Random House.

Mueller, John. 1994. *Policy and Opinion in the Gulf War*. Chicago: University of Chicago Press.

Neuman, Russell W. 1986. *The Paradox of Mass Politics*. Cambridge, MA: Harvard University Press.

Neuman, Russell W. 1991. *The Future of the Audience*. New York: Cambridge University Press.

Neustadt, Richard E. 1990. *Presidential Power*. New York: Free Press.

Page, Benjamin I., and Robert Y. Shapiro. 1992. *The Rational Public*. Chicago: University of Chicago Press.

Pole, J. R. 1983. *The Gift of Government*. Athens: University of Georgia Press.

Price, Vincent. 1992. *Public Opinion*. Newbury Park, CA: Sage Publications.

Ricci, David. 1993. *Transformation of American Politics*. New Haven, CT: Yale University Press.

Schuman, Howard, and Stanley Presser. 1981. *Questions and Answers in Attitude Surveys*. New York: Wiley.

Steele, Richard W. 1974. "The Pulse of the People: FDR and the Gauging of American Public Opinion." *Journal of Contemporary History* 9:195–216.

Stimson, James A. 1991. *Public Opinion in America*. Boulder, CO: Westview Publishing.

Tulis, Jeffrey K. 1987. *The Rhetorical Presidency*. Princeton, NJ: Princeton University Press

Warner, Lucien. 1939. "The Reliability of Public Opinion." *Public Opinion Quarterly* 3:376–90.

Warren, Kenneth F. 2001. *In Defense of Public Opinion Polling*. Boulder, CO: Westview Press.

Will, Garry. 1995. *Certain Trumpets*. New York: Touchstone Books.

Zaller, John R. 1992. *The Nature and Origins of Mass Opinion*. New York: Cambridge University Press.

Zaller, John R. 1998. "Monica Lewinsky's Contribution of Political Science." *PS: Political Science & Politics* 31:182–9.

7

Uncertainty and American Public Opinion

R. Michael Alvarez
John Brehm
Catherine Wilson

ARE AMERICANS UNCERTAIN ABOUT ISSUES?

Early research on American political knowledge began with a strong normative assumption – that Americans are well-informed about political issues. Consider Berelson, Lazarsfeld, and McPhee (1954): "The democratic citizen is expected to be well-informed about political affairs. He is supposed to know what the issues are, what their history is, what the relevant facts are, what alternatives are proposed, what the party stands for, what the likely consequences are" (1954, 308). Current research in this field has not moved much beyond such expectations. Delli Carpini and Keeter open their book on the political knowledge of Americans by asserting that "democracy functions best when its citizens are politically informed (because) a broadly and equitably informed citizenry helps assure a democracy that is both responsive and responsible" (1996, 1).

Unsurprisingly, when measured against these standards, most Americans fall quite short. Scholars who assume that Americans are well informed about politics are often disappointed when they find that the public knows very little about most important political issues of the day. We contend that research that assumes that Americans are well informed about politics suffers from a paternalistic view of our fellow citizens: the reality of life is that there are too many pressing and competing concerns for the time, energy, and

Associate Professor of Political Science, Division of Humanities and Social Sciences, California Institute of Technology, MC 228-77, Pasadena, CA 91125, rma@hss.caltech.edu.

Professor of Political Science, Department of Political Science, 5828 S. University, University of Chicago, Chicago, IL 60637, jjbrehm@uchicago.edu.

Ph.D. Candidate, Division of Humanities and Social Sciences, California Institute of Technology, MC 228-77, Pasadena, CA 91125, chw@hss.caltech.edu. We thank Mark Hansen and Barry Burden for their comments on an earlier version of this research. Alvarez thanks the IBM Corporation for their support of his research through their University Matching Grants program.

cognitive capacity of most individuals for this assumption to be realistic. What is important for democracy is accounting for why some people are poorly informed about issues and how they may become better informed, and demonstrating how the informed and uninformed interact to produce what we observe as public opinion.

In previous research, we have explored how information matters for understanding public opinion about political issues (Alvarez and Brehm, 2002). Our analysis has focused on three ways in which information matters. Building from theories based in economics and rational choice, we have discussed how information influences popular political opinion because it can reduce the *uncertainty* that people have about political issues and because it can *persuade* them to change their opinions. Drawing from research in psychology, we have discussed how information about an issue can *activate or make relevant core values and predispositions for issue opinions*. Through each of these mechanisms, information controls the opinions or survey responses we observe as researchers.

However, documenting the impact of information on public opinion is not simple. Researchers typically have at their disposal only survey data that has been collected by others, often for purposes far removed from the academic study of public opinion. This makes the measurement of uncertainty difficult, the documentation of persuasion even harder, and the study of the activation of core values and predispositions arduous. The innovation in our previous research is our exposition of inferential statistical techniques that allow us to study uncertainty in a straightforward manner, using survey data previously collected for other purposes.

We wish to be explicit about the form of uncertainty modelled in this chapter: individual citizens are uncertain about their own opinions about policies. They may have stable and enduring values and beliefs, but the meaning of specific policies in terms of those beliefs might be unclear. Consider the respondent who is asked about group-led prayer in school. Is this a problem of free speech, permitting the student groups to express their religious values in a public setting? Or is this a problem of establishment of religion, keeping clear the boundaries between church and state? By contrast, consider some alternative forms of uncertainty. Respondents might be uncertain about where a candidate falls along a spectrum of political issues (as per Alvarez 1997). The ambiguity of the candidate's positions creates uncertainty on the part of the respondent not for where the respondent stands on policy, but where the candidate's true position falls. Respondents might be uncertain about the consequences of policy choices. Nearly everyone favors a reduction in violent crime, but there are ambiguities about the effect of certain policies (e.g., mandatory minimum sentencing, penal reform, parole limits) on violent crime. Instead, we wish to focus on the abilities of the respondent to assess what he or she feels about the policy choices before him or her.

We begin the remainder of this chapter by discussing in more detail our conceptualization of uncertainty. Then we develop in brief outline our inferential statistical techniques. Following our conceptual and methodological discussions, we turn to our empirical applications drawn from survey data collected in 1998. We present a series of analyses, showing uncertainty in the opinions of Americans about four important and socially divisive issues. We conclude with a discussion of our findings here, and how they fit into the larger mosaic of our research agenda.

CONCEPTUALIZING UNCERTAINTY IN PUBLIC OPINION

Two important political scientists were early advocates of the notion that the American public is uncertain in its knowledge of political issues. In his classic book *The Responsible Electorate* (1966), V. O. Key noted that not only were voters poorly informed about issues but that much of the blame for this lack of information lay in the hands of political parties and candidates: "The voice of the people is but an echo. The output of an echo chamber bears an inevitable and invariable relation to the input. As candidates and parties clamor for attention and vie for popular support, the people's verdict can be no more than a selective reflection from among the alternatives and outlooks presented to them" (1966, 2). Thus, when parties and candidates are ambiguous about issues, Americans will be poorly informed about the same issues.

Downs, in *An Economic Theory of Democracy* (1957), also posited that Americans were uncertain about politics. But Downs's argument was much more centered on citizens, as he rooted this uncertainty in the costs to individuals of information gathering. Downs noted that there are two forms of information costs in a democratic society: transferable and nontransferable costs. Transferable costs are those that can be passed on to others; they include the costs of gathering, summarizing and evaluating informational data about a political issue or candidate. Nontransferable costs are those that have to be picked up by each individual, and they include the costs of actual decision making as well as going to the polls to vote. Downs noted, furthermore, that both types of costs will be distributed unequally throughout society, with some citizens having high transferable costs while others have low transferable costs. This implies that there is heterogeneity in informedness in American politics, with some being well informed and others being poorly informed.

Both of these contributions are important for our analysis. Beginning with Key, an entire literature has arisen that is focused on spatial issues and how much voters know about candidate policy positions (Achen 1975; Alvarez 1997; Alvarez and Franklin 1994; Bartels 1986; Enelow and Hinich 1984; Franklin 1991). An insight we have gained from this research is that candidates have strong incentives to be ambiguous about their policy positions, as reflected in voter uncertainty about these same candidate positions (Alvarez 1997; Page 1978; Shepsle 1972).

In general, researchers in this literature assume that voter perceptions of candidate policy positions can be represented by probability distributions, which have central tendencies and distributions of points around the central tendency. In this approach, the central tendency of the voter's perception is usually assumed to be the voter's best guess about the position of the candidate, and the distribution of points around that best guess is taken to represent the voter's uncertainty about the exact location of the candidate's position.

In our research, we extend this conceptualization out of the realm of electoral competition and into the more general arena of opinions about all political issues. Thus, we think about citizens as having opinions that can be represented as statistical distributions with a best guess or central tendency, and a variance around that central tendency. These differences between citizens in the size of this variance are our concern in this chapter.

The central tendency of these distributions is governed by a set of predispositions, or inclinations to evaluate policy in terms of enduring and stable beliefs, and can be traced to a variety of different sources. Over a century ago, Tocqueville commented on the recurrence of libertarian and egalitarian values in the American public. More recently, Milton Rokeach (1973) documented the multiplicity of instrumental (means) and terminal (ends) values in his subjects, and the power of these "core values" as a metric for making political and social judgments. Chong (2000), Feldman (1988), Hochschild (1981), Kinder and Sanders (1996), and Sniderman and Piazza (1993), among many others, employ the idea of core values as bases of public opinion. At the same time, core values are not the sole form of predispositions; Alvarez and Brehm (2002) explore identities, expectations, and affective evaluations as supplementary predispositions.

We posit that there are three determinants, however, of response variability. The first is caused by uncertainty, which is distinguished from other forms of response variability in that additional information helps the respondent sharpen his or her opinions. As previous research has shown, uncertainty about public policies is a function of a lack of information, either stemming from the respondent's own personal information costs or from deficiencies in the transmission of information from elites to citizens (Alvarez 1997; Alvarez and Franklin 1994; Bartels 1986). Uncertainty can always be resolved, and hence survey response variation diminished, when citizens acquire more information.

The second form of response variability is ambivalence, wherein additional information only heightens internalized conflict (Liberman and Chaiken 1991; Tetlock 1986), making the policy choices more difficult and responses more variable. Ambivalence arises in a choice situation when the choice disallows compromise, such that opting for one alternative precludes the other. An ambivalent person is subject to simultaneously existing values or predispositions that conflict with one another. The role of additional information is not to reduce the number of factors relevant in an ambivalent choice situation; instead, additional information makes the simultaneous factors more salient. If two of a respondent's core values conflict in their relation to a policy choice, no amount of additional information can narrow the response variance (Alvarez and Brehm 1997).

The third form of response variability is equivocation (Alvarez and Brehm 1998, 2002). Equivocation is the logical opposite of ambivalence, in that equivocation arises when conflicting core beliefs or predispositions act to reduce response variability. This occurs when core beliefs impact an individual's opinion on a policy issue in a unified way. By reinforcing another value's effect on an individual's survey response, such core beliefs cause a reduction in the associated variance. In previous work, we have argued that information has no impact on equivocal beliefs (Alvarez and Brehm 2002).

Although our method is clearly intended to serve as a diagnostic tool to separate out the different forms of response variability, we also wish to establish the theoretical conditions whereby respondents fall into the three forms. (A fuller treatment of this issue appears in Alvarez and Brehm [2002].)

Let us be clear about what this method permits: it is an inferential means to ascertain whether *survey* respondents are ambivalent, uncertain, or equivocal about policy. We expect that the vast majority of policy domains *as measured by surveys* will fall under the uncertainty condition, that some highly familiar domains will be equivocal, and that very few domains will be ambivalent. What does it take for a respondent to be seen as ambivalent by our method? The respondent has to simultaneously invoke competing and irreconcilable beliefs when questioned about policy. Given the very rapid pace of public opinion surveys, in a context that is not conducive to reflection or deliberation, we expect that it is unusual for respondents to invoke more than one belief and, furthermore, not to be particularly attentive to any potential conflicts. Indeed, as we show in our analysis of attitudes toward the IRS (Alvarez and Brehm 1998), even logical contradiction is not sufficient to induce ambivalence, if respondents (apparently) do not realize the inconsistency. Ambivalent survey response requires comprehension of fundamentally irreconcilable and equally maintained values.

Likewise, relative to uncertainty, equivocation is less frequent. While not requiring the irreconcilability of core values and beliefs, it does require that the respondent be able to elaborate on a policy domain beyond what is sufficient to provide an answer. The incentives for the respondent to do so are minimal, and the pressures from the interviewer to proceed to the next topic are palpable. However, for topics that are widely discussed and highly familiar to respondents, thinking of policy in terms of multiple, mutually reinforcing dimensions is possible. Equivocation requires elaboration of these

multiple dimensions, which in turn requires that the respondent be motivated and able to think of policy from multiple angles (Petty and Cacioppo
1986).

Uncertainty, then, is the most likely of the three response categories. For
one, it simply requires that the respondent interpret a policy question along
the lines of a single value or belief. It is cognitively easy, and does not imply
elaboration.

Uncertain respondents attempt to understand policy questions in terms of
their values, but this "understanding" may be very probabilistic, where those
respondents who are more in contact with elite discourse would be more
likely to come to conventional understandings than those who are withdrawn
from regular discussions of these policy problems.

Alternative modes for assessing policy preferences might well demonstrate
a greater frequency of ambivalence. In particular, the intensive interviewing
approach should be more likely to demonstrate ambivalence, because it requires reflection and deliberation, and because the interviewer engages the
subject along the lines of potential conflict, whether logical, ethical, moral,
or otherwise.

Thus, a citizen who is certain, unambivalent, or is equivocal about a given
policy has a very compact distribution around the central tendency, while a
citizen who is uncertain, ambivalent, or is not equivocal has a widely spread
distribution around the central tendency. So, however we approach the analysis of public opinion, we must take into account both the strong likelihood
of heterogeneity caused by uncertainty, ambivalence and equivocation in the
minds of the American public. We will discuss our method of doing so in the
following section.

A STATISTICAL MODEL FOR UNCERTAIN OPINIONS

If we were not concerned about the problem of unequal survey response
variability across individuals in our surveys, it would be relatively simple
for us to examine the effects of predispositions on public policy preferences
using our survey response data. This is because both the binary and ordinal probit choice models are well understood and easy to implement in
virtually all major statistics packages. However, such models assume survey opinion responses have equal variance. If the process that causes them
to have unequal variance is not accounted for in an empirical model of
a given survey question, the model is likely to produce incorrect results.
Moreover, the underlying variance in a respondent's answers yields direct
information about the degree of certainty that a respondent has in his or
her opinions. When there is the possibility that uncertainty, ambivalence
or equivocation are operative for some individuals, then these three different sources of response variability must be included in models of issue
preferences.

Yet, the problem of unequal variance across observations is familiar to every analyst of regression models as heteroskedasticity. In the least squares regression model, if the errors are heteroskedastic, the estimator is unbiased and consistent but is also inefficient, and the typical estimate of the parameter covariance matrix is incorrect. Unfortunately, unequal variance is a worse problem for both binary and ordinal choice models. In the specific case of the probit model, for example, heteroskedasticity makes the maximum likelihood estimates *inconsistent* and the estimate of the covariance matrix of the model estimates incorrect (Yatchew and Griliches 1985). Unlike the case of linear models (where heteroskedasticity only leads to inefficiency), in non-linear choice models it leads to both inconsistent and inefficient coefficient estimates because the heteroskedasticity effects both the coefficient estimates and the estimated variances of the parameters. Therefore, if heteroskedasticity is suspected in a probit model, it must be tested for and included in the model if one expects to obtain consistent estimates.

In maximum likelihood terms, the idea behind modeling dichotomous choice is to specify the systematic component of some probability (π_i) of individual i adopting the choice (y_i). In conventional probit and logit estimations, the analyst assumes that the π_i were generated by a homogeneous process, or that the data are identically and independently distributed. This permits the analyst to write the likelihood function in a relatively simple form:

$$\log L(\pi|y) = \sum_{i=1}^{n} [y_i \log \pi_i + (1 - y_i) \log(1 - \pi_i)]$$

(where π_i is reparameterized as a function, in this case the probit function, of a set of explanatory variables). Our argument is that preferences for public policy choices are *not* identically distributed, but that the process of generating responses to policy choices is heterogeneous: some respondents will be more uncertain, more ambivalent, or more equivocal than other respondents and this will cause them to have a wider underlying distribution of choices. This means that the standard probit model will yield inconsistent estimates (see Greene 1993, 649–50). Note, however, that we still assume independence of observations; this is perfectly plausible, bordering on the mundane, with probability samples of the public.

We can address this source of inconsistency by modeling the heterogeneity. A plausible choice for the functional form of the heterogeneity is a variation of Harvey's "multiplicative heteroskedasticity" approach (1976):

$$y_i^* = X_i\beta + \epsilon_i \tag{1}$$
$$\text{var}(\epsilon_i) = [\exp(Z_i\gamma)]^2$$

where y_i^* is a binary response to the policy question, X_i and Z_i are matrices of independent variables, ϵ_i is an error term and β and γ are coefficient vectors to estimate. The first equation is a model of choice, in which a person's policy beliefs are a linear combination of interests leading the respondent to opt for a particular choice. (In this equation, we also will add sets of control variables that allow us to obtain accurate estimates about the effects of the core values and predispositions on preferences and to test alternative hypotheses about what determines particular policy preferences.) The second equation is a model for the error variance, where we introduce variables accounting for alternative explanations (the multiplicative heteroskedasticity idea). This means that the systematic component now describes an identically distributed process for π_i^*:

$$\pi_i^* = g\left(\frac{X_i\beta}{e^{Z_i\gamma}}\right)$$

where $g()$ is an appropriate link function bounded between zero and one such as the probit function ($\Phi()$). The only identifying assumption in this model is that the variance equation cannot have a constant.

This leads to a log-likelihood function very similar to the usual probit log-likelihood:

$$\log L = \sum_{i=1}^{n}\left(y_i \log \Phi\left(\frac{X_i\beta}{\exp(Z_i\gamma)}\right)\right.$$
$$\left. + (1 - y_i)\log\left[1 - \Phi\left(\frac{X_i\beta}{\exp(Z_i\gamma)}\right)\right]\right) \tag{2}$$

The significant difference between the likelihood above and the conventional probit is the inclusion of the variance model in the denominator in Equation 2.

As we have the term $\frac{X_i\beta}{\exp(Z_i\gamma)}$ in the log-likelihood of Equation 2, it is easy to gain an intuition for why it is important that heteroskedasticity in discrete choice models must be dealt with explicitly. Given that we have the systemic component of the choice function $X_i\beta$ divided by the variance function $\exp(Z_i\gamma)$ we clearly have a nonlinear model. That is, the estimated effect of each component of the choice function (each β) is conditional on the elements of the denominator of this fraction ($\exp(Z_i\gamma)$). If the denominator takes a different value for each individual, then the parameters of the choice function will be incorrectly estimated unless this individual variation is taken into account in the estimation of the model parameters.[1]

---

[1] This can also be seen in the derivatives of the log-likelihood function given in Equation 2 for the two sets of coefficients. First, the derivative of the log-likelihood function with respect to β is:

$$\frac{\partial \log L}{\partial \beta} = \sum_{i=1}^{n}\left[\frac{\phi_i(y_i - \Phi_i)}{\Phi_i(1 - \Phi_i)}\right]\exp(-Z_i\gamma)X_i$$

PUBLIC OPINION ON DIVISIVE ISSUES

We begin this section by discussing the four dependent variables we take from the 1998 American National Election Studies (NES): how we code them for our analysis and what the opinions of Americans were about these four divisive dimensions of public policy. We then turn our attention later in this section to our independent variable measures, and discuss them fully.

Dependent variables

We chose the 1998 American National Election Studies because it contains the appropriate components for our analysis: variables with which to construct core value scales, variables measuring uncertainty and informedness, and variables representing respondents' opinions on a wide variety of political issues. From these issues we selected four that together are representative of the types of issues considered by Americans in recent years. These issues are whether English should be made the official language of the United States, whether schools should be allowed to lead prayers in class, whether blacks should be given preference in hiring and promotion, and whether the government should ban the type of abortion known as "partial birth abortion."

These issues aid our analysis because they differ from one another in important respects. Some, such as English-only and school prayer, are more highly divisive than others, thus making it more likely that conflicting core values may shape public opinion on them. Another, the partial-birth abortion ban, is a fairly new addition to the debate surrounding the abortion issue. For this reason, individuals are likely to have not considered it as much as other issues and so be more uncertain of their opinion on it. They also are likely to be uncertain about their opinion on affirmative action, not because it is a new issue but because it is one that may be addressed by a variety of relatively complicated policies. By differing from one another in these important ways, these issues combine to form a representative and diverse sample.

The variable measuring the opinions of respondents on the English-language-only law is formed from the following survey question, "Do you favor a law making English the official language of the United States, meaning

And the derivative of the log-likelihood function with respect to γ is:

$$\frac{\partial \log L}{\partial \gamma} = \sum_{i=1}^{n} \left[\frac{\phi_i (y_i - \Phi_i)}{\Phi_i (1 - \Phi_i)} \right] \exp(-Z_i \gamma) Z_i (-X_i \beta)$$

Thus, from the derivative in the above equations, it is easy to see that the estimates of β depend on the variance function, in that $Z_i \gamma$ is part of the equation for the rate of change in β: This implies that if there is heteroskedasticity in the data that is ignored the coefficient estimates would be biased.

government business would be conducted in English only, or do you oppose such a law?" For a respondent that favored such a law, the dependent variable is coded a 1, whereas for a respondent that opposed such a law the dependent variable is coded a 0.

The variable indicating the preferences of respondents on the school prayer issue is formed from a more complicated survey question. Respondents were asked to choose the policy they prefer most out of four given selections. The question was, "Which of the following views comes closest to your opinion on the issue of school prayer?" The four possible answers have a clear order along the issue dimension. For the first two, the dependent variable is coded a 0. These are (in order), "By law, prayers should not be allowed in public schools," and, "The law should allow public schools to schedule time when children can pray silently if they want to." The second two correspond with a coding of 1 for the dependent variable. These are (also in order), "The law should allow public schools to schedule time when children as a group can say a general prayer," and "By law, public schools should schedule a time when all children would say a chosen Christian prayer." The distinguishing feature of these two sets of issue positions is that in the former schools are not legally allowed to lead the children in prayer, whereas in the latter schools may lead an organized prayer for the entire class.

The variable measuring respondent's opinions on affirmative action is formed from the following question, "Some people say that because of past discrimination, blacks should be given preference in hiring and promotion. Others say that such preference in hiring and promotion of blacks is wrong because it gives blacks advantages they haven't earned. What about your opinion – are you for or against preferential hiring and promotion of blacks?" The dependent variables of respondents who said they were against such hiring and promotion preferences are coded with a 1 and those of respondents that said that they were for such preferences are coded with a 0.

The variable indicating the position of respondents on the partial birth abortion ban were based on the question, "There has been discussion recently about a proposed law to ban certain types of late-term abortions, sometimes called partial birth abortions. Do you favor or oppose a ban on these types of abortions?" Respondents that said they favor a ban on this type of abortion correspond with a dependent variable that is coded a 1 whereas those that said that they oppose a ban on this sort of abortion correspond with a dependent variable that is coded a 0.

We present the frequency distributions of survey responses for each of the four questions in Table 7.1. Beginning with the question regarding English-only being the official language of the United States, we see that there is strong support for this notion in the American public – two thirds of Americans surveyed in 1998 supported this proposal, and one third opposed it. By contrast,

TABLE 7.1 *Distributions of Responses for Policy Questions*

Response	English–Only Law	Group Led School Prayer	End Affirmative Action	Abortion Ban
Favor	66.6% (853)	30.8% (394)	77.0% (981)	57.4% (723)
Oppose	27.6% (353)	66.4% (848)	17.0% (217)	35.6% (448)
Other	5.5% (70)*	1.9% (24)	3.2% (41)	
Don't Know	.3% (4)	.9% (12)	2.7% (35)	7.1% (89)

Correlation Matrix of Generated Core Value Scales

Variable	Egalitarianism	Antiblack Attitudes	Traditional Morality
Egalitarianism	1.00		
Antiblack Attitudes	−0.34	1.00	
Traditional Morality	−0.28	0.32	1.00

* Answered "Neither favor nor oppose."

in the second column of Table 7.1 we see that two thirds of Americans surveyed opposed group-led school prayer, with 31 percent supporting this policy change. Ending affirmative action was strongly supported by Americans in 1998, as 77 percent of those surveyed favored this policy position and only 17 percent opposed ending affirmative action. Last, 57 percent favored banning late-term abortions, with 36 percent in opposition.

Independent Variables: Core Values

We construct three core values scales using principle factor analysis. Each scale measures types of values that scholarly analysis indicates have significant influence on political beliefs. The survey questions that make up the basis of the factor analysis are intended to reveal respondents' deeply held values about social norms – in this case egalitarianism, anti-black attitudes and moral traditionalism.

Each of these questions was prefaced by the survey administrator saying the following:

I am going to read several statements. After each one, I would like you to tell me whether you agree strongly with the statement, agree somewhat, neither agree nor disagree, disagree somewhat, or disagree strongly.

In our data, the subjects' answers are coded 5 (agree strongly) to 1 (disagree strongly) and enter likewise into the factor analysis.

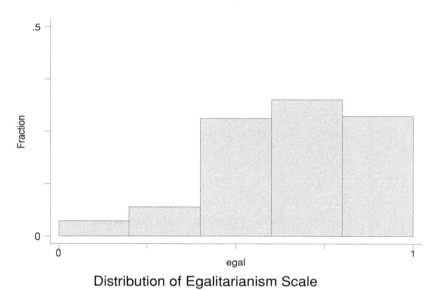

Distribution of Egalitarianism Scale

FIGURE 7.1. Egalitarian Predispositions

The egalitarianism scale is formed from two statements that the respondents replied to in the above fashion. The first is "If people were treated more equally in this country we would have many fewer problems." People who agreed strongly with this statement are likely to rate high on the egalitarianism scale. Conversely, people who agreed strongly with the second statement, "We have gone too far in pushing equal rights in this country" are more likely to rate low on the egalitarianism scale. The two questions have oppositely signed factor loadings of equal magnitude (the former being 0.30 and the latter being −0.30).

We present a histogram of the distribution of our egalitarianism scale in Figure 7.1. The distribution of this measure is skewed toward the positive end, with few respondents scoring low on the egalitarianism scale. Instead, most respondents in the 1998 NES data score on the higher ends of this egalitarianism measure, implying more positive predispositions toward egalitarian beliefs in this dataset.

The second scale measures antiblack attitudes and is formed from two questions which tap into racist or antiblack beliefs. The first is "Irish, Italians, Jewish and many other minorities overcame prejudice and worked their way up. Blacks should do the same without any special favors." People who agreed strongly are more likely to rate high on the antiblack scale. Conversely, people who agreed strongly with the second statement, "Over the past few years, blacks have gotten less than they deserve" are less likely to rate high on the antiblack scale. As with the egalitarianism scale, the two

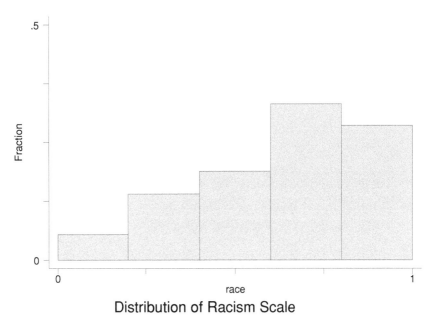

Distribution of Racism Scale

FIGURE 7.2. Antiblack Predispositions

questions used to form this scale have oppositely signed factor loadings of equal magnitude (the former being 0.35 and the latter being −0.35).

We present in Figure 7.2 the distribution of the antiblack or racism measure. Given the way in which we have scaled the variables in the principle factor analysis, respondents who score nearer 1 on this measure are less antiblack or racist than respondents who score near 0. With that in mind, it is interesting to note that most respondents in the sample do fall into the higher ranges of this measure, thus most of the respondents in the sample do report less antiblack predispositions.

Finally, the moral traditionalism scale is composed from five questions that the NES respondents replied to by stating their agreement level. The first is, "The world is always changing and we should adjust our view of moral behavior to those changes." The factor loading for this question is −0.38, indicating that the more a respondent agreed with this statement the more likely he/she rates low on the morality scale. The subsequent two questions are ones with which agreement indicates a high rating on the morality scale. These are, "The newer lifestyles are contributing to the breakdown of our society" (with a factor loading of 0.64) and "This country would have many fewer problems if there were more emphasis on traditional family ties" (with a factor loading of 0.63). The fourth question, "We should be more tolerant of people who choose to live according to their own moral standards, even

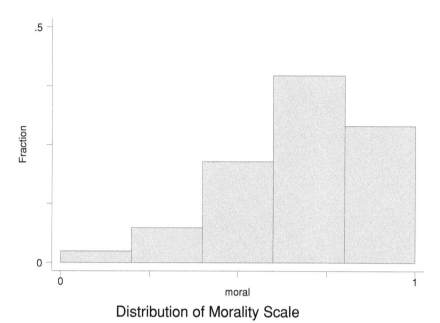

Distribution of Morality Scale

FIGURE 7.3. Moral Traditionalism Predispositions

if they are very different from our own" is one for which higher agreement corresponds with a lower rating on the morality scale, as the factor loading is −0.39. Finally, the last question on the scale is "It is always wrong for a married person to have sexual relations with someone other than their marriage partner." For this question, the more a respondent agreed the more likely he/she is to rate high on the morality scale (with a factor loading of 0.38).

In Figure 7.3 we provide the distribution of the moral traditionalism measure in the 1998 NES data. Like the other two predisposition measures, we find that there is a decidedly positive skew to our measure of this particular predisposition. Most respondents score in the upper ranges of this measure, meaning that they have stronger moral traditionalism predispositions than respondents at the bottom range of the scale.

Furthermore, it is important to note that these scales are not highly correlated with one another. The relative independence of the three predisposition measures can easily be seen in Table 7.2. It is quite clear that the antiblack predisposition measure is relatively independent of moral traditionalism (the correlation is .32). The antiblack and egalitarianism predispositions, and the moral traditionalism and egalitarianism predispositions, both have negative but relatively weak correlations (−.34 and −.28, respectively). The lack of strong correlation among these value scales demonstrates that they are separate and distinct values, and that we are not measuring interrelated sets of core beliefs.

TABLE 7.2 *Heteroskedastic Probit Estimates – 1998 Policy Opinions*

Variable	English–Only Law	Group Led School Prayer	End Affirmative Action	Abortion Ban
Choice Model				
Constant	−1.12(.80)	−.52*(.19)	.29(.31)	−.05(.17)
Egalitarianism	−.31(.28)	.01(.04)	−.38*(.22)	−.05(.08)
Antiblack Attitudes	1.40**(.64)	.09(.07)	1.47**(.57)	.09(.11)
Traditional Morality	1.14**(.52)	.36**(.16)	.23(.25)	.55*(.33)
Liberal	.01(.11)	.02(.02)	−.35**(.15)	−.05(.04)
Conservative	.06(.12)	.01(.02)	−.18(.12)	.04(.04)
National Economy	.02(.06)	−.01(.01)	−.13**(.06)	.02(.02)
Religion	.03(.09)	.06*(.04)	−.02(.07)	.04(.04)
Age	1.04**(.47)	.21**(.10)	−.37*(.22)	−.32*(.18)
Married	−.04(.09)	−.02(.02)	−.03(.07)	−.02(.03)
Male	.07(.10)	−.03(.02)	−.05(.07)	−.05(.04)
White	−.16(.13)	−.00(.03)	.43**(.16)	−.00(.04)
Education	.01(.04)	−.00(.01)	−.02(.03)	−.03**(.01)
Variance Model				
Informedness	−.61**(.28)	−.89**(.30)	−.46**(.20)	−.70*(.36)
Education	−.03(.05)	−.12**(.06)	−.09**(.04)	−.10(.07)
Egal*Moral	.56(.53)	.16(.70)	−.23(.38)	−1.51**(.65)
Egal*Antiblack	.07(.55)	.14(.54)	.89**(.40)	1.67**(.75)
Antiblack*Moral	.58**(.25)	−1.31**(.45)	.02(.29)	−.66*(.39)
Log-Likelihood	595.23	670.45	383.75	658.13
N	1142	1177	1143	1124

** indicates $\rho < .05$ and * indicates $\rho < .10$

Independent Variables: Information and Education

The amount of political knowledge held by a respondent has been shown by a number of scholars to influence the policy positions he/she espouses in surveys and the polling booth (Alvarez 1997, Alvarez and Franklin 1994, Bartels 1986). We use two variables to indicate a respondent's level of political knowledge. The first of these is a categorical measure of the level of education that he/she has attained. Although education is a somewhat indirect measure of political knowledge, the two variables are strongly correlated and education is thought to be a means of lowering the costs of becoming politically informed. Thus, more highly educated people are hypothesized to be able to easily find out about political leaders and issues and thereby to readily become informed about important events.

We also generate a measure of informedness using four relevant questions in the 1998 NES survey. These questions were designed to elicit whether or not a survey respondent could identify the office held by various prominent American and foreign leaders. In each question, respondents were given a leader's name and asked to state the title of his current job or political office. The first of these was Al Gore (who was correctly identified by 1,133 of 1,281 as the vice president). Next, was William Rehnquist (who was correctly identified by only 136 respondents), Boris Yeltsin (who was correctly identified by 637 respondents), and Newt Gingrich (who was correctly identified by 767 respondents).

The overall measure of informedness was generated by weighting each answer (correct or incorrect) equally. This produced a variable that would equal 1 if a survey respondent correctly identified the title of all four politicians, a corresponding fraction (.75, .5, or .25) if he/she correctly identified some subset (3, 2, or 1) of the leaders, or zero if he/she identified none of the leaders' titles correctly.

Other Independent Variables

We have included an array of other variables that have been shown in much of the voting literature to predict political issue preferences. Among these are the respondent's age and dummy variables that represent whether or not an individual is a liberal (places self left of center on the ideology scale), a conservative (places self right of center on the ideology scale), married, male, white, or attends religious services. We also measure how respondents feel about the economy using a three point scale that indicates if he/she thinks the economic situation in the United States has improved, remained the same, or worsened over the last year's time.

HETEROSKEDASTIC PROBIT AND UNCERTAIN ATTITUDES

With the heteroskedastic probit we are able to specify and estimate simultaneously two related equations, one for the probability of a choice, the other for the variance of the error residual. We refer to the first equation as the "Choice Model" and to the second equation as the "Variance Model." Note that the variance modeled by this approach is the individual respondent's variance in choice, not the variance across the sample. Our approach employs inferential statistics to model and estimate this variance in choice.

The heteroskedastic probit model is well suited to testing our current hypotheses about the role of uncertainty, ambivalence and equivocation in determining individual preferences on political issues. Ambivalence as a form of response variability entails two criteria; that individuals who are better informed exhibit greater response variability, and also that those individuals display conflict between core beliefs or values. Conversely, uncertainty and equivocation as forms of response variability entail only one criteria each. The uncertainty criteria posits that individuals who are less informed exhibit greater response variability, whereas the equivocation criteria posits that individuals whose core values reinforce their impact on a policy opinion exhibit less response variability.

Specification of the Choice Function

The specification of the choice function is largely driven by the existing literature in this field. We include several dummy variables that are expected to help predict an individual's basic political preferences, which have been shown by previous research on voting and political opinion (Campbell, Converse, Miller, and Stokes 1960; Lazarfeld, Berelson, and Gaudet 1944) to correlate strongly with ideology, age, education, one's perception of economic conditions, and traits such as whether or not one is white, married, male, or religious. Also expected to influence political preferences (as described earlier) are the three core value scales, which shape individuals' perceptions of issues and policy choices. These scales have each been normalized to the [0, 1] interval, so as to make the interpretation of their effects easier.

Specification of the Variance Function

The specification of the variance function reflects our desire to test three competing explanations for differences across Americans in the variation of their policy issue beliefs. Variation in policy beliefs may reflect fundamental uncertainty about the policy choice under discussion. In other words, people may simply lack information about the policy choices and what they imply, and that uncertainty will be reflected in the variance function of the heteroskedastic probit model.

To control for the effect of uncertainty, we include in the specification of the variance function two variables which measure the cost of becoming generally informed and knowledgeable of current political affairs. The first of these is a simple ordinal categorization of the level of education of the respondent, such as whether or not he/she finished high school, enrolled in college courses, earned a junior college or four-year college degree or earned some sort of postgraduate degree. The second of these is a linear [0,1] variable that increases with the number of political leaders (out of a total of four possible) that a respondent correctly identifies.

The rival explanations for variability in policy attitudes are ambivalence and equivocation induced by conflicting core beliefs. We set two criteria in order to identify ambivalence. The first is that additional information should not reduce, and may in fact heighten, the response variability. The second criterion is that response variability should increase as core beliefs and values conflict. If both of these are satisfied, the impact of ambivalence on response variability is clear. In contrast, we set one criterion in order to identify equivocation. This criteria stipulates that conflicting core beliefs should reinforce one another in influencing an individual's policy choice, thereby reducing response variability.

To test for the core belief conflict or reinforcement we include interaction terms for each of the three core beliefs that we have measured. Each interaction term is simply the value of one core belief multiplied by the value of another core belief. As we have estimated three core value measures, we have three interaction terms specified in the variance function of each policy model. The first of these is the egalitarianism scale multiplied by the traditional morality scale, the second of these is the egalitarian scale multiplied by the antiblack scale, and the last of these is the traditional morality scale multiplied by the antiblack scale. The higher one's belief in any two of these core values, the greater will be the magnitude of the interaction term between the same two core values; thus the interaction terms operationalize the concept of clashing or reinforcing values.[2] Hence, if ambivalence is the appropriate characterization, we expect that the coefficients on the political knowledge variables are positive or not significantly different from zero and the coefficients on the interaction terms are positive and statistically significant, whereas if equivocation is the appropriate characterization, we expect that the coefficients on the interaction terms are negative and statistically significant.

RESULTS

The results of the four issue models are presented in Table 7.2. For each of the dependent variables we present the probit estimates for the choice function

---

[2] Of course, there are alternative ways to measure conflicting or reinforcing values. In particular, given sufficient resources, one approach would be to employ experimental designs within survey instruments to attempt to invoke conflicing or reinforcing values (e.g., Alvarez and Brehm 2000; Sniderman and Piazza 1993). In the current analysis, however, such experiments were not included in the original survey design. Thus, interaction terms for value conflict or reinforcement are the best available measures.

component of the model in the top rows of the table, and the estimates for the variance function component in the bottom rows of the model.

Our estimates of the choice function shed some light on the types of values that shape policy choices for different political issues. Unsurprisingly, opinions on the two issues that are related to minorities are strongly affected by an individual's antiblack attitudes. One is much more likely to support an English language–only law and the ending of affirmative action policies the greater one's antiblack attitudes.

One's level of traditional morality also influences in an expected manner one's opinions on a number of these issues. The higher an individual rates on the traditional morality scale, the more he or she is likely to support an English language–only law, school-led prayer, and a partial birth abortion ban. Conversely, the variable measuring the egalitarianism value has little impact on one's choice in any of the models except the affirmative action model. In this case we find that an individual who rates low on the egalitarianism scale is likely to support repealing affirmative action laws. Given that of all of the policies we consider this is the one most closely related to the issue of race equality, this result makes intuitive sense.

Of primary interest are the estimates on the variance specification of the model. We find that for all four issues modeled, more informed respondents have smaller variances in their policy choices than less-informed respondents. The effect of political informedness in the variance model is always negative and statistically significant for each issue. The effect of education is also always negative but is only statistically significant for two of the four issues: school prayer and affirmative action.

The distinction between ambivalence and uncertainty is that additional information reduces uncertainty, but does not neccessarily reduce ambivalence. If the respondent is in a state of internalized conflict, then additional information only heightens the state of conflict. The consistently negative sign on political informedness and education implies that for these policy issues high variance in opinion is due to low information. This and the fact that only three of the twelve coefficients estimated for the conflicting core value measures are positive and significant indicate that the variance in opinion may be best characterized by uncertainty and not by ambivalence.[3]

In addition to this strong support for the uncertainty hypothesis, we find some slightly weaker support for the equivocation hypothesis. The variance of opinions on both school prayer and abortion is reduced as the value of

---

[3] This is consistent with our previous research. For certain types of abortion policies we have shown that variance in citizens' opinions is due to ambivalence. Unlike the abortion policy considered in this chapter (regarding a ban of partial birth abortions), the policies considered previously were related to the legality of various reasons women have for wanting abortions. Reasons that did not include health or rape (such as not wanting more children) generated higher degrees of ambiguity among citizens' opinions.

an individual's antiblack and traditional morality interaction scale increases. This is shown by the fact that the coefficients on this variable in the two models are each negative and significant. This indicates that both uncertainty and equivocation influence public opinion on these two issues. Our understanding of the relative importance of each explanation of response variability is improved by studying the magnitude of each estimated impact on both choice and variance, a subject we discuss in the next section.

Magnitude of Estimated Effects

The magnitude of the effect of each of the independent variables on the likelihood that an individual chooses to support a given political policy is indecipherable from the results shown in the previous table. The reason for this is the probability that an individual chooses an option in the probit model is determined by the cumulative normal distribution function of the expected utility generated by the independent variables. Thus, while the most salient aspects of a coefficient – its sign and whether or not it is statistically different from zero are immediately knowable from looking at results such as those shown in the previous table – an understanding of the impact of each of the independent variables on the individual's choice, is not so easily gained.

For this we turn to another way of presenting the results of a probit model, the "first differences" for each of the independent variables shown in the table below. The "first difference" methodology is relatively simple (King 1989). Here we set each independent variable to the sample mean value and determine with this the probability that a hypothetical "representative respondent" would choose a particular action (to abstain, vote for the Democrat or vote for the Republican). Then, for any given independent variable (for example: education level) we increase the value of that variable by one sample standard deviation and calculate the probability that the hypothetical respondent chooses each possible action and then decrease the value of that variable by one sample standard deviation and calculate the probability that the hypothetical respondent chooses each possible action. The difference between these two probability estimates provides our "first difference," which can be thought of as an estimate of the impact on the outcome of a two standard deviation change in one independent variable, holding all other effects in the model constant.

The "first differences" are presented for selected variables in the Table 7.3. This presents strong evidence that the greater the level of one's antiblack attitudes the more likely one is to support both an English language–only law and the end of affirmative action practices. The likelihood that one supports the former policy is increased by 21 percentage points and the likelihood that one supports the latter policy is increased by 12 percentage points from a two standard deviation increase in one's antiblack attitudes.

TABLE 7.3 *Effects of Values and Uncertainty on Choice*

Variable	English–Only Law	Group Led School Prayer	End Affirmative Action	Abortion Ban
Informedness	.06	−.07	.04	.05
Education	.04	−.09	.05	−.05
Egalitarianism	−.04	.01	−.03	−.02
Antiblack Attitudes	.21	.07	.12	.04
Traditional Morality	.14	.20	.01	.22

Each cell entry is the change in probability of a positive response due to two standard deviation change around the mean.

TABLE 7.4 *Effects of Uncertainty and Ambivalence on the Variance of Choice*

Variable	English–Only Law	Group Led School Prayer	End Affirmative Action	Abortion Ban
Informedness	−0.73	−0.06	−0.22	−0.09
Education	−0.31	−0.07	−0.38	−0.11
Egal*Moral	0.50	0.01	−0.08	−0.15
Egal*Antiblack	0.07	0.01	0.35	0.19
Antiblack*Moral	0.67	−0.09	−0.01	−0.08

Each cell entry is the change in total variance due to two standard deviation change around the mean.

One's degree of traditional morality has less impact than the antiblack attitudes measure, although it also makes one more likely (by 14 percentage points) to support the English language–only law. Unsurprisingly, its impact on the probability that one supports organized school prayer and a ban on the partial-birth abortion procedure is fairly large. A two standard deviation increase in one's rating on the traditional morality scale increases the likelihood one supports the former by 20 percentage points and increases the likelihood one supports the latter by 22 percentage points.

The estimated parameters in the variance function are also difficult to interpret. In Table 7.4 we present calculations that will allow us to discuss the magnitude of the estimated effects on the variation in respondent policy choices. Here we again employ the "first difference" approach by estimating the underlying error variance for the same hypothetical respondent (using the mean value of all of the right-hand side variables), with one of the error variance terms set to the mean minus its standard deviation. We then estimate the error variance again, after changing the same variable to its mean plus its standard deviation. In Table 7.4, we give the difference between these two calculations. As with Table 7.3, this may be thought of as an estimate of the impact on the variance of a two standard deviation change in one independent variable, holding the other variables constant.

This exercise demonstrates that political informedness and education have strongly negative effects on respondents' opinion variance for each of the four issues studied. For each policy except abortion, a two standard deviation increase in one of the variables measuring an individual's uncertainty leads to a decrease in the variance of his or her opinion that is greater in magnitude than shifts caused by the same increases in variables measuring core value conflict. For all four of the policies modeled, the negative and significant effects of the uncertainty variables indicate that it is uncertainty and not ambivalence that is the cause of individuals' response variance. In addition, the results for the school prayer and abortion models indicate that on these issues equivocation acts with uncertainty to reduce response variability. The magnitude of the effects of informedness and education show us that for the first three issues modeled (the English–only law, organized school prayer and ending affirmative action) the influence of uncertainty on the distribution of responses is particularly large.

CONCLUSION

The new research we present in this chapter demonstrates that uncertainty, in the way we have conceptualized it, is indeed an important characteristic of American public opinion. This underscores previous research (Alvarez and Brehm [2002]) on public opinion, and should serve as an important corrective to the public opinion literature that has often been mired in a debate about extremes – whether Americans are perfectly informed about public affairs or totally ignorant about public affairs.

Rather, our work suggests that the questions should be *how well informed* are Americans about issues generally, *why is uncertainty high on some issues but not others*, and *why some individuals are better informed than others*. These are all important questions, and providing a research agenda aimed at answering these questions should be the focus of research in the field of public opinion. That is, instead of constructing straw man arguments about how citizens fail to live up to the standards of perfect information, we argue that our focus should be on the variation in that information.

That the research here demonstrates a condition of uncertainty rather than ambivalence should be informative for other debates. Contrary to much of the longer tradition in the field, we found little evidence that multiple predispositions are in conflict over these diverse areas of policy. While there may be a good reason to find moral traditionalism, egalitarianism, and racial aversion all logically incompatible with one another, we find that single values tend to dominate. This is well worth note, because all four of the topics we cover have been the subject of intense campaigns to "frame" the discussion. Pro-choice activists won the "partial birth abortion" debate because they were successful in framing the debate in those terms, rather than the clinical ("dilation and curetage") terms preferred by medical practitioners (Freedman 1997). Note that in our prior work on attitudes toward abortion that we found evidence of internalized conflict only when the subjects were unable to rationalize a largely one–sided and asymmetrical problem (i.e., under the most pro–choice of conditions). Under the most widely supported conditions (i.e., when the mother's health is in danger, rape, incest, and birth defects), attitudes toward abortion are clearly *uncertain*, not ambivalent. Likewise, antiaffirmative action activists were only successful in their campaigns once the frame shifted from one of unearned advantages to that of reverse discrimination, inviting egalitarians to reverse their support for such pro–black policies.

The implication from the success of the frames and the finding of uncertainty might then be that such radical shifts of frames are only possible if political elites are able to convincingly portray the policy in terms that tend toward one-sided, asymmetrical politics. That is not to say that pro–choice and pro–affirmative action advocates have not been persuasive in their own counts, but that the pro–choice and pro–affirmative action sides faced very difficult debates to counter: pro–choice advocates could no more be supporters of partial birth abortions than pro–affirmative action advocates could be supporters of reverse discrimination. To the extent that these sides hope to influence future debates, it will surely be by casting the problem in one-sided terms favorable to their own causes.

In fact, the most important component of the variance models is information, measured in two forms: chronic political informedness and education. It is a standard feature of public opinion research that those who are better educated tend to have better "crystallized" belief systems. This program of research documents that information is the best predictor of response variance, an inference about the potential range of survey responses.

Our research also has an important methodological dimension as well. In the past, research on uncertainty has been stymied by a lack of appropriate measures of uncertainty. This spawned innovative attempts in the field of electoral politics to operationalize and measure uncertainty (Alvarez 1997; Bartels 1986) using existing survey data, as well as work on direct survey measures of uncertainty (Alvarez and Franklin 1994). As we have discussed in this chapter, our research agenda has been to develop inferential statistical models that can be used to study uncertainty and other types of variability in public opinion, along the lines taken by Franklin (1991). These inferential statistical models are now widely available in popular statistical software packages making them more accessible and easy to use than ever before. For this reason and because we have shown that they are often essential for generating accurate results, we hope that they are used more frequently in the study of public opinion.

References

Achen, C. H. 1975. "Mass Political Attitudes and the Survey Response." *American Political Science Review* 69:1218–23.

Alvarez, R. Michael. 1997. *Information and Elections*. Ann Arbor: University of Michigan Press.

Alvarez, R. Michael, and John Brehm. 1995. "American Ambivalence Toward Abortion Policy: A Heteroskedastic Probit Method for Assessing Conflicting Values." *American Journal of Political Science* 39:1055–82.

Alvarez, R. Michael, and John Brehm. 1997. "Are Americans Ambivalent Toward Racial Policies?" *American Journal of Political Science* 41:345–274.

Alvarez, R. Michael, and John Brehm. 1998. "Speaking in Two Voices: American Equivocation About the Internal Revenue Service." *American Journal of Political Science* 42:418–52.

Alvarez, R. Michael, and John Brehm. 2000. "Binding the Frame: How Important are Frames for Survey Response." Paper presented at the 2000 Annual Meeting of the American Political Science Association.

Alvarez, R. Michael, and John Brehm. 2002. *Hard Choices, Easy Answers: Values, Information and American Public Opinion*. Princeton, NJ: Princeton University Press.

Alvarez, R. Michael, and Charles H. Franklin. 1994. "Uncertainty and Political Perceptions." *Journal of Politics* 56:671–88.

Bartels, Larry M. 1986. "Issue Voting Under Uncertainty: An Empirical Test." *American Journal of Political Science* 30:709–23.

Berelson, Bernard, Paul Lazarsfeld, and William McPhee. 1954. *Voting*. Chicago: University of Chicago Press.

Campbell, A., P. E. Converse, W. E. Miller, and D. E. Stokes. 1960. *The American Voter*. Chicago: University of Chicago Press.

Chong, Dennis. 2000. *Rational Lives: Norms and Values in Politics and Society*. Chicago: University of Chicago Press.

Delli Carpini, Michaelx, and Scott Keeter. 1996. *What Americans Know About Politics and Why It Matters*. New Haven: Yale University Press.

Downs, Anthony. 1957. *An Economic Theory of Democracy*. New York: Harper and Row.

Enelow, James M., and Melvin J. Hinich. 1984. *The Spatial Theory of Voting*. New York: Cambridge University Press.

Feldman, Stanley. 1988. "Structure and Consistency in Public Opinion: The Role of Core Beliefs and Values." *American Journal of Political Science* 32:416–40.

Franklin, Charles H. 1991. "Eschewing Obfuscation? Campaigns and the Perceptions of U.S. Senate Incumbents." *American Political Science Review* 85: 1193–214.

Freedman, Paul. 1997. "Framing the 'Partial Birth' Abortion Debate: A Survey Experiment." Paper presented at the 1997 Midwest Political Science Association Annual Meetings.

Greene, William H. 1993. *Econometric Analysis*. 2nd ed. New York: Macmillan Publishing Company.

Harvey, Andrew. 1976. "Estimating Regression Models with Multiplicative Heteroskedasticity." *Econometrics* 44:461–465.

Hochschild, Jennifer L. 1981. *What's Fair? American Beliefs about Distributive Justice*. Cambridge, MA: Harvard University Press.

Key, V.O., Jr. 1966. *The Responsible Electorate*. New York: Vintage Books.

Kinder, Donald R., and Lynn M. Sanders. 1996. *Divided by Color: Racial Politics and Democratic Ideals*. Chicago: University of Chicago Press.

King, Gary. 1989. *Unifying Political Methodology: The Likelihood Theory of Statistical Inference*. New York: Cambridge University Press.

Lazarfeld, P., B. Berelson, and H. Gaudet. 1944. *The People's Choice*. New York: Columbia University Press.

Liberman, Akiva, and Shelly Chaiken. 1991. "Value Conflict and Thought-Induced Attitude Change." *Journal of Experimental Social Psychology* 27:203–16.

Page, Benjamin I. 1978. *Choices and Echoes in Presidential Elections*. Chicago: University of Chicago Press.

Petty, R. E., and J. Cacioppo. 1986. *Communication and Persuasion: Central and Peripheral Routes to Attitude Change*. New York: Springer-Verlag.

Rokeach, M. 1973. *The Nature of Human Values*. New York: Free Press.

Shepsle, Kenneth A. 1972. "The Strategy of Ambiguity." *American Political Science Review* 66:555–68.

Sniderman, Paul M., and Thomas Piazza. 1993. *The Scar of Race*. Cambridge, MA: Harvard University Press.

Tetlock, Philip E. 1986. "A Value Pluralism Model of Ideological Reasoning." *Journal of Personality and Social Psychology* 1986:819–27.

Yatchew, A., and Z. Griliches. 1985. "Specification Error in Probit Models." *Review of Economics and Statistics* 18:239–40.

8

Risk and Uncertainty as Sources of Incumbent Insecurity

Cherie D. Maestas

The concept of electoral insecurity plays a central role in theories of incumbent behavior and representation as we strive to understand how incumbent legislators respond to their political environment. A broad and influential body of research is rooted in the belief that incumbents' insecurity over reelection can explain a variety of political phenomenon such as roll call votes, incumbent district service, fundraising, institutional features of Congress, and the changing strength of political parties.[1] Yet, how we define the concept of "insecurity" affects the type of political conditions we focus on when analyzing or predicting incumbent behavior and affects our views of the conditions that are necessary or sufficient for representation. Accordingly, the concept of insecurity deserves careful scrutiny.

Typically, incumbent insecurity is defined as a form of risk, based on incumbents' assessments of their chances of winning reelection. Not surprisingly, the chance of winning is often treated as synonymous with the level of competition or vote share in a district. Incumbents who face strong, well-funded challengers, or have only "marginal" vote support risk losing their seats when they run for reelection and are expected to alter their behavior while in office to reduce that risk. Sources of electoral risk, such as previous vote margin, district party balance, opinion heterogeneity or challenger quality, are placed at the center of analyses because we believe that incumbents estimate their chances of reelection by assessing these types of factors. From this perspective, the vast majority of incumbents should

[1] See, for example, Arnold 1990; Cox and McCubbins 1993; Fenno 1978; Fiorina 1974; Johannes and McAdams 1981; Kingdon 1989; Mayhew 1974a; Parker 1992; Rivers and Fiorina 1989; Rohde 1991.

I appreciate the suggestions given by Barry Burden and Mark Hansen. Their questions and comments helped to clarify several key points in this chapter. I also thank Walter Stone, Ron Rapoport, Scott Adler, and John McIver for their many helpful comments on earlier drafts. All remaining errors are, of course, my own.

feel quite secure. The number of "marginal" elections at both the state and congressional level has declined (Jewell and Breaux 1988; Mayhew 1974b; Weber, Tucker, and Brace 1991) and studies show that the probability of incumbent reelection is extremely high, particularly for legislators who have access to resources to help insulate themselves from political or economic tides (Berry, Berkman, and Schneiderman 2000; Carey, Niemi, and Powell 2000).[2]

Yet, despite the high probability of reelection, many incumbents do not act as if they feel secure. Instead, we often find that even legislators in the "safest" districts still focus a substantial amount of time on reelection seeking activities. This anomaly suggests that we must explore new avenues to identify the full range of factors that shape incumbents' feelings of insecurity and, ultimately, their behavior while in office.

This chapter argues that to understand fully the concept of incumbent insecurity, we must explicitly recognize the uncertainty incumbents face when trying to forecast future events. Hence, the concept of incumbent insecurity should be broken down into two separate dimensions: risk, the chances that an incumbent will win or lose, and uncertainty, the confidence that an incumbent feels when trying to "guesstimate" his future chances. The reason for this is quite simple; incumbents must assess a range of conditions and anticipate the actions of many actors, including prospective challengers, potential voters, interest groups, and media. This multipart calculation is complex. Uncertainty over any single aspect of the district environment can lead an incumbent to doubt his best guess.

Indeed, some scholars suggest that weak partisanship combined with new campaign technologies and candidate centered elections create a more volatile and unpredictable electoral climate (see, for example Jacobson 1987a, 1987b, 1997; King 1997; Schlesinger 1991, 187–99). When vote patterns are not stable from one election to the next, it is more difficult for incumbents to assess their chances of reelection because they must rely heavily on prospective information rather than retrospective information about past voter support or vote margins. How *certain* incumbents feel about their assessed chances of winning can vary considerably across districts, depending on the type and quality of information available to incumbents when they assess their chances. Even incumbents who estimate their chances to be quite high might feel a sense of uncertainty over whether their favorable estimate is correct and niggling doubts could have the largest effects where we expect them least: seemingly safe districts.

---

[2] Although scholars note that fewer congressional elections are marginal, some question whether this translates into greater security for incumbents. Jacobson (1987a, 1987b) and Collie (1981), for example, argue that the there is not a clear relationship between marginality and the probability of being reelected. For different perspectives on this debate, also see Gross and Garand (1984) and Garand, Wink, and Vincent (1993).

Exploring the concept of uncertainty, distinct from risk, offers a different way of thinking about the electoral forces incumbents respond to and can help us discern important differences in the degree of insecurity felt by incumbents, even among incumbents we typically think of as "safe." Indeed, treating risk and uncertainty as separate dimensions offers an alternative perspective to the question of whether incumbents are more secure now than in the past. Jacobson's (1987a, 1987b) work, for example, suggests that even though electoral *risk* might be declining, incumbent *uncertainty* might be increasing. So, while the general level of insecurity incumbents feel might not have declined, the reasons for insecurity might have changed, and this change could have significant implications for how incumbents respond to conditions in their districts. This is important because insecurity that is derived from known risks associated with competitive elections and insecurity derived from uncertainty over the ability to forecast the future may prompt different behavioral responses from incumbents.

INSECURITY IN TWO DIMENSIONS

Differentiating uncertainty from risk begins by clearly defining both concepts in a decision-making context. The most basic model of decision making assumes that individuals have ordered preferences for alternative "states of the world" and that they select the alternative that is most highly ranked. However, it is rare that an individual can directly choose the preferred outcome or state of the world. Instead, the individual must choose actions that he or she believes will lead to the preferred outcome. Here, the decision maker is operating under conditions of risk because actions and outcomes do not have a one to one correspondence. As one action may lead to more than one outcome, the decision maker cannot know ahead of time whether the chosen action will lead to the preferred outcome. He or she must select a course of action based on *probabilistic* outcomes, thus assuming some *risk* that the outcome will be undesirable.

When risks are known and depend on a set of objective conditions, such as the probability of drawing an ace from a fair deck of cards, the decision maker faces *uncertainty over outcomes* but not *uncertainty over probabilities*. Risk is really just another way of describing uncertainty over outcomes because it is the numeric expression of the chances that different events will occur. This is very different from uncertainty over probabilities, where the decision maker is unsure of the correct probability to assign to events. Although uncertainty over probabilities can occur in any situation where a decision maker lacks full information, it is common in situations in which decision makers rely on subjectively estimated probabilities. This is precisely the situation that incumbents are faced with – subjectively estimating the chance of winning reelection.

Historically, uncertainty over probabilities has been treated as synonymous with uncertainty over outcomes because scholars assume that decision makers who are uncertain about the probability of some future outcome will *equalize* their subjective probability estimates (see, for example, Cioffi-Revilla 1998; Hey 1979; Hirshleifer and Riley 1992; Niemi and Weisberg 1972; Shepsle and Bonchek 1997). An uncertain individual assessing the probability of two outcomes would assess the chances of each at 1/2; an uncertain individual assessing the probability of three possible outcomes would simply assign 1/3, and so on. Applied to the reelection calculus, this approach assumes that incumbents who are completely uncertain about the chance of reelection would assess their chances of winning to be fifty-fifty, where winning is as probable as losing.[3] In contrast, incumbents who are certain would assess their chances of winning at the ends of the probabilistic scale at zero, certain to lose, or one, certain to win.

This definition of uncertainty makes no formal distinction between risk and uncertainty because theorists assume that a decision maker's subjective estimate of risk fully embodies the uncertainty in the decision context. However, as Alpert (1980, 211) aptly points out "the use of equal probabilities of events arising from ignorance or uncertainty may have different implications for political decision making compared with the use of equal probabilities based on knowledge." In other words, incumbents who rate their chances as low because they are uncertain about district conditions might behave quite differently than those who rate their chances as low because they *know* they face a tough reelection campaign against a well-known challenger. Similarly, incumbents who view their chances as high yet still feel uncertain because they lack information about challengers, voters or both, might choose different actions than incumbents who are certain their chances are high because they know they will not face a challenger. To account for this type of variation, we must define risk and uncertainty separately. Only then can we explore their relationship to district conditions and their relationship to each other.

Uncertainty can be distinguished from risk by making two simple but plausible assumptions. The first assumption is that an incumbent can arrive

---

[3] This is very different from assuming that an incumbent will receive 50 percent of the vote. Indeed, if an incumbent was certain that he would win 50 percent + 1 vote, he would estimate the chances of reelection at 1 and be highly confident about that assessment. In other words, the expectation of a low vote margin does not necessarily imply that an incumbent would assess odds of reelection at 50/50. Generally speaking, incumbents in districts where the vote is likely to be close are thought to have a lower chance of winning because the probability of a vote shift large enough to unseat an incumbent with a 52 percent margin is greater than the probability of a vote shift large enough to unseat an incumbent with a 72 percent margin. It is important to note, however, this view is disputed by scholars who find evidence that higher margins do not translate into lower chances of turnover (Collie 1981; Jacobson 1987a, 1987b).

at some subjective estimation of the probability of winning reelection. Regardless of the district or personal conditions, incumbents, if pressed, could offer a numeric estimate of their chances of winning their upcoming election. Second, and perhaps more controversial, is the assumption that this estimate takes on the characteristics of a random variable. In other words, I assume that subjective probabilities contain some element of randomness where an incumbent offers a slightly different estimate of the chances of reelection if repeatedly asked (e.g. "sampled"), even if nothing about the district or campaign context had changed.

These two assumptions give rise to a distribution that is similar to what Savage (1954) calls a "secondary distribution of probabilities," which expresses the decision maker's view of the chances that any given probability estimate is the "true" probability of an outcome.[4] The mean of the secondary distribution is the probability of winning that the incumbent believes is "most likely" and, indeed, is most likely to offer if asked. The variance of this distribution reflects the range of probabilities that is plausible.[5] These probabilities, while perhaps not the most likely, also might be consistent enough with district conditions that the incumbent would view them as possible, but to lesser degrees. Alternatively stated, an incumbent who was repeatedly "sampled" is also likely to offer other estimates than the mean, and the secondary distribution reflects the range and likelihood of different subjective probabilities. Greater confidence, or certainty, in estimating the probability of reelection is associated with lower variance in this secondary distribution of probabilities.

Figure 8.1 illustrates the differences in uncertainty reflected in secondary probability distributions for two hypothetical incumbents. Although both incumbents assess their probability of reelection as quite high (.9), one incumbent is much more uncertain about that assessment than the other. The "very uncertain" incumbent believes probabilities of reelection ranging from 0 to 1 to be possible while the "somewhat uncertain" incumbent sees his likely chances of winning as ranging from around .6 to one. This difference in uncertainty arises because incumbents must estimate their chances of reelection

---

[4] Savage (1954) cautions that adopting such an approach opens the door to an infinite series of prior probability distributions, and cautions readers to resist such an approach. Nevertheless, this formulation captures an essential element of the decision environment that is lacking when limiting the focus to the "primary" probability distribution. Moreover, the series of probability distributions prior to the "secondary" distribution serve only to amplify uncertainty and need not be treated separately in conceptualizing risk and uncertainty as separate dimensions.

[5] For simplicity's sake, I assume that subjective probability is normally distributed, so that greater uncertainty leads to an increased chance that probabilities both above and below the mean estimate are likely. An alternative, and perhaps more accurate approach might be to assume a skewed distribution where the direction of skew depends on whether the decision maker is risk averse or risk acceptant. A normal distribution, then, would be associated with risk neutrality.

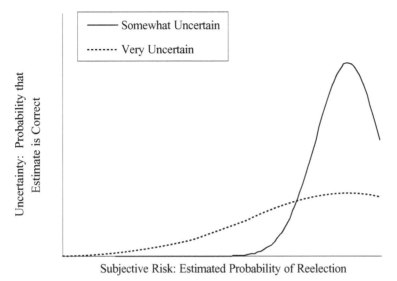

FIGURE 8.1. Distribution of Subjective Probability Estimates of an Outcome, with Uncertainty about Estimated Probability

based on different levels of information or under different district conditions. For example, one incumbent might have substantial knowledge about the quality of his challenger and the likely effect of campaign information on voters, while another incumbent might know very little about the challenger or potential voter reactions. Thus, the latter incumbent is likely to feel much less confident in assessing future chances.

This conceptualization of risk and uncertainty allows the uncertainty dimension to differ across incumbents, even if they face a similar degree of risk. At the same time, it is important to recognize that uncertainty and risk can be related. Distinguishing risk from uncertainty at the theoretical level helps to clarify how greater uncertainty can cause incumbents to act as if they face great risk. Experimental and theoretical work by several economists suggests that uncertainty might cause risk averse decision makers to over-weight lower end probabilities and make decisions based on the "worst case scenario" (Ellsberg 1961; Gilboa 1987; Gilboa and Schmidler 1989; Raiffa 1961). This implies that incumbents who are uncertain would have lower "effective" estimates of their chances of reelection. This view is consistent with the anecdotal evidence that "safe" incumbents often still feel insecure.[6]

In sum, distinguishing risk from uncertainty allows us to trace *why* incumbents feel insecure and behave as if they are more at risk. Does their

---

[6] Note, uncertainty might not necessarily lead to a downward bias. For risk acceptant agents, uncertainty could create an upward bias in the subjective probability. However, it seems reasonable to assume that incumbents are risk averse with respect to losing their seats.

apprehension stem from a true "wolf at the door" or does it stem from seeing shadows in the district? Moreover, it allows us to explicitly incorporate each aspect into theoretical and empirical models of incumbent behavior and can help us develop more complete explanations of how different types of district forces shape political outcomes.[7]

MEASURING RISK AND UNCERTAINTY

The more important question is whether risk and uncertainty can be distinguished empirically, and if so, whether they are related to different district or personal conditions. If not, the theoretical distinction is of little substantive significance. I explored these questions empirically using data gathered from a survey of state legislative incumbents running for reelection in 1998 in eight states: Connecticut, Delaware, Florida, Massachusetts, Minnesota, Oklahoma, Wisconsin, and Vermont. Because state legislators are accessible, data can be obtained through a mail survey directly asking them to assess their chances of reelection and to indicate the degree of certainty they felt about that estimate. In addition, the survey asked for their views on their district environment, the characteristics of potential challengers, the responsiveness of voters to different stimulus, and their plans to devote time and resources to a range of campaign and office activities.[8] Notably, state legislative races have become increasingly candidate centered and similar to congressional races, where state legislators' efforts to secure their seats mimic the tactics used at the congressional level (Salamore and Salamore 1989). Thus, although most state legislatures are not as professional as Congress, the similarities are sufficient to test general hypotheses about legislator perceptions and behavior. Moreover, this is the best possible means of testing theories based on subjective data since similar data cannot be easily obtained at the congressional level.

Respondents were asked to rate their chances of reelection on a scale of 0 to 100 percent, in 10 percent increments.[9] As one would expect from incumbents who have chosen to run for reelection, most rate their chances as quite high. Over half (60 percent) rated their chances at 90 or 100 percent,

---

[7] The use of both dimensions in an expected utility model of incumbent behavior can be found in Maestas (2000), Chapter 3.

[8] The survey was conducted during the summer of 1998 prior to the primary election in each state. I selected this time frame for the survey so that incumbents would be actively involved in assessing their electoral prospects but would not yet have full information on their general election challenger. The survey yielded a response rate of 35 percent as 430 of the 1,224 incumbents surveyed returned completed questionnaires.

[9] Respondents were asked, "Thinking about the next election you will face, what is your best estimate of your chances of winning the general election? (0 percent means no chance of winning while 100 percent means you are sure to win. A 50 percent chance would indicate that you have about the same chance of winning as you do of losing)."

while only 9 percent rated their chances in the 40 to 60 percent range. The remaining respondents rated their chances at 70 percent or 80 percent.

The certainty question was designed to determine whether respondents believe that their estimate was generally correct and stable, or whether respondents thought it would change in response to new information. The format follows the pioneering work of Michael Alvarez and Charles Franklin in designing survey questions to directly tap a respondent's certainty about a previous survey response (Alvarez and Franklin 1994).[10] Their approach allows researchers to differentiate between individuals who place themselves at the same point on an item scale, but do not feel equally certain about that placement. The format of this question suits the purpose at hand nicely because it provides a way to tap the second dimension of insecurity. Incumbents could indicate that they were "very certain," "pretty certain," or "not very certain" about their estimated chances of reelection.[11] A slight majority of incumbents feel "very certain" about their estimated chances and do not expect those estimates to change. However, 45 percent of respondents were not fully certain about their estimates and believed that their estimates could change.

RISK AND UNCERTAINTY: A DISTINCTION WITHOUT
A DIFFERENCE?

The fact that there is such a close theoretical link between risk and uncertainty leads to the question of whether, in practice, risk and uncertainty are identical. In other words, are the empirical measures of risk and uncertainty so highly correlated that the theoretical distinction between them collapses into a single dimension in survey responses?

Figure 8.2 clearly shows a negative relationship between chances of reelection and the incumbent's uncertainty in estimating those chances. The proportion of incumbents who feel uncertain decreases from 100 percent to 11 percent as their estimates of chances increase from .5 to 1. Notably, the strongest relationship between the two measures occurs at the very ends of the scale. Eighty-nine percent of incumbents who believe they are sure to win are also very certain about that estimate, while none the incumbents who see their race as a toss-up feel very certain about their estimate. Certainly, this pattern in the data is consistent with the proposition that uncertainty affects

[10] Pretests of a question format prompting uncertain respondents to offer a range of probabilities was unsuccessful. Less than 3 percent offered a range of probabilities. For details on the pretest results, see Maestas 2000, pp. 72–88.

[11] Respondents were asked, "Since elections differ in how predictable they are, I would also like to know how certain you are about your estimated chances." The following three response categories were offered: Very certain, I doubt my estimates will change; Pretty certain, although my estimates might change some; Not very certain, my estimate is likely to change a great deal.

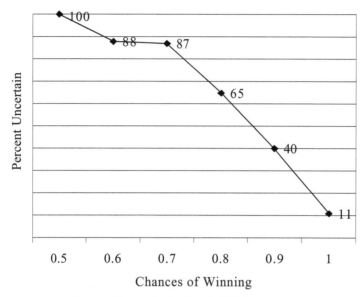

FIGURE 8.2. Percent Uncertain, by Level of Risk

risk perceptions. That is, incumbents who are more uncertain also tend to feel more at risk of defeat.

However, there is another simple explanation for this pattern that suggests the relationship between the two might be partially spurious. Both chances and uncertainty depend heavily on the presence of a challenger. Incumbents who do not expect to face a challenger are both sure to win and can feel confident when they estimate their chances of winning. Accordingly, 64 percent of respondents rating their chances of winning reelection at 1.0 did not expect to face a challenger in the general election. In contrast, incumbents who did expect to face a challenger in the general election generally rated their chances as lower. Moreover, the introduction of a challenger to the race brings into play a number of factors that can affect the chances an incumbent will win, namely, the strength and quality of the challenger.

At the same time, the likely effect of these variables is often not known at the outset of a race. Incumbents are left to estimate their odds of winning without full knowledge of how the qualities of a challenger might affect the outcome. As such, the presence of a challenger has the dual effect of reducing the chances that an incumbent will win *and* introducing uncertainty into the estimates of the chances of reelection. So, at the broadest level, the competitive environment affects both risk and uncertainty, leading to correlation between the two measures.

Nevertheless, it also is clear from Figure 8.2 that uncertainty and risk are less tightly tied in the middle categories of estimated chances than they are in the extreme categories. Although in general, incumbents who view their

TABLE 8.1 *Combinations of Risk and Uncertainty*

	Low Risk of Losing Seat (Chances ≥ .8)	*High Risk* of Losing Seat (Chances < .8)
Certain About Estimate of Risk	• No challenger • Definite weak challenger • Stable or predictable vote patterns	• Definite strong challenger • Stable or predictable vote patterns
	52% ($n = 202$)	2% ($n = 9$)
Uncertain About Estimate of Risk	• Probable weak challenger • Unstable or unpredictable vote patterns	• Probable strong challenger • Unstable or unpredictable vote patterns
	30% ($n = 115$)	16% ($n = 62$)

chances as lower are also more likely to be uncertain, a good number of incumbents who rate their chances high also express uncertainty about their estimates. A full 50 percent of incumbents who rate their chances at .8 or .9 are uncertain about their estimate. In addition, 13 percent of individuals who rate their chances of winning at near a toss up (.6 or .7) are very certain about their estimate. This implies that incumbents' assessments of risk are neither necessary nor sufficient for incumbents to feel uncertain about their expectations, nor is uncertainty necessary or sufficient for incumbents to feel at risk. Even though the two are correlated, they are not synonymous and exploring the potential sources for each will prove enlightening.

CAUSES OF RISK AND UNCERTAINTY

If risk and uncertainty truly reflect different dimensions of the incumbent environment, then we should expect different factors to give rise to each. Table 8.1 summarizes the electoral conditions that might affect each dimension and provides the percentage of all respondents that fall into each of the four categories. Notably, this table indicates that a fair percentage of respondents (30 percent) fall into the category that Jacobson's research suggests could be on the rise – seemingly safe, but uncertain incumbents. Not surprisingly, however, the largest percentage of incumbents expect to win and are quite certain about their expectation.

As suggested earlier, the common feature underlying the low risk dimension is the expectation that the general election challenger will be weak or nonexistent. The uncertainty dimension, however, is rooted in the amount of information that the incumbent has to help him assess the quality of the challenger and the voter reactions to that challenger. The more information the incumbent has to determine the identity and characteristics of the challenger, the easier it is to assess how that challenger will impact the chances of reelection, and, the more confident he or she will feel in making that assessment. Similarly, the more stable and predictable voters are in the district, the easier it is to determine how they might react to campaign events. Hence, it is possible to model incumbents' estimates of chances as a function of the characteristics of competitive environment, but model incumbents' uncertainty as a function of the level of knowledge about the competitive environment. The survey of incumbents provides measures of both aspects of the environment and can be used to test the hypothesis that risk and uncertainty, although related, spring from different district factors.

Measures of District "Risk" Factors

The central factors that should influence incumbent chances of winning are the strength of the challenger and the ability of the incumbent to build support among constituents. Challenger strength is measured by an index created from a series of survey questions asking incumbents to rate the qualities of their *most likely* challenger. The survey asked each incumbent who expected to face a challenger to indicate whether they believed their challenger was "strong," "average," or "weak," in the following areas: ability to gain media attention, potential support from the political party organization, ability to raise funds, ability to increase turnout, potential support from his or her own party voters, potential support from independent voters, and ability to sway the issue opinions of voters.[12] The index is simply the arithmetic mean of the scores for these seven questions and ranges from a low of zero to a high of three.[13] The mean for respondents expecting a challenger is 1.85,

---

[12] This battery of questions was designed to tap the incumbent's perceptions of both the strengths of the challenger and the incumbent's uncertainty about those strengths. Respondents were given a six point scale that allowed them to indicate that the challenger was "probably weak," "definitely weak," "probably average," "definitely average," "probably strong," or "definitely strong." This scale was divided into two separate measures, a measure of item strength and a measure of item uncertainty. The strength measure is scaled from 0 to 3, where no challenger scores 0, a weak challenger scores a 1, an average challenger scores a 2 and a strong challenger scores a 3. I am implicitly assuming that any challenger presents more of a threat than no challenger. Interpolating a 0 score on the strength measure allows me to include incumbents without challengers in the same analysis as incumbents with challengers.

[13] A principle components analysis indicates that a single factor underlies the covariation of these seven strength measures. Thus, when missing values occur in one or more of the questions in this battery, I compute the mean from the remaining strength measures given by the incumbent. This reduces the number of cases lost as a result of missing data on individual items.

indicating that, on average, incumbents expect to face a weak to average strength challenger.

The ability of incumbents to build a stable base of support among voters should be an important determinant of chances. Office holders have access to a range of resources and political goods that they can use to help mitigate their chances of defeat (Johannes 1984; Johannes and McAdams 1981; Mayhew 1974b; Parker 1992; Rivers and Fiorina 1989; to name just a few). Monopoly controlled resources include the incumbent's ability to provide distributive or substantive policy benefits to district interests, and the incumbent's ability to provide personal assistance to constituents (Parker 1992). Incumbents who believe they can use their legislative service to enhance their ability to win or who make a special effort to provide constituent services are likely to rate their chances of winning as higher than those who do not. Two measures are used to capture variation along these dimensions: how frequently constituents contact the incumbent for assistance with problems and the extent to which incumbents believe their policy work affects the vote in their district.[14] Incumbents who score higher on each of these measures should assess their chances of reelection as higher than incumbents who score lower on these measures.

Measures of District Uncertainty Factors

While I expect incumbents' assessments of chances to be related to factors that directly influence the vote, I expect uncertainty to be related to the level or quality of information about those factors. As with the model of chances, I expect the challenger to be a central force in creating uncertainty for the incumbent. Empirically, I measure uncertainty about challenger strength through an index that averages how uncertain the incumbent is about each of the seven strength assessments listed in the previous section.[15]

---

[14] Constituent contact is measured by a question asking "On average, how many times *per week* is your office contacted by constituents asking for help with a problem?" Response categories include "0–5 times," "6–10 times," "11–20 times," "21–30 times," and "more than 30." Influence of policy work on vote is measured as the mean of two questions. The first asks how much voter knowledge of the incumbent's past legislative accomplishments affect his or her percentage of vote. The second asks how much voter knowledge of the incumbent's position affects his or her percentage of the vote. As with the challenger questions the scale is designed to tap strength and certainty, thus is given a 6-point scale. The strength categories include "little or no effect on vote," "moderate effect on vote," and "large effect on vote." As with the challenger questions, the respondent could choose between "probably" or "definitely" for each strength response.

[15] Individuals who did not expect to face a challenger or chose the response of "definitely" were scored a 0 on this measure. Incumbents who rated their challenger using the "probably" category were scored a 1 for this category. Finally, incumbents who responded in the "don't know" category for the item were scored a 2. This latter category is assigned a missing value for strength, because the incumbent had so little knowledge that they were unable or

This measure ranges from 0 to 2 with a mean of .52. On this scale, 0 represents complete certainty about challenger characteristics while 2 represents complete uncertainty. This should be positively related to uncertainty about estimated chances.[16]

In addition to being sensitive to the amount of information about the challenger, I expect incumbents to be concerned with the predictability of voter behavior. In fact, Jacobson's argument that nonmarginal incumbents are also insecure about reelection centers on this point as he suggests that voter volatility drives incumbent insecurity (Jacobson 1987a, 1987b). Incumbents who believe that the vote patterns in their district are stable over time might find it relatively easy to predict how voters will respond to competitive conditions. By contrast, if voters are unusually volatile, incumbents might find it very difficult to predict voter reactions and, ultimately, vote choice. Given this, incumbents in districts with a high proportion of unpredictable voters should feel more uncertain about their estimates of chances as compared to incumbents in districts with few unpredictable voters. To measure this, the survey directly asked incumbents to indicate what percentage of the voters in their district vote unpredictably. Interestingly, responses ranged from a low of 0 percent to a surprising high of 100 percent, although the mean was just over 11 percent.[17]

A second source of uncertainty about voter behavior could stem from the incumbent's knowledge about how voters react to broader political events or conditions. Incumbents who have some sense of how reactive voters are to react to partisan tides, economic conditions, or more prominent political races should feel more confident in predicting voter behavior.[18]

---

unwilling to rank the challenger for that item. Thus, this represents the highest degree of uncertainty that an incumbent can express about a challenger. The uncertainty score was averaged across the seven questions to yield the uncertainty index score for each incumbent.

[16] See Footnote 12 for a fuller description of the scaling of the challenger strength measures.

[17] This question was part of a larger question asking incumbents to give the percentage of voters in the districts into those that "always vote for you," "always vote against you," "usually vote for you," "usually vote against you," and "vote unpredictably." This measure was designed to sum to 100 percent, and the majority of respondents (85 percent) answered this question correctly. Individuals whose responses did not sum to 100 percent were excluded from the analysis. Finally, where the "unpredictable" response was left missing but the remaining answer summed to 100 percent, I interpolated a response of 0 percent for the percent of unpredictable voters.

[18] This is measured by a question asking respondents about how much out of district conditions affect the vote in their district that taps both the strength and the uncertainty dimension. The uncertainty dimension is coded 0 for individuals who responded in the "definitely" categories, 1 for individuals who responded in the "probably" categories and 2 for those that responded "don't know." This variable has a mean range of 0 to 2 and a mean of .71. Note, the strength of the effect of outside conditions is not included in as a risk factor because the direction of effect cannot be determined. Some outside conditions will have positive effects, others will have negative effects, depending on the specifics of each race (e.g., party of incumbent, state of residence, specific statewide political shocks, etc.)

Finally, incumbent uncertainty should be directly related to past efforts to learn about the preferences of voters. Incumbents who have made some effort to gather information about voter opinions and preferences in their district should feel more confident when trying to assess how campaign events might affect the election. Past informational efforts were measured by asking incumbents to indicate how often, generally, they have analyzed their phone calls, mail, or fax transmissions to determine voter opinions during their time in office.[19]

Simultaneity of Risk and Uncertainty Perceptions

To this point, the emphasis has been on how risk and uncertainty differ from one another. However, as discussed earlier, risk and uncertainty might be related to one another so we should account for this relationship explicitly in the model. At the same time, how certain or uncertain an incumbent feels can stem, in part, from the expected chances. Although the theoretical reasons that lower chances should directly induce uncertainty are not as compelling as the theoretical reasons for the reverse relationship, there is still reason to suspect simultaneity. Incumbents who rate their chances as 100 percent could do so because they face no challenger, thus there are no "unknowns" in the process of estimating chances, hence, no uncertainty either. However, the processes that lead an incumbent to estimate his or her chances near a toss-up, or around 50 percent, also tend to generate more uncertainty, as the number of possible unknowns in the competitive situation grow. For example, incumbents in districts with marginal vote support and a strong challenger also might feel more uncertain because they have to make estimates of both the strength of the challenger *and* the loyalty of the voters. Multistep estimation processes are more complex, leading to reduced certainty about the overall estimate of chances. The empirical model, then, must recognize and account for the possible simultaneity of risk and uncertainty.

Two-Stage Model of Risk and Uncertainty

The empirical models for risk and uncertainty take the following form:

$$c_i = X_{1i}\,\beta_{11} + X_{2i}\,\beta_{12} + \tau_1\,u_i + \varepsilon_{1i}$$
$$u_i^* = X_{1i}\,\beta_{21} + X_{3i}\,\beta_{22} + \tau_2\,c_i + \varepsilon_{2I}$$

---

[19] Response categories range from a low of "less than once per year" to a high of "several times each week." The mean of this variable falls at 4.54, between the categories of "several times every 3–6 months" and "several times each month." However, the modal response fell in the highest category, with just over 35 percent of incumbents responding that they analyzed their voter communications several times a week.

where

$$u = 1 \text{ if } u^* > 0$$
$$u = 0 \text{ otherwise}$$

C is the chances of reelection as estimated by the incumbent. The term u is the incumbent's uncertainty about the estimated chances of reelection. Although theoretically, uncertainty can be thought of as a continuous measure, the full range of values is not observable. Instead, only the survey responses can be observed. Since the uncertainty measure has so few observations in the "not very certain" category, it is collapsed into a dichotomous measure of uncertainty, where responses of "pretty certain" and "not very certain" score a 1. Responses of "very certain" score a 0.

In these models, X_1 represents those factors that cause both risk and uncertainty. This includes the number of terms served, service in the minority party, service in the upper chamber, and holding a seat in a multimember district. In addition, I include a set of state level dummy variables as controls to account for any differences in state electoral contexts. X_2 includes factors outlined above thought to only affect chances, and X_3 includes factors thought to affect only uncertainty.

The τ terms indicate the effect of the endogenous variables. Since simultaneity is suspected, it is inappropriate to simply enter uncertainty or chances as independent variables into right hand side of the equations listed above.[20] Doing so would cause the error term of each model to be correlated with the endogenous regressor, leading to inconsistent estimates (Alvarez and Glasgow 1999; Greene 1997). Instead, the endogeneity in the model must be accounted for using a two stage model. A combination of estimation techniques, the two stage probit least squares model (2SPLS) and the two stage conditional maximum likelihood model (2SCML), are employed, as suggested by Alvarez and Glasgow (1999). Through Monte Carlo simulations, they show the first model, 2SPLS, to be superior to the 2SCML model for small sample estimates. However, only the 2SCML model offers an explicit test for endogeneity, so they suggest estimating both to capitalize on the strength of each model.[21]

---

[20] Alvarez and Glasgow (1999) point out that a two-stage procedure is appropriate even if the model is thought to be hierarchical. If a common cause is left out of the specification of the two models, the coefficients will be inconsistent even if the model is not fully recursive because the error terms will be correlated. This is certainly a plausible scenario in the model in this chapter. So, even if τ_2 is 0, there is still an important reason to use a two stage model to test these hypotheses.

[21] Here, I treat the chances variables as continuous, although it is an interval level measure. As such, the precise statistical properties of the two-stage estimators are not known. The greatest potential problem stems from the fact that OLS regression on a polychotomous variable is heteroskedastic. If so, this could bias the Rivers and Vuong test of exogeneity. However, heteroskedasticity in OLS becomes minimal as the number of categories in the

Results from the Two-stage Models of Risk and Uncertainty

Table 8.2 shows the reduced form equations for the two models that serve to generate the instrumental variables. While the purpose of the reduced form equations is to create instruments for the two stage analysis, these models also shed some light on the question of whether risk and uncertainty spring from different sources. The models show that even though risk and uncertainty have overlapping causes, as would be expected with two variables that are related, they also have distinct causes. The OLS model of chances shows that constituent contact has a positive impact on how incumbents rate their chances. Similarly, incumbents who believe that their legislative positions and past accomplishment will have a large effect on voters estimate their chances of reelection higher, as well. Neither of these has any impact on uncertainty. The probit model shows that incumbents who are unsure about their competitor or do not know how outside political conditions will affect voters are more likely to be uncertain. The same variables have no impact on estimated chances, however. The model shows that although risk and uncertainty share common causes, each also has a set of distinct causes. This lends credence, empirically, to the idea that risk and uncertainty are not wholly identical.

The instrument from the reduced form probit model is the predicted probit score, not the predicted probability (Alvarez and Glasgow 1999, 7). For the 2SPLS model, only the predicted values from the reduced form equations are included as regressors. For the 2SCML model, I also obtain the residuals from the reduced form regression model of chances to enter into the second stage equation along with the predicted value. Rivers and Vuong (1988) show that this addition facilitates a direct test of exogeneity using a standard likelihood ratio test of the form:

$$LR = -2(\ln L_R - \ln L_U).$$

The restricted log likelihood value ($\ln L_R$) comes from the probit model without the residuals while the unrestricted value comes from the probit model that includes those residuals. This statistic is distributed chi-square, with the degrees of freedom equal to the number of endogenous variables included in the equation.

The results in Table 8.3 are generally consistent with my expectations. Notably, this model provides individual level support for Jacobson's argument that voter volatility plays an important role in incumbent uncertainty. Incumbents in districts where voters are more volatile tend to feel less confident about their estimates of chances. Similarly, incumbents who do not know how outside political conditions will affect voters are also more uncertain.

data increases. In the absence of an alternative estimator, I proceed with caution. Clearly, this is an area where additional research on the properties of estimators would be helpful, but such analysis is beyond the scope of this chapter.

TABLE 8.2 *Reduced Form Models of Incumbent Perceptions of Uncertainty and Chances*

	Uncertainty (Probit)	Chances (OLS)
Constituent Factors		
Uncertainty Factors:		
Percent unpredictable voters	.025**	−.012**
	(.009)	(.005)
Previous informational efforts	−.064	.0278
	(.06)	(.050)
Uncertainty about effect of out	.279*	−.017
of district conditions on vote	(.177)	(.136)
Risk Factors:		
Frequency of constituent contact	−.060	.113*
	(.096)	(.072)
Effect of legislative service	−.012	.262*
	(.224)	(.175)
Challenger Characteristics		
Challenger Strength Index	.622**	−.715**
	(.147)	(.114)
Uncertainty about Challenger	.583**	.228
Strengths	(.325)	(.261)
Incumbent Characteristics		
Risk and Uncertainty Factors		
Member of minority party	−.079	.002
	(.211)	(.165)
Multimember district	.300	.128
	(.437)	(.346)
Number of terms served	−.084	−.045
	(.076)	(.059)
Senator	−.073	−.033
	(.293)	(.224)
Dummy variables for individual states not reported	−	−
Constant	−1.555**	9.216**
% Correctly Predicted	77%	
χ^2(df)	100.73 (18)	F(18, 232)
sig.	p < .000	7.98
	ROE: 49%	p < .000
N	251	Adj R ^{2}: .33
		251

** $p < .05$, * $p < .10$ (one-tailed tests)

TABLE 8.3 *Two-Stage Probit Model of Uncertainty*

	Uncertainty 2SPLS	Uncertainty 2SCML
Chances of winning	−.817**	−.861**
	(.188)	(.211)
Error from reduced form chances model	−	−.529**
		(.098)
Constituent Factors		
Uncertainty Factors:		
Percent unpredictable voters	.016*	.022**
	(.010)	(.011)
Previous informational efforts	−.039	−.049
	(.064)	(.068)
Uncertainty about effect of out of district conditions on vote	.217*	.303**
	(.169)	(.182)
Challenger Characteristics		
Uncertainty about Challenger Strengths	.811**	1.02**
	(.326)	(.327)
Incumbent Characteristics		
Risk and Uncertainty Factors		
Member of minority party	−.085	−.058
	(.21)	(.231)
Multimember district	.399	.448
	(.437)	(.477)
Number of terms served	−.114*	−.101
	(.074)	(.082)
Senator	−.107	−.087
	(.291)	(.318)
Dummy variables for individual states not reported		
Constant	6.64**	6.83**
% Correctly Predicted	76.49	77.29
χ^2(df)	99.72 (16)	132.75 (17)
sig.	p < .000	p < .000
N	251	250
Rivers and Vuong LR Test for Exogeneity		34.24 ∼ χ^2 (1) (p < .00)

** $p < .05$, * $p < .10$ (one-tailed tests)

Finally, the incumbent's degree of knowledge about the likely competitor has a significant effect on the probability of feeling uncertain. Surprisingly, past informational efforts did not decrease the probability of uncertainty, and the effect of the number of terms served was not robust across specifications.

This model does show that lower estimated chances increase the probability that the incumbent will feel uncertain about those estimates. In both equations the instrument has a negative and statistically significant effect. Moreover, the Rivers and Vuong test reported provides further evidence of the endogeneity between risk and uncertainty.

The model of incumbent chances in Table 8.4 indicates that, as expected, uncertainty depresses incumbents' views of their chances of reelection. As with the previous model, however, we still see independent effects of incumbent perceptions about their competitive environment. The coefficients for challenger strengths are negative and significant, while the coefficient for the effect of legislative service remains positive and significant.

The substantive conclusions that can be drawn from these models echo the theoretical expectations. The district context affects incumbents' perceptions of risk and uncertainty in different ways. Even after accounting for the simultaneity of risk and uncertainty, we still see that each is related to different characteristics of the electoral context. This supports the hypothesis that risk and uncertainty are distinct dimensions of the electoral environment.

Graphical portrayals of the relationships among variables provide a clearer picture of how sensitive incumbents are to conditions in their district environment. Figure 8.3 shows how the probability of being uncertain changes in response to challenger strengths and the percent of unpredictable voters in the district. The simulated probabilities are based on the coefficients from the 2SPLS model in Table 8.3, using mean and modal values for the remaining independent variables.[22] Here, we see evidence that as the strength of the challenger increases, fewer unpredictable voters are needed to generate uncertainty in the minds of incumbents. Thus, incumbents who anticipate a weak challenger are likely to feel uncertain about their estimated

---

[22] The values for the independent variables are based on the mean, mode, or category closest to the mean and are set at the following values: a. Previous information = 5 (analyze mail/calls several times each month); b. Uncertainty about effect of out of district conditions on vote: .68 (certain – somewhat certain about effect); c. Frequency of constituent contact = 3 (contacted by constituents 11–20 times per week); d. Effect of legislative service on vote = 2.58 (moderate to strong effect); e. Minority party = 0 (majority party member); f. Multimember district = 0 (not in multimember district); g. Number of terms served in position = 3 (3–4 terms); h. Senator = 0 (member of lower chamber); i. index of uncertainty about challenger strength was set at .44 (certain – somewhat certain). The state dummy variables were set to 0 for all states expect Minnesota, which is set equal to one. Minnesota falls at about the midpoint of professionalization and resources for the states included in this survey. The variables allowed to vary to predict outcomes were the percent independent voters, which was varied from 1 to 100 percent; the strength of the challenger, which took on three values: 1 = Weak, 2 = Average, 3 = Strong.

TABLE 8.4 *Two Stage Least Square Model of Incumbent Chances*

	Chances (2SLS model)
Uncertainty about chances	−.299** (.177)
Constituent Factors	
Risk Factors:	
Frequency of constituent contact	.089 (.073)
Effect of legislative service	.221* (.171)
Challenger Characteristics	
Challenger Strength Index	−.442** (.174)
Incumbent Characteristics	
Risk and Uncertainty Factors	
Member of minority party	−.127 (.164)
Multimember district	.206 (.350)
Number of terms served	−.061 (.061)
Senator	−.044 (.224)
Dummy variables for individual states not reported	
Constant	8.938**
F (15, 235)	9.30
sig.	p < .000
Adj. R square	.33
N	251

** $p < .05$, * $p < .10$ (one-tailed tests)

a: uncertainty is the instrument from the reduced form regression.

b: Standard errors are corrected by multiplying each times a weighting factor of :

$$\sqrt{\frac{\sigma_p^2}{\sigma_u^2}}$$

where the numerator is the variance from the residual from the second stage chances model and the denominator is the variance of the residual from the second stage regression model using the endogenous variable in place of the instrument. The weighting factor is just over 1.01.

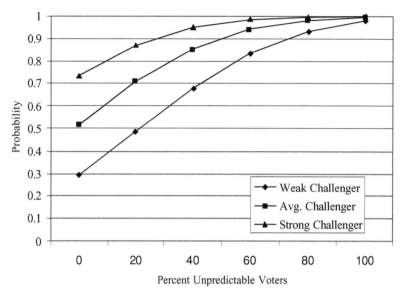

FIGURE 8.3. Predicted Probability of Feeling Uncertain

chances only if their district tends to have a high percent of volatile voters. In contrast, incumbents who anticipate an average or strong challenger are likely to be uncertain, even with very few unpredictable voters. At the same time, the chart also shows that highly volatile conditions make it likely that incumbents facing even the weakest opponents will feel uncertain.

Furthermore, it is important to note that the slope of the "weak challenger" line, especially at low levels of unpredictable voters, is steeper than slopes of the lines for stronger challengers. This indicates that the marginal effect of a change in district volatility is greater for incumbents expecting a weak challenger than those expecting a strong challenger. This primarily stems from the fact that incumbents in competitive districts are already fairly likely to feel uncertain. Hence, a marginal change in the unpredictable vote does not have a large effect on the uncertainty probabilities. By contrast, incumbents in noncompetitive districts might feel quite secure as long as they believe that they can predict the patterns of voters. However, if vote patterns become unpredictable, the probability of being uncertain when estimating reelection chances increases dramatically.

Interestingly, one implication of this is that if districts are becoming more volatile over time, as Jacobson suggests, the increased volatility will have the greatest effect on incumbent perceptions where we least expect it – in the least competitive districts. Given that incumbents in strong to moderately competitive districts are already quite likely to feel uncertain as well as feel at risk, changes in behavior resulting from the increased volatility would be most apparent among incumbents in noncompetitive districts. The differential impact of volatility offers one explanation for the puzzling increase in the time and resources devoted to reelection efforts such as fundraising among seemingly safe incumbents.

DISCUSSION

This research has implications for how we think about the effect of electoral conditions on both micro and macro political outcomes. This section offers both an overview of preliminary findings about the effect of uncertainty, distinct from risk, on incumbent behavior and offers some thoughts on the types of questions that we should explore through the lens of uncertainty.

At the individual level, the central question is what type of response might uncertainty prompt from incumbents? Incorporating uncertainty as well as risk into a formal model of decision making suggests that uncertainty imposes significant direct and indirect utility losses on incumbents thinking about running for reelection.[23] As a result, we should expect uncertain incumbents to dedicate a portion of their office, personal and campaign resources to reducing uncertainty about voters, challengers or both. In fact, analysis of the survey data from incumbent state legislators suggests that uncertainty influences a range of incumbent choices related to information gathering, office activities, and fundraising (Maestas 2000). Such findings are significant because they demonstrate that the district conditions that spark uncertainty also affect representation efforts in important ways.

In one sense, this suggests that uncertainty might have positive effects on representation because uncertainty prompts incumbents to increase their efforts to gather information about constituent preferences. Indeed, incumbents can be more certain than ever of citizen preferences through the use of sophisticated polling techniques (Geer and Goorha, this volume). Thus, increased potential of electoral volatility can reinforces the exchange of ideas between citizens and their representatives. Similarly, incumbents who view voters as more unpredictable appear to dedicate more time to constituent service: another important form of representation.

However, uncertainty could also stimulate a number of less desirable outcomes. For example, incumbents who face unstable voters might prefer to reduce uncertainty through the challenger side of the calculus and focus their efforts on preemptive fundraising or other tactics to deter the entry of challengers. Of course, the absence of a challenger is the surest way to ensure that potential volatility does not become a genuine threat. Preliminary evidence from the survey responses from state legislators suggests that the percentage of unpredictable voters affects the amount of time incumbents dedicate to fundraising (Maestas 2000).

---

[23] For models of incumbent behavior under uncertainty and risk, see Maestas 2000, Chapter 3.

While early findings are suggestive, many questions remain to be answered. For example, when uncertain incumbents are challenged, how do
they respond? Perhaps uncertain incumbents approach the campaign process differently that those who are more certain. For example, when challenged, incumbents in districts dominated by unstable voters could shy away
from presenting informationally rich campaigns due to their uncertainty over
how voters might respond to campaign messages. Instead, they might opt
for "name recognition" campaign themes rather than policy themes. Alternatively, uncertain incumbents could alter their mobilization efforts to carefully
craft narrow campaign messages targeted to single issue interests to maximize the certainty of their mobilization efforts. Thus, rather than develop
broad policy themes designed to inform and attract a wide range of citizens,
incumbents need only address issues in a piecemeal fashion. Political polling
and mass mail technologies make this a viable strategy since narrow interests
can be targeted at low cost. Individual strategies such as these would reduce
the prospects for strong representation of broad interests in conditions of
uncertainty.

Perhaps the most interesting and challenging questions, however, occur
at the macro political level. What are the potential effects of a more volatile
political environment on political institutions and parties? If uncertainty is
costly to incumbents, as suggested, and if the electoral forces that create
uncertainty are widespread, legislators might collectively seek institutional
changes designed to mitigate uncertainty. Certainly, volatile conditions
could create broad incentives to transfer the individual costs of uncertainty
to the institution in some way. In particular, we might expect collective
demands for greater informational infrastructure in institutions, more staff,
or institutional mechanisms to limit challenger entry. The latter response
would be most troubling because it limits the potential for representation at
a systemic level. Nevertheless, for uncertain incumbents, policy changes to
campaign finance laws, candidate filing deadlines, primary election rules or
other institutional aspects of elections that reduce the chances of a challenger
could prove to be irresistible because they reduce both risk and uncertainty.
The research here suggests that it might be fruitful to explore changes in electoral rules in light of how the level of uncertainty or volatility has changed
over time.

In addition, we should explore the role of political parties in mitigat-
ing uncertainty. Many theories of the development and strength of political parties focus on how parties mitigate risk for their members through
services or policy output (cf. Aldrich 1995; Cox and McCubbins 1993;
Rohde 1991; Schlesinger 1991). However, changes in macro-political volatility could prompt incumbents to shift some of the uncertainty burden to
their institutional parties as well. Aldrich (1995), for example, notes the
role that political parties play in reducing uncertainty in a variety of ways,
including regulating the career paths of candidates. Campaign committees

and legislative leadership can provide many tools to assist members who face potentially turbulent conditions ranging from assistance with polling and fundraising to directly discouraging primary election challengers. In this light, increased electoral uncertainty could encourage members to strengthen the resources and role of the party within the legislature since a collective party solution to uncertainty might be superior to an individual solution, even if the cost to the incumbent is reduced autonomy. Hence, a theory of parties based on electoral uncertainty offers an alternative view of the resurgence of political parties in the last few decades. One rather puzzling aspect of party redevelopment is that it occurs during a time when electoral risk was supposedly on the decline. However, if Jacobson is correct and the macro-political environment is more turbulent, it is plausible that party development is driven by widespread response to uncertainty rather than widespread response to risk.

Finally, on a more practical note, if the concept of uncertainty is to be useful as an explanatory variable, we must develop objective indicators of electoral uncertainty rather than rely on subjective measures such as the survey data used here. While the concept of uncertainty is attractive theoretically, it is not very tractable if it can only be measured through survey questions. Broad scale surveys of members of Congress are near impossible for the average researcher and in depth interviews do not allow for broad scale testing of hypotheses about the effects of uncertainty. Moreover, if we wish to use the concept of uncertainty to link changes in the electoral environment to changes in institutions or parties, it is not possible to go back in time and obtain firsthand perceptions. Thus, a natural extension of this work is to explore how the subjective perceptions of incumbents are related to objective indicators of their electoral environment.

At the same time, we also must recognize that uncertainty complicates linking subjective perceptions with objective measures such as vote share or vote swings. Preliminary work in this area shows that incumbents who are certain do much better at forecasting election outcomes than incumbents who are uncertain (Maestas 2000). For example, 86 percent of certain incumbents accurately predict whether or not they would have a marginal election, whereas only 63 percent of uncertain incumbents did so.[24] As we might expect, the majority of "errors" stem from incumbents who underestimated their level of support. Similarly, 88 percent of certain incumbents correctly predicted whether or not they would have a strong challenger; only 49 percent of uncertain incumbents correctly predicted challenger

---

[24] State legislators planing on running for reelection in 1998 were asked to estimate their expected vote percentage in the general election. By dichotomizing the expected vote and actual vote at 60 percent, I could compare the number of incumbents who expected to receive less than 60 percent with those who actually received less than 60 percent. The overall percentage of correct predictions was 76 percent.

strength.[25] These findings imply that objective indicators of electoral risk are less accurate for incumbents who are in situations of uncertainty and highlights the importance developing indicators of uncertainty to use in conjunction with indicators of risk.

At the same time, identifying uncertainty indicators may prove to be a difficult task. The subjective measures of volatility do not correspond closely to the vote swing from 1996 to 1998, nor is there evidence that vote swings are higher for uncertain incumbents. The correlation between state legislators' estimates of the percentage of voters who vote unpredictably and the magnitude of the vote swing in their districts from 1996 to 1998 is only .13 ($p = .052$) and there is no difference in the average vote swing for certain and uncertain incumbents. The absence of a relationship between the objective indicators and subjective perceptions could stem from the fact that incumbents are estimating *potential* volatility, much of which was never realized because of ineffectual challengers. More complex measures are no doubt necessary to capture the concept of potential volatility and, ultimately uncertainty. Certainly, these findings underscore the need for future research to identify how subjective perceptions of both risk and uncertainty are related to objective indicators.

References

Aldrich, John H. 1995. *Why Parties. The Origins and Transformation of Political Parties in America*. Chicago: University of Chicago Press.

Alpert, Eugene J. 1980. "Risk and Uncertainty in Political Choice." *Uncertainty, Behavioral and Social Dimensions*, ed. S. Fiddle. New York: Praeger Publishers.

Alvarez, R. Michael, and Charles H. Franklin. 1994. "Uncertainty and Political Perceptions." *The Journal of Politics* 56:671–88.

Alvarez, R. Michael, and Garrett Glasgow. 1999. "Two Stage Estimation of Non-Recursive Choice Models." Working paper, California Institute of Technology.

Arnold, R. Douglas. 1990. *The Logic of Congressional Action*. New Haven, CT: Yale University Press.

Berry, William D., Michael B. Berkman, and Stuart Schneiderman. 2000. "Legislative Professionalism and Incumbent Reelection: The Development of Institutional Boundaries." *American Political Science Review* 94: 859–74.

Carey, John M., Richard G. Niemi, and Lynda W. Powell. 2000. "Incumbency and the Probability of Reelection in State Legislative Elections." *Journal of Politics* 62:671–700.

Cioffi-Revilla, Claudio. 1998. *Politics and Uncertainty: Theory, Models and Applications*. New York: Cambridge University Press.

---

[25] A race was considered to have a strong challenger if the incumbent received less than 60 percent of the vote. This measure was compared to survey responses regarding expectations of challenger strength. Overall, 72 percent of incumbents accurately forecast the strength of the challenger.

Collie, Melissa P. 1981. "Incumbency, Electoral Safety and Turnover in the House of Representatives, 1952-76." *American Political Science Review* 75:119–31.

Cox, Gary W., and Matthew D. McCubbins. 1993. *Legislative Leviathan: Party Government in the House.* Los Angeles: University of California Press.

Ellsberg, Daniel. 1961. "Risk, Ambiguity and the Savage Axioms." *Quarterly Journal of Economics* 75:643–69.

Fenno, Richard F. 1978. *Home Style: House Members in Their Districts.* Boston: Little Brown.

Fiorina, Morris P. 1974. *Representatives, Roll Calls and Constituencies.* Lexington, KY: Lexington Books.

Garand, James C., Kenneth Wink, and Bryan Vincent. 1993. "Changing Meaning of Electoral Marginality in U.S. House Elections, 1824-1978." *Political Research Quarterly* 46:27–48.

Gilboa, Itzhak. 1987. "Expected Utility with Purely Subjective Non-Additive Probabilties." *Journal of Mathematical Economics* 16:65–85.

Gilboa, Itzhak, and David Schmeidler. 1989. "Maxmin Expected Utility with Non-Unique Prior." *Journal of Mathematical Economics* 18:141–53.

Greene, William H. 1997. *Econometric Analysis.* 3rd ed. Upper Saddle River, NJ: Prentice Hall.

Gross, Donald A., and James C. Garand. 1984. "The Vanishing Marginals, 1824–1980." *Journal of Politics* 46:224–37.

Hey, John D. 1979. *Uncertainty in Microeconomics.* New York: New York University Press.

Hirshleifer, Jack, and John G. Riley. 1992. *The Analytics of Uncertainty and Information.* Cambridge: Cambridge University Press.

Jacobson, Gary. 1987a. "The Marginals Never Vanished: Incumbency and Competition in Elections to the U.S. House of Representatives, 1952–1982." *American Journal of Political Science* 31(1):126–41.

Jacobson, Gary C. 1987b. "Running Scared: Elections and Congressional Politics in the 1980's." *Congress: Structure and Policy.* M. D. McCubbins and T. Sullivan, eds. Cambridge: Cambridge University Press.

Jacobson, Gary C. 1997. *The Politics of Congressional Elections.* New York: Longman.

Jewell, Malcolm E., and David Breaux. 1988. "The Effect of Incumbency on State Legislative Elections." *Legislative Studies Quarterly* 13:495–514.

Johannes, John R. 1984. *To Serve the People: Congress and Constituency Service.* Lincoln: University of Nebraska Press.

Johannes, John R., and John C. McAdams. 1981. "The Congressional Incumbency Effect: Is it Casework, Policy Compatibility or Something Else?" *American Journal of Political Science* 25:512–42.

King, Anthony S. 1997. *Running Scared: Why America's Politicians Campaign Too Much and Govern Too Little.* New York: Martin Kessler Books, Free Press.

Kingdon, John W. 1989. *Congressmen's Voting Decisions.* 3rd ed. Ann Arbor: University of Michigan Press.

Maestas, Cherie D. 2000. *Uncertain Calculations: Incumbent Perceptions and Behavior in a Volatile World.* Unpublished dissertation. University of Colorado.

Mayhew, David R. 1974a. *Congress: The Electoral Connection.* New Haven, CT: Yale University Press.

Mayhew, David R. 1974b. "Congressional Elections: The Case of the Vanishing Marginals." *Polity* 6:295–317.

Niemi, Richard G., and Herbert F. Weisberg. 1972. *Probability Models of Collective Decision Making.* Columbus, OH: Charles E. Merrill Publishing Co.

Parker, Glenn R. 1992. *Institutional Change, Discretion, and the Making of the Modern Congress.* Ann Arbor: University of Michigan Press.

Raiffa, Howard. 1961. "Risk, Ambiguity, and the Savage Axioms: Comment." *Quarterly Journal of Economics* 75:690–5.

Rivers, Douglas, and Morris P. Fiorina. 1989. "Constituency Service, Reputation, and the Incumbency Advantage." *Home Style and Washington Work. Studies of Congressional Politics.* Morris P. Fiorina and David W. Rhode, eds. Ann Arbor: University of Michigan Press.

Rivers, Douglas, and Q. H. Vuong. 1988. "Limited Information Estimators and Exogeneity Tests for Simultaneous Probit Models." *Journal of Econometrics* 39:347–66.

Rohde, David W. 1991. *Parties and Leaders in the Postreform House.* Chicago: University of Chicago Press.

Salmore, Barbara G., and Stephen A. Salmore. 1989. *Candidates, Parties and Campaigns.* 2nd ed. Washington, DC: CQ Press.

Savage, Leonard J. 1954. *The Foundations of Statistics.* New York: John Wiley and Sons.

Schlesinger, Joseph A. 1991. *Political Parties and the Winning of Office.* Ann Arbor: University of Michigan Press.

Shepsle, K. A., and M. S. Bonchek. 1997. *Analyzing Politics. Rationality, Behavior and Institutions.* New York: W.W. Norton and Company.

Weber, Ronald E., Harvey J. Tucker, and Paul Brace. 1991. "Vanishing Marginals in State Legislative Elections." *Legislative Studies Quarterly* 16:29–47.

9

Uncertainty, Experience with Black Representation, and the White Vote

Zoltan L. Hajnal*

Two questions have commanded much of the attention of scholars interested in black political representation in the United States. The first asks whether white Americans will vote for black candidates (and why or why not this is the case). The second asks whether black representatives, once elected, can improve the economic standing of African Americans. Answers to both of these questions have generally been discouraging. First, given the choice, the vast majority of white Americans will vote for a white candidate, even if it means switching parties.[1] Despite the success of a number of highly visible black candidates such as former Governor Douglas Wilder, former Mayor Tom Bradley, and Congressmen J. C. Watts, and despite the increasingly popular belief that race no longer plays a major role in the voting booth (Swain 1995; Thernstrom and Thernstrom 1997), extensive empirical studies suggest that 70 to 90 percent of white voters will still vote for the white candidate rather than the black candidate in a typical black/white contest (Lieske and Hillard 1984; Loewen 1990; McCrary 1990). Race still matters when white voters are faced with a black office seeker.

Second, even if black candidates can get elected, their leadership has not greatly improved the economic well-being of African Americans in their cities, regions, or states. Studies suggest that black incumbents can modestly

[1] Although the vast majority of whites say in surveys that they would vote for a qualified black candidate for office (Schuman et al. 1997), experimental studies suggest that a candidate's race can and does affect the white vote in important ways (Reeves 1997; Sigelman et al. 1995).

* The author wishes to thank Barbara Walter, Amy Bridges, Charles Bullock, Nancy Crowe, Michael Dawson, Richard Deleon, Jamie Druckman, Kevin Esterling, Claudine Gay, Mark Hansen, Karen Hoffman, Andrew Grant-Thomas, Liz Gerber, Jim Glaser, Donald Green, Anna Greenberg, Karen Kaufmann, Thomas Kim, Taeku Lee, Paul Lewis, Roger Larocca, Hugh Louch, Arthur Lupia, Donald Norris, Lynn Sanders, Lee Sigelman, Raphael Sonenshein, Robert Stein, and William J. Wilson for their invaluable assistance. Please direct all comments or questions to: Department of Politics, UCSD, La, Jolla, CA, 92093-0521. zhajnal@weber.ucsd.edu. Phone: 858-822-5015.

change local hiring policies and spending priorities (Browning, Marshall, and Tabb 1984; Eisinger 1982; Mladenka 1989), but these and other changes have not been dramatic.[2] The overall substantive impact on most members of the black community has been negligible (Reed 1988; Singh 1998). Either because black incumbents consciously choose to follow a conservative, prodevelopment agenda or because they are forced by the constraints of local politics (Peterson 1981), the end result is very little change. "Their elections," in the words of Manning Marable, "can be viewed as a psychological triumph, but they represent no qualitative resolution to the crises of black poverty, educational inequality, crime, and unemployment" (quoted in Perry 1996, 6).

Scholars have interpreted these results as a sign of a lack of progress for blacks and proof of the ineffectiveness of black leaders (Reed 1988; Smith 1996). This conclusion, however, ignores the potentially positive impact black representation can have on the *white* community and the effect this might have on the uncertainty surrounding black candidates and future voting behavior.[3] In what follows, I shift the focus of attention away from black politicians' impact on the African American community and onto their impact on white constituents. Electing blacks into public office might not improve the condition of blacks to the degree many people had hoped, but it might have the less visible but equally consequential effect of educating white voters about black leaders, reducing uncertainty, and changing the way whites vote in black/white elections.[4]

OVERVIEW

The rest of this chapter is broken down into four parts. I begin with a description of the information model in which I hypothesize that experience under black incumbents should alter white voter behavior by reducing the fear and uncertainty associated with black candidates. I contrast this with two competing hypotheses: a racial prejudice model and a white backlash model. The next section provides a brief summary of the data, measures, and methodology. The findings section then shows how the white vote changes between

---

[2] Studies at the Congressional level indicate that the voting patterns of black incumbents are different than those of white representatives but these studies also fail to demonstrate any significant change in black well-being as a result (Canon 1999; Lublin 1997).

[3] It also ignores the symbolic impact black representation has on the black community (Bobo and Gilliam 1990; Gay 2001).

[4] Few systematic empirical studies directly assess changes in white behavior under black incumbents. The most common view, based largely on the end of black leadership in New York, Chicago, and Los Angeles, is that white residents continue to respond negatively to black incumbents (Abney and Hutcheson 1981; Sleeper 1993; see also Gay 1999 on Congressional incumbents). Accounts from a few cities do, however, contradict this more prevalent, negative view (Eisinger 1980; Pettigrew 1976; Watson 1984).

black challenger and black incumbent elections, it illustrates changes over time in the nature of black challenger elections, and it shows how the racial balance of power in a city can affect uncertainty and consequently alter white reactions to black incumbents. The last section highlights three major implications of this research and notes a number of larger questions that it leaves unanswered.

HYPOTHESES

The Information Model

I argue that experience with a black incumbent should significantly change the way white Americans think about black candidates and their voting behavior in subsequent elections (even if the black incumbent runs against a white challenger), because it imparts critical information that greatly reduces uncertainty and dispels white fears about blacks and black leadership. When black challengers run for office, many white residents fear that black leadership will favor the black community over the white community. By redistributing income, encouraging integration, and generally channeling resources toward the black community, the white fear is that there will be a reversal of the racial status quo. Yet, as the existing research shows, this does not happen. For the vast majority of the white community, their world under black leadership is almost identical to their world under white leadership. Once black leaders have the opportunity to prove that black leadership does not harm white interests, white fear should decline and whites should be more willing to consider voting for black candidates.

UNCERTAINTY AND WHITE FEARS IN BLACK CHALLENGER ELECTIONS. To understand the important informational role black leadership plays for the white community, one must first understand why white Americans fear black leadership. When blacks challenge for offices they have never held, whites do not know what to expect. Normally voters have less information about a challenger than an incumbent (Popkin 1991). When that challenger is black, information is even more sparse. In most cases, white residents have had little firsthand experience with black leadership. They have not lived under a black mayor, a black representative, a black senator, or a black president. They do not know what the consequences of black leadership are likely to be.

Having little or no personal experience with black leadership, white voters are forced to rely on racial stereotypes for information about how black leaders are likely to behave once elected to office (Conover and Feldman 1989). This, however, inevitably hurts black candidates' chances for white support. Knowing little about a candidate other than race, white respondents rate black candidates worse than white candidates on nineteen out of twenty leadership and personality characteristics, viewing a black candidate as less trustworthy, less able to "get things done," and even less intelligent (Williams 1990).

Black challengers can, and usually do, try to counter these stereotypes and the uncertainty surrounding their candidacies by running "deracialized" or prowhite campaigns. Thirman Milner, the first black mayor of Hartford, was typical of black challengers in that he proclaimed: "There is no such a thing as black legislation." Similarly, in Cleveland, Carl Stokes promised to be "Mayor for all the people." Wilson Goode maintained, "My campaign is not a drive to elect a black mayor." Unfortunately for black challengers, these efforts are often lost in the face of campaigns by white opponents who attempt to garner white support by playing on white fears. Richard Epton's slogan in Chicago, "Epton for mayor – before it's too late" epitomized this type of campaign. Others are more subtle – as with Richard Hackett's commercials in Memphis, "A steady hand for changing times" – but the notion that black challengers pose a real risk is clear enough. The media tends to make matters worse for black candidates by continuously highlighting the historic nature of a possible black victory (Mendelberg 1994; Reeves 1997). Even in a city like Seattle in which blacks make up only 10 percent of the population, coverage of the campaign between Norm Rice and Doug Jewett mentioned the race of the candidates 63 percent of the time (Reeves 1997, 53).

In the end, the limited information that whites have, the inflammatory campaigns that white opponents often run, and the stereotypes that whites rely on, all trigger a host of negative projections about the impact of a black victory.[5] For many, the fear is that if the black challenger wins and the black community is able to take control of the neighborhood, district, or city, the white community will lose out in countless ways (Rivlin 1992; Sonenshein 1993).[6] In short, heightened uncertainty in black challenger elections is likely to lead most whites to fear the black candidate and to vote to prevent a black victory.

WHY DOES BLACK INCUMBENCY MAKE A DIFFERENCE? Incumbency is critical for any office holder (King and Gelman 1991). Aside from the role it plays in helping candidates acquire resources like money and endorsements, incumbency plays a vital informational role that greatly helps candidates get reelected (Popkin 1991). Put simply, what incumbency and time in office

---

[5] Underlying this account is the notion that uncertainty, rather than ambivalence, is at the heart of white views toward blacks (Alvarez and Brehm 1997).

[6] In its most basic form the fear is simply that a black leader will serve black interests at the expense of white interests. In more specific forms, white residents express fear about things like racial integration, school busing, and the flight of white businesses. A truck driver in Chicago described his fears of a black victory this way, "I don't know how to say this but I am afraid [Harold Washington] is going to exert all of his powers for the black community and the white community is going to get nothing. My fear is that he is going to try to push racial integration, which is fine as long as I don't lose money on my house . . . because I just can't take the loss" (quoted in Coleman 1983).

does is reduce uncertainty. As residents become more and more familiar with an incumbent and his or her actions, the uncertainty about what a challenger might do as new issues come forward slowly fades away.

This process is all the more important for black candidates where uncertainty is that much greater and fears about the consequences of black leadership are likely to be widespread. Once an African American is elected into office whites obtain important information about the impact black representation has on their lives. Whites can now base their assessments of black leadership on an incumbent's track record rather than on stereotypes, exaggerated fears, or incendiary predictions of white candidates. When white residents do not lose their jobs, when blacks do not move into white neighborhoods in large numbers, and when black crime does not proliferate, white residents learn that they have less to fear from blacks and black leadership.

Black political leadership is especially important in the minds of white residents because it marks one of the first times that blacks have authority or control over the white community. When blacks have the power (or are perceived as having the power) to inflict harm on the white community and they choose not to do so, white residents learn for the first time that black control does not mean white downfall. In most cases, the contrast between white fears and the reality of black leadership is so stark that white residents are forced to reevaluate black leadership.[7]

If this information model is valid, we should see a distinct pattern in elections with black and white candidates opposing each other. In black challenger elections, the white vote should be largely based on racial threat (the size of the black population) and few whites should end up supporting the black candidate. In black incumbents elections, racial threat should play much less of a role and white voters should begin to base their votes on the track record of the incumbent and the specifics of the campaign. Finally, as more and more blacks are elected to leadership positions over the years, uncertainty regarding black leadership should decline and whites should become more and more inclined to consider supporting black challengers.

Enduring Racial Stereotypes: The Racial Prejudice Model

These predictions could be naively optimistic. A plausible argument could be made that black representation – no matter how positive its effect on the white community – will have no effect on white behavior toward black incumbents. If racial prejudice is the primary factor behind white opposition

---

[7] There are some exceptional cases when the information provided by a black incumbent confirms white fears. For example, Marion Barry's tenure in Washington, DC, may have done little to improve white views of black leadership. However, as long as the policies of black incumbents are significantly better than the fears of white residents, views of black leadership should improve.

to black empowerment, as many have suggested, then there is little reason to suspect that white behavior will change (Allport 1954; Hurwitz and Peffley 1998). Racial stereotypes are simply too deeply ingrained (Fazio et al. 1995) and too stable (Rothbart and John 1993) to be swayed by a single black politician who wins public office. Even if the words and actions of black incumbents do not fit whites' racial stereotypes, whites can use an array of tactics to try to maintain their current stereotypes and create cognitive consistency (Hamilton 1981).

A White Backlash: The Racial Threat Model

It is also possible that black leadership could have a third, more alarming effect on white behavior. If, as researchers from Blumer (1958) to Bobo (1983) have suggested, white Americans identify as a group and feel threatened whenever blacks endanger the wealth and political power of the white community, then white Americans are likely to respond negatively to black incumbency. In this light, black electoral victories can be seen as a direct threat to white power, disrupting the traditional balance of power. Indeed, this is essentially what happened during Reconstruction when for the first time African Americans were elected to important leadership positions. In response, over a thirty-year period, whites used poll taxes, registration requirement, violence, and a host of other tools to reduce the number of black elected officials in state legislatures and Congress from a high of 325 down to 5 (Foner 1984).

DATA AND METHODOLOGY

To determine which of these three theories is most accurate, I look at changes in white voting behavior before and after the transition from a white to a black *mayoralty*. Although each of the three models of white behavior should apply to any level of political leadership, I focus on the transition from a white to a black mayoralty because the information model of white behavior is likely to be most pronounced at the mayoral level. First, most people know who their mayor is (Cole 1976). If white residents are to obtain information through direct experience with black leadership, they must know who their leader is. Second, as an executive of a city, mayors can often act unilaterally, unlike legislators at the local, state and federal level who must obtain the support of a majority of their colleagues before acting. This allows citizens to track a mayor's impact on policy outcomes more directly. If the streets are cleaned, the mayor has done her job. If garbage piles up, the mayor can be blamed.[8] A black mayoralty, therefore, provides more information to white

---

[8] A poll assessing residents' views of the power of their mayor found that even in Washington, DC, a city with limited local control, a large majority of city residents believe the mayor "can

residents than would a black legislator and should therefore have a greater effect on white behavior.

Data

To test these hypotheses I gather data on a series of mayoral contests with both black and white candidates in large American cities. Since I want to look at changes in white behavior as a black candidate moves from challenger to incumbent, I collect data from two elections in each city – the election in which a city elects its first black mayor and the election immediately following in which a black mayor runs for reelection. In addition, I only include cases in which a black candidate runs against a white opponent in both the challenger and incumbent elections to isolate white reactions to black representation. Including cases in which two black candidates run against each other would reveal nothing about white preferences for black over white leadership or their general acceptance of black leadership. Finally, I confine my analysis to general or run-off elections rather than primaries to avoid complications from multiple candidacies and voter disinterest.

The data set includes all cities over one hundred thousand in population that fit these criteria. Specifically, the data set includes fifty-two elections in twenty-six cities. While admittedly a small number, this actually represents two thirds of the cases of white-black transition in large American cities. In other words, what is happening here is more or less what happens in the world when a white mayor is replaced by a black mayor in a large American city.

The dependent variable in each case is the percentage of white voters who support the black candidate. These data come either from exit polls (half of the cases) or precinct level analysis. For the latter, I use estimates from existing studies when they are available and the methodology is appropriate (1/4 of the cases). In the rest of the cases, I undertake analysis of aggregate ward or precinct voting results myself. Depending on the extensiveness of the available data, I either perform ecological inference (see King 1997) or analyze homogenous precincts using the 'complementary percentages' method described by Loewen and Grofman (1989). Whenever possible, I have tried to obtain multiple estimates of white voting behavior for the same election. Most estimates vary by only a few percentage points. In each city, the data for both elections are compiled in the same manner (i.e., the same firm is conducting the exit poll or the same precincts are analyzed).

To see if the role of race and racial threat declines under black incumbents, I include three measures in the analysis. First, in line with a long line of research, I include percent black in the city as a measure of racial threat (Giles

---

control" or "exact influence" on almost every issue of concern to the city (*Washington Post*, June 11, 1978:A1).

and Hertz 1994; Key 1949).[9] Third, because many scholars have claimed that "deracialization" is one of the keys to attracting white support (Hamilton 1977; Henry 1992; Perry 1996), I break down black candidates' campaigns into three categories: (1) campaigns that had any sort of explicit, problack focus; (2) campaigns that addressed the black community implicitly through a generally problack policy agenda or by actively mobilizing black voters and speaking before black audiences; and (3) campaigns that never mentioned black interests and were fairly race neutral.[10]

To see if the impact of what might be called 'traditional' politics increases under black incumbents, I include a number of the factors most often cited in the literature as being important in the voting booth. To gauge the overall impact of incumbency, I include a dummy variable measuring whether or not the white opponent in the black challenger election was the incumbent mayor (see Bullock 1984; King and Gelman 1991; Vanderleeuw 1991 for details on incumbency effects at various levels of office). Since candidate quality is also clearly related to voting outcomes, I included a measure of the political experience of the white opponent and the black challenger (Jacobson and Kernell 1981; Krasno and Green 1988; Lieske 1989).[11] Several scholars have also demonstrated the importance of money in both local and federal elections (Cox and Munger 1989; Gierzynski 1998). To assess the role of campaign spending, I collected data on the black and white candidates' total spending in each election. Political endorsements also have been shown to play a role in a variety of elections (Lieske 1989). For each election, I noted whether or not the local Democratic party endorsed the black candidate and

---

[9] Others have argued that interracial contact (or at least certain forms of interracial contact) should lead to less rather than more racial antagonism (Jackman and Crane 1986). Still others maintain that the relationship between the black population and white threat is curvilinear (Blalock 1967; Longshore 1988). Unfortunately, due to the limited number of cases and the extremely high correlation between percent black and percent black squared ($r = .98$) both variables could not be included as independent variables.

[10] To code black campaigns I focused on three factors: (1) the policy platform, (2) the presence or absence of racial rhetoric, and (3) the extent to which the candidate disproportionately addressed black audiences. In practice, most black candidates ran dual campaigns with different tactics and different issues depending on the racial makeup of the audience. Few campaigns were overtly racial. Fewer still were clearly race neutral. In the end, the range of campaigns was not that wide. Tom Bradley, who is seen as having the quintessential deracialized campaign talked about affirmative action and how he could address the problems of the black community. On the opposite end of the spectrum, Harold Washington did make the famous "It's our turn" comment but the vast majority of time he avoided mentioning black interests and instead talked about serving the whole city. Very few campaigns were coded as explicitly racially focused. In black challenger campaigns there was an even split between implicitly pro-black and race neutral campaigns. In black incumbent elections, race neutral campaigns were a slight majority.

[11] Candidate quality was measured on the following scale. (4) candidates with current or past citywide or statewide positions, (3) city council members or state representatives, (2) other local elected office, and (1) local appointed office or otherwise well known figure.

whether or not the major local daily newspaper endorsed the black candidate in each contest.[12]

To see whether the policy programs of black incumbents affected the white vote, I focus on the area where black mayors could impact the largest number of white residents – government spending. Specifically, I include a measure of the degree to which black incumbents shifted spending away from developmental spending (highways, airports, and streets) and onto redistributional functions (social services, housing and education). This shift would presumably disproportionately aid the black community.[13] Also, since white residents may be concerned about the fiscal health of a city, I include a measure of the city's debt as a percentage of the city's overall revenue.

One possible confounding factor in this analysis is white flight from the city. The rapid out-migration of a large number of anti-black white residents under black mayors could clearly affect the remaining mix of white voters under black incumbents. Several factors suggest that this is not a primary factor here. First, only a small number of whites leave these cities in the first few years following the election of the city's first black mayor. On average, percent white declines by only 1.9 percent in these cities (Bureau of the Census 1994, 1990, 1978). This fits with other analysis, which indicates that the rapid outmigration of whites was largely stemmed by the time most of these cities had elected their first black mayors (Brown 1997). Second, existing research suggest that due to the costs of moving, whites who leave cities tend to be younger, wealthier, and better educated (Deane 1990). The poor, older, and less educated who are left behind are the people who are most likely to be racially intolerant (Bobo 1983; Rieder 1985). Finally, while race is often important for moves from neighborhood to neighborhood, studies of intermetropolitan migration suggest that racial motivations are seldom relevant for moves into and out of metropolitan areas (Long 1988). Nevertheless, to ensure that changes in the white vote are not a function of white flight, I include a measure of the change in the city's white population as a control.

Another possibility is that whites who oppose black leadership might simply give up and not bother to vote when faced with an overwhelming black voting bloc. To test for this possibility, I include a measure of voter turnout in

---

[12] Half of the cities are nonpartisan, but in twenty-five of twenty-six cases, the black candidate was mostly closely aligned with the Democratic party or with Democratic voters. The support or opposition of the Democratic party was almost always seen as an important factor in the progress of the election campaign. If there was no formal endorsement by the Democratic party, I determined whether there was active opposition, mixed support or active support of the black candidate from leaders and workers of the local Democratic party.

[13] In each case, I used the change in the percentage of the city's annual expenditures that went to redistributive functions minus the change in the percent going to development functions between the first and last year of the mayor's first term.

each election. I use overall turnout rather than white turnout because turnout by race is only available in twelve of the cities. The reality is that white turnout and overall turnout are nearly identical. Aggregate white, black, and overall turnout are extremely highly correlated in these elections ($r > .9$).

Election results and registration data have been gathered from city, county and state offices and from Lublin and Tate's (1995) data set. Data on candidate quality, the racial focus of the black candidate's campaign, campaign spending and Democratic party endorsements are derived from newspaper coverage and other secondary accounts. Local government spending patterns are from the census' annual local government finances report. City demographics are from the relevant census publications.

To test the implications of the information model across a broader range of cases, I also collected data on the outcome of every black incumbent reelection bid in every city over fifty thousand for the years 1965 to 1999. This data set, which includes the race of the candidates and the outcome of the election, was compiled using the National Roster of Black Elected Officials and local newspapers reports in each city.

FINDINGS

Does the calculus of white voters change under black incumbents? In Table 9.1, I test this proposition by comparing aggregate voting patterns in black challenger and black incumbent mayoral elections. A brief glance at the table reveals a dramatic change between the two sets of elections. As predicted by the information model, when black candidates challenge for the mayoralty for the first time, aggregate white voting patterns are tied almost exclusively to race and racial threat. In contrast, after a few years of black representation and with a lot more information available to them, the calculus of white voters changes. When black incumbents run for reelection campaigns, race remains important but traditional political factors like endorsements, candidate quality, and policies also begin to matter.

The Importance of Race in Black Challenger Elections

As the first half of Table 9.1 shows, race is the dominant factor in black challenger elections. First, the larger the black population, the less willing whites are to support a black challenger. Racial threat, as measured by the size of the black population, accounts for almost all of the variation in aggregate white behavior (adding percent black and percent black squared increases the adj. R-squared of the model by .53). Even considering the selection bias inherent in these cases, it is impressive how closely the white vote is tied to the size of the black population. The regression results suggest that a ten percentage point increase in percent black leads to a 6.9 percentage point drop in white support for the black candidate. Birmingham offers an

TABLE 9.1 *Determinants of White Voting in Black Challenger and Black Incumbent Elections*

	Percentage of White Voters Who Voted for the Black Candidate	
	Black Challenger Elections	Black Incumbent Elections
RACE		
Percent Black in the City	−.68 (.11)***	−.65 (.08)***
Racial Focus of Black Candidate's Campaign[a]	−12.6 (5.5)**	12.1 (6.6)
TRADITIONAL POLITICS		
White Incumbent (1 = yes)	−4.8 (6.1)	−
Quality of the Black Challenger	−.76 (1.7)	−
Quality of the White Opponent	−.94 (1.6)	−5.2 (.97)***
Democratic Party Endorsement	.88 (4.5)	14.5 (4.1)**
Local Newspaper Endorsement	1.9 (3.8)	22.7 (7.0)**
Redistributive Spending	−	−.54 (.24)*
City Debt	−	−.07 (.04)
WHITES EXITING		
Percent Change in White Population	−	−.47 (.70)
Percent Turnout	−.19 (.11)*	−.29 (.08)***
Constant	72.6 (10.0)***	45.5 (13.4)***
N	24[b]	17[b]
adj. R^2	.76	.93

OLS regression. Figures in parentheses are standard errors.

[a] Coded as follows: 0-race neutral, .5-implicit racial appeal, 1-explicit racial appeal.

[b] The number of cases varies because the variable redistributive spending is only available for 17 cases. When it is excluded from the model in column, none of the other relationships is significantly altered.

*** $p < .01$, ** $p < .05$, * $p < .10$.

example of this preoccupation with the black community: "Whites worried not so much about Richard Arrington Jr, but about blacks, the group they believed he represented. Had that day now come when 'the last shall be first, and the first shall be last?" (Franklin 1989). This strong relationship further confirms research connecting racial threat to the size of the black population (Giles and Hertz 1994; Key 1949).

The only other factor other than voter turnout that is related to the white vote in black challenger elections is the racial focus of the black candidate's campaign. Black challengers who run less racially focused campaigns, tend to get more white support – confirming the accounts of Perry (1996) and Hamilton (1977).

In contrast, all of the other factors traditionally associated with political success fail to have any noticeable impact on aggregate white voting

behavior in these elections. Despite the overwhelming evidence that incumbency provides candidates with enormous advantages, it seems that
incumbency makes little difference here (King and Gelman 1991). In the
seven cases in which black challengers face a white incumbent, they do
no worse than in the other nineteen cases where they run in an open-
seat contest. Candidate quality and political endorsements also are not
significantly tied to the white vote in black challenger elections. Even
the political experience of the black candidate does not matter in these
elections.

Moreover, the impact of all these factors is not being masked by some sort
of correlation with the percentage of blacks in the city. Even when percent
black is omitted from the regression, none of the remaining independent
variables is significantly related to white voter behavior in black challenger
elections. In short, when blacks challenge to become the first black mayor
of a city, all that seems to matter is race.

These empirical findings conform closely to media accounts of most of
these black challenger elections. In Detroit, for example, the focus was not
on issues or endorsements but race: "The unions were for [Coleman Young].
The business and political establishments were for him. The liberal, money-
laden suburbs were for him. But when they tallied the votes, none of that mat-
tered. The only issue that counted when Coleman Young became Detroit's
first black mayor in 1973 was race" (Cantor 1989). Accounts of Cleveland
came to the same conclusion: "Both [candidates] took nearly identical and
liberal positions on almost every important issue like law enforcement, public housing, and the curtailment of air and water pollution, but by election
day, the contest for mayor was a tossup, and race was clearly the central
issue" (Levine 1974, 58). And in Chicago, even though Harold Washington
faced an unknown Republican who began his bid with limited campaign experience, no campaign funds, no organization, and a record that was almost
identical to Washington on civil rights, equal rights for women, and a host
of other issues, 88 percent of white Chicago voted against Washington. In
short, when uncertainty is great and whites fear a black takeover, little other
than race matters.

The Second Time Around

However, as predicted by the information model, the nature of the white
vote changes dramatically once black incumbents have been given a chance
to prove themselves and uncertainty surrounding blacks and black leadership
has declined. As the second column of Table 9.1 demonstrates, race appears
to diminish in importance in black incumbent elections. The aggregate white
vote is no longer significantly related to the racial focus of the black candidates' campaign. Also, the white vote is not as closely tied to racial threat.
Although the coefficients changes only marginally, percent black accounts

for only 34 percent of the variation in these elections. As one reporter put it in Chicago, "Something has changed. The paranoia and ugly racism that ripped the city apart [four years ago] are largely absent this time" (Bose 1987).

Even more important, as uncertainty and fear about black leadership declines, "politics" begins to play a primary role. In these black incumbent elections, the quality of the white opponent, whether or not the newspaper endorses the black candidate, whether or not the local Democratic party endorses the black candidate, and the spending patterns of the black incumbent's administration are all significantly or nearly significantly ($p < .05$) related to the percentage of white voters voting for the black incumbent.[14] In each case, the relationship is in the expected direction. When black incumbents face less experienced opponents, when they get endorsed by the local newspaper, and when they get endorsed by the local Democratic party, they tend to get more white votes.[15] Additional analysis reveals that campaign spending also seems to play a significant role in these contests. In particular, as the spending of the white opponent increases, white support for the black incumbent tends to significantly decline ($p < .05$).[16]

Moreover, the policies of local government under black mayors also matter. Black incumbents who shift resources toward redistributive functions such as welfare, housing, and education get greater white support. While one may not have predicted the direction of this relationship at first, it begins to make sense when one considers the fact that white Democrats (as opposed to white Republicans) are the voters who are most likely to begin to change their minds about black leadership under black incumbents (Hajnal, 2001). In other words, liberal white voters may be more likely to support black mayors who are more proactively addressing what they see as the major problems of a city. In contrast, increasing

[14] This type of OLS regression clearly cannot tell us about the causal directions of these relationships. Given that Jacobson (1980) and others have demonstrated the endogeneity of campaign spending, challenger quality and other resources in campaigns, it is possible that the causal arrows could be reversed. For the present purposes, however, all that matters is that conventional politics plays a primary role in these black incumbent elections (and not in the challenger elections).

[15] It is important to note that in each case the change between black challenger elections and black incumbent elections is statistically significant. When all of the challenger and incumbent elections are combined in one regression and interaction terms are included, candidate quality, newspaper endorsements, and party endorsements are all significantly more important in incumbent elections. It is also important to note that the change in the nature of the white vote is not directly related to a change in the variance of these independent variables. As Appendix Table A-3 shows, variance actually declines for most of these measures in black incumbent elections.

[16] Spending totals for the black incumbent and the white opponent were included in an alternate specification. However, since data on spending is only available in slightly over half of the cases, these variables were not included in the final model.

or decreasing the size of the city's debt doesn't appear to affect the white vote.

The key point to make is that the calculus by which many white residents make their decisions appears to change. In black incumbent elections voting decisions are much less likely to be based blindly on the race of the candidate and white fears of a black "take over." Rather, when black incumbents run for reelection, white residents seem to more deliberately assess the pluses and minuses of their candidacies. As Sharon Watson put it in her account of eight cities, "Race as an issue appeared neutralized somewhat while the black incumbent's record in office became the focus" (1984, 172).

Are White Residents Giving Up?

Table 9.1 also indicates that changes in the size of the white population living in the city are not significantly related to the white vote in black incumbent elections. This could be because relatively few white residents actually leave these cities in the short period between elections, or it could be because white outmigration is unrelated to the racial politics of the city. Whatever the reason, white flight does not appear to be an important factor in these incumbent elections.

By contrast, there are some signs that changes in white voter turnout do play a role in these elections. In the twelve cases in which turnout by race is available, white turnout drops significantly from an average of 64 percent in black challenger elections to 54 percent in black incumbent elections. Moreover, as Table 9.1 indicates, overall voter turnout (which is correlated with white turnout at .97 in black incumbent elections) is significantly related to the white vote in black incumbent elections. Lower turnout is associated with greater white support of black incumbents. Unfortunately, it is not clear what this relationship means. White voters who oppose black leadership could be giving up in the face of an overwhelming black voting bloc or it could be that as whites learn that black leadership makes little difference, they choose not to vote in an election that has limited consequences for their well-being.

Without attitudinal data it is difficult to test these alternatives. Nevertheless, several indirect tests are available. If whites are giving up when they have little chance of reversing the outcome, white voter turnout should be lowest where blacks makeup most of a city's population and can presumably determine the outcome of the election. This is, however, not the case. White residents are no more apt to give up in cities where blacks are the majority and could presumably determine the outcome of the race than they are elsewhere. White turnout actually drops less in majority black cities (5.5-point drop) than it does in minority black cities (8.7). More generally, changes in white turnout are unrelated to the size of the black population in the city ($r = .05$; $p = .89$). Finally, changes in white turnout are not significantly related to the margin of victory in the black challenger election. Even if the first election was close and whites had a real chance of reversing the outcome, white turnout dropped at about the same rate as it did elsewhere.

Two other pieces of evidence provide at least some support for the notion that a cross-section of white voters is dropping out rather than a select group of antiblack white voters. First, in the few cases where preelection surveys are available in black incumbent elections, the data indicate that white support for black incumbents among the entire registered voter population ends up being fairly close to the eventual election results. This suggests that white nonvoters are not that different from white voters. Second, in cities where data are available by precinct or district, turnout falls at about the same rate across neighborhoods. White neighborhoods that were more opposed to the black challenger generally lost voters at about the same rate as white neighborhoods that had been more supportive of the black challenger (Sonenshein 1993).

All of this suggests that selective voter decline is not the driving force behind the growing importance of nonracial factors in black incumbent elections but it is certainly not definitive. More direct evidence of just who is dropping out and why they do so will have to be acquired before we can know whether white voters are losing interest in elections because black leadership no longer poses the threat it once did or whether white voters are simply giving up when outnumbered.

A New Type of Election

Perhaps the biggest change in these elections cannot be seen in the regression table. As black candidates move from the position of challenger to that of incumbent, there is an often dramatic change in the tone of the elections.

Black challenger elections tend to be intense, racially polarized affairs. These challenger elections are characterized by the media with phrases like, "black versus white" (Flint 1983), "race dominated" (Chicago 1983), or "highly polarized" (Memphis 1991). These challenger elections are replete with highly provocative campaigns that only serve to heighten racial fears. In Chicago, for example, Harold Washington's opponent ran on the slogan, "Epton, Now Before It's Too Late." In Memphis, when Willie Herenton ran, his opponent's ads proclaimed, "A Steady Head For A Changing Time." And in Philadelphia, one of Wilson Goode's opponents simply exclaimed at one point, "Vote white!" In many of these black challenger elections, turnout reaches record or near record levels. In the end, very few white voters end up supporting the black challenger. Overall, 71 percent of all white voters vote against the black challenger. This is all the more remarkable given that these black candidates are generally liberals or Democrats running in overwhelmingly Democratic cities.[17]

But after a period of only four years, these bitter, polarized elections give way to more dull affairs. In sharp contrast to black challenger elections, electoral contests with black incumbent elections are described with phrases like, "low-key, almost dignified politicking" (Atlantic City 1986), "ho-hum voters" (Memphis 1995), or "a lusterless campaign" (Cleveland 1969), or "a humdrum affair" (Denver 1999). In Newark, for example, a black challenger election that had included numerous incidents of racial heckling, bomb threats, and even racial violence was replaced four years later by a black incumbent election that was characterized as "a surprisingly uneventful campaign"(New York Times, May 12, 1974). Similarly, in Birmingham four years after Richard Arrington's election bid "brought racial animosities in the city to their highest pitch since the civil rights demonstrations of 1963" (Raines 1979), his reelection bid ended "with a biracial coalition and the largest victory margin in city history" (Russakoff 1983).

"The Black Candidate" becomes "The Candidate"

Another equally important change is in how black candidates are perceived. Challengers who are seen as black are replaced by incumbents who are viewed less through the lens of race and are judged more by their record. This shift in perceptions is epitomized by Tom Bradley's tenure in Los Angeles.[18] A few months after his racially divisive electoral victory in 1973, the Los Angeles Times starting referring to him as "the mayor" rather than as "the black mayor." White voters in Los Angeles experienced the same transition. A white resident of Los Angeles put it this way: "A lot of people were very suspicious and fearful before Bradley got in. But they never say anything now. I'm sure they have changed their opinions.... Most important, he is a good person. Whether he is black or white is immaterial" (US News and World Report 1975). A local newspaper editor described the change in the following way, "Tom Bradley is beyond black in the eyes of most of the people of L.A. Most of us think of him simply as our mayor" (US News and World Report 1975).

---

[17] Percent Democrat is positively and significantly related to the white vote in black challenger elections, however, it is difficult to know whether this is the result of greater support among white Democrats than among white Republicans or whether it is caused by blacks in the Democratic party. Interestingly, whether a city is partisan or not has no independent effect in either the challenger or the incumbent elections.

[18] Bradley is only one among many black elected officials who have talked about changes in white perceptions. Thirman Milner's comments are typical: "I ran up against racial issues in my first election with all the talk that crime would go up, the city would go down and I would only address black issues. But people began to see there are no racial distinctions when it comes to operating as a mayor" (Hagstom and Guskind 1983).

Interestingly, the value of Bradley's 'blackness' itself underwent a tremendous change. In Bradley's challenger elections, his race was seen by most as a huge liability. At that point one prominent pollster claimed "Tom Bradley contributed to the [white] backlash sentiment by being black in a de facto segregated society" (Maullin 1971, 51). But Bradley's race eventually became one of his greatest assets. Ten years later, without a hint of irony, another prominent pollster would proclaim "Bradley is the kind of guy that a lot of whites who fear they might be prejudiced would like to vote for – a kind of reverse discrimination" (from Ingwerson 1981).

Bradley felt that this shift in white perceptions was one of the greatest accomplishments of his career, both for the city and the country:

Race, in my judgment, was not a relevant issue. Never should have been. But it took the experience of the people to be convinced that it should not and would not become a factor in how you serve the interests of this city. (Ingwerson 1981)

Bradley's statement may have been overly positive, but these changes do show black representation can have a real impact on the views and votes of many white Americans.

Changes Over Time

If the information model is accurate, we should also see changes over time. As more and more blacks are elected to leadership positions over the years, uncertainty regarding black leadership should decline. White voters across the country should gain more and more information about black leadership and new black challengers should pose less and less of a threat.[19]

Table 9.2 suggests that this is what happens. Support for black candidates who run as challengers markedly increases over time. The number of cases

---

[19] Anecdotal evidence suggests that learning *within* cities also takes time. Black incumbents have to prove themselves before white residents begin to change their minds about black leadership. Maynard Jackson's mayoral victory in Atlanta, for example, was followed by a period of bitter racial confrontation. It was only after Jackson played a pivotal role in breaking a strike of low-paid, mostly black garbage workers that he began to receive more support from the white community. According to one advisor, Jackson's actions helped make whites "less paranoid" (Scott 1977). Similarly, in Detroit, whites elites only began to support Coleman Young after he successfully quelled a potential riot in one of the city's black neighborhoods (Eisinger 1980). Young's "decisiveness in cutting expenditures and ordering layoffs" that cut the city payroll by almost twenty-five thousand (Eisinger 1980, 93) only served to further allay white fears and expand his white support. Survey data in Birmingham suggest that racial tension actually increased in the first two years after the election of Richard Arrington as mayor (Russakoff 1983). By the time he ran for reelection, however, Arrington and other local politicians were complaining that the national news media no longer covered the campaign because Birmingham's mayoral politics lacked the racial animosity of old (Russakoff 1983).

TABLE 9.2 *Changes in Voting Behavior Over Time:*
Black Challenger Elections

Decade (N)	Average White Support for Black Challenger	Average Turnout
1960s (2)	17%	76%
1970s (5)	21	67
1980s (13)	33	54
1990s (6)	34	41

Source: Exit polls and analysis of precinct voting data as described
in text.

in each decade may be small, but the change is clear. Black challengers in
the 1960s faced almost unanimous white opposition (83 percent of white
votes). In the 1970s, white support for black challengers was, on average,
four percent higher. White support in the 1980s grew another 12 percent. By
the 1990s, the average black challenger received the support of 34 percent
of all white voters.[20]

At the same time, turnout rapidly declined. Whereas black challengers
in the 1960s and 1970s sparked record turnout, by the 1990s black challengers faced only moderate opposition. Overall, turnout dropped from an
average of 76 percent in the 1960s all the way down to 41 percent in the
1990s. For the cases where turnout is broken down by race, it is also clear
that turnout declined over time for both whites and blacks at roughly the
same rate. While one can only speculate on the reasons for this decline,
it is clear that in recent years the arrival of a serious black challenger no
longer spurs whites into action. It may be that the election of a black
candidate to office does not mean as much in the 1990s as it did in the
1960s.[21]

One of the most dramatic changes over time is in the types of campaigns
that white candidates run. Early black challengers faced white opponents
who tried to play on white fears and uncertainty about black leadership.

[20] The correlation between the white vote and the year of the election is .41 ($p < .05$). If the
year of the election is included in the regression model in Table 9.1, it is positively but not
quite significantly related to the white vote in black challenger elections.

[21] A similar process seems to be at work for African American residents in these cities. There is
little change in the black vote. On average, 94 percent of blacks support black incumbents –
essentially no different from the figure of 93 percent black support in black challenger elections. Nevertheless, it is clear that for many black residents, their views of black leadership
and their expectations do change over time. Black residents interviewed in these cities repeatedly expressed frustration and disappointment with the lack of real change under black
representation (Keiser 1997; Wildstrom 1998). The fact that black turnout dropped just
as quickly as white turnout in these cities may be a sign that "the reality of governance
generated less enthusiasm than its prospect" (Peterson 1994, 2).

So, for example, in Los Angeles when Sam Yorty ran against Tom Bradley in 1973, he attempted to spark white fears by asking:

You know what kind of city we've got. We don't know what we might get. So we'd be taking quite a chance with this particular kind of candidate.... Will your city be safe with this man?

In Newark, the white police chief simply stated, "Whether we survive or cease to exist depends on what you do on [election day]" (quoted in Eisinger 1980, 15). Similarly, in Atlanta, when Maynard Jackson ran, the slogan was, "Atlanta is too young to die."

By the 1990s, these types of scare tactics have faded out of existence. They are simply no longer credible. It is no longer possible to claim, as white candidates did in Los Angeles in 1969 or Birmingham in 1976, that the city's police force would quit en masse if a black man were elected mayor. Too many black mayors have been elected in too many places, for whites to continue to believe these types of threats.

Learning Across Cities

Beyond these changes over time, there also likely to be real differences across cities. For a number of reasons, the information that white residents get from their experience with blacks and black leadership is likely to vary dramatically from city to city.

For whites to learn anything from black representation, whites must be able to connect the lack of change under a black mayor to black leadership itself. That means two things. First, whites must believe that blacks had some measure of control over local events. If whites are unsure whether the lack of change is due to the newly elected black mayor, or due to an obstructionist, primarily white city council, they have gained no additional information about black leadership and their vote is unlikely to change. Second, race must be a relevant concern and whites must fear that black leadership will hurt them. If whites know that a black leader will be unable to enact any significant problack policies (as would be the case when whites are the majority and they dominate the city council and other political offices) they will have little to fear from the black challenger. Under these conditions, white opposition may be limited and any change in white behavior under a black incumbent is likely to be less dramatic.

Thus, I hypothesize that the racial balance of power in a city will play a critical role in altering white behavior. In cities where blacks are the clear majority and where blacks are perceived to have real control over the local political arena, whites should get the most information about the consequences of black leadership under a black incumbent. As a result, changes in white behavior should be most dramatic in majority-black cities.[22] In contrast, if whites and blacks are fairly evenly numbered and control of the local political arena is hotly contested between black and white elites, whites should get much less information about the true consequences of black leadership. Moreover, since the reelection of a black incumbent in these racially balanced cities may mean that blacks are that much closer to consolidating power, there may be even more reason for whites to oppose a black incumbent than a black challenger. Finally, in cities where whites are the clear majority, race is much less likely to play a major role in either the black challenger or the black incumbent election. Whites in majority white cities can be fairly certain that a black mayor will have little opportunity to "take over" the policy making process. This lack of black control means both that whites will have little reason to oppose a black challenger and that whites will not learn a lot from their experience with black mayoral leadership. The end result is that there should be only moderate change in white behavior in majority white cities.

If this account is true, the change in white behavior between black challenger and black incumbent elections should be most positive in black majority cities, less positive in white majority cities, and slightly negative in racially balanced cities.

Table 9.3 tests these propositions by looking both at changes in the white vote as well as at black incumbent reelection rates across different types of cities. Cities are divided in the following manner: majority white (greater than 55 percent white), racially balanced (45 to 55 percent white) and minority white (less than 45 percent white).[23]

The importance of the racial balance of power is clearly evident in Table 9.3. First, whether or not white support grows in black incumbent elections depends critically on the racial demographics of a city. In minority white cities, where blacks have the most control over the local political arena, white support for the *same* black candidate increases by an average of 16.3 percentage points, which roughly doubles the level of white support in

---

[22] An alternate hypothesis is that whites are most likely to give up and stop voting in majority black cities. However, as Table 9.3 indicates, turnout drops only marginally more in majority black cities than it does in other cities.

[23] Two important points should be made here. First, the exact cutoffs distinguishing each type of city are not critical. Alternate measures of racial balance (i. e., 40 to 60 percent white) also illustrate the distinct behavior of the white electorate under racially balanced conditions. I chose these cutoffs because they adhere to previous empirical research (Cameron et al. 1996; Grofman and Handley 1989). Second, this coding largely ignores the role that Latino and Asian American voters could play in these elections. Unfortunately, given that, on average, 90 percent of the residents of these cities are black or white, this is clearly not the best data set to try to understand the impact of Latino or Asian American voters in this process. In cases like Chicago, where Latinos can provide the margin of victory for either a white- or black-led coalition, the nonblack, nonwhite vote is likely to be critical.

TABLE 9.3 *The Importance of the Racial Balance of Power*

City Makeup	Change in White Support[1] (Challenger to Incumbent Election)	Black Incumbent Reelection Rate[2]
Minority White	+16.3	81% (61 of 75 cases)
Racially Balanced	−2.9	67% (14 of 21 cases)
Majority White	+6.2	79% (23 of 29 cases)

[1] Includes data from 26 challenger and incumbent elections detailed in the Appendix.
[2] Includes data for all black incumbents in all cities over fifty thousand (1970–1998).
Source: Wolman et al. (1990), National Roster of Black Elected Officials (1970–1994), and exit polls and precinct vote data as described in text.

these cities (from 16.1 percent in black challenger elections to 32.4 percent in black incumbent elections). In majority white cities where blacks have much less control and where racial learning should be more limited, white support increases by an average of only 6.2 percent (from 42.2 percent to 48.4 percent). Finally in racially balanced cities where learning is also limited and where the threat of blacks gaining control of the city's political arena goes up, white support actually *decreases* by an average of 2.9 percent. Chicago is perhaps the best example of this type of city. In 1983, almost 90 percent of all white voters opposed Harold Washington when he won the mayoralty for the first time. The election was followed by three years of the famous "City Council Wars." Each piece of significant legislation that Washington proposed was blocked by the white city council coalition. Even though Washington had been mayor for four years, white residents still had little idea what would happen if blacks actually gained control of the local political arena. In Washington's reelection bid, white opposition stayed at almost 90 percent.

This same pattern across cities is evident even in multivariate tests, which control for the same list of election specific factors included in the regressions in Table 9.1. The racial balance of power is, in fact, the only factor to significantly predict change in the white vote between black challenger and black incumbent elections (see Table A-1 in Appendix).

Moreover, as the second column of Table 9.3 demonstrates, this pattern is not confined to large cities or to the first reelection bid of the first black mayor of a city. Rather than focusing on the same twenty-six black challenger and black incumbent elections, the second column of the table tabulates the outcomes of every black incumbent election between 1970 and 1998 for every city over fifty thousand in population. Using the expanded data set, we get much the same pattern. Over the past three decades, black incumbent success has been strongly related to the racial balance of power. In minority-white cities, black incumbents win almost all of their reelection bids (81 percent). In majority-white cities, black incumbents are slightly less successful – they win 79 percent of their reelection bids. By contrast, in racially balanced cities black incumbents win only 67 percent of their reelection bids. There seems little doubt that the racial balance of power is central to the electoral process in these black/white contests.[24] These findings also provide further support for the notion that racial threat is not always linearly associated with the proportion black but at times curvilinearly (Blalock 1967; Longshore 1988).

What all of this suggests is that if black leaders can be held accountable for the lack of change that occurs under their watch, then their tenure in office will provide valuable information to white voters about the effects of black leadership on their interests. This, in turn, will lead to greatly increased white support and almost certain reelection. In contrast, for a select group running in racially balanced cities control is too precarious and racial competition too intense for white residents to know who is to blame or credit for their continued well-being. In these racially balanced cities, white fears will remain, elections remain highly racialized, and black politicians will have a more difficult time getting reelected.

IMPLICATIONS

Three lessons in particular can be drawn from this study. The first is that uncertainty and information are critical in the voting process – especially when racial politics are involved. When whites are uncertain about black leadership, they tend to vote against black challengers. In contrast, when white voters have information about the consequences of black leadership – when they know what they are about to get – their calculus of voting changes. Racial threat declines in importance and things like candidates, endorsements, and policy positions begin to play a much more central role in voting decisions.[25]

This research also clearly shows that black representation does matter. Previous research has bemoaned the fact that black representation has failed to resolve the crises of black poverty, educational inequality, crime, and unemployment and scholars have interpreted this as a sign of ineffectiveness (Marable 1992; Reed 1988; Singh 1998; Smith 1996). What the present research shows is that the "politics as usual" that occurs under black representation can have a positive impact on white Americans. Black representation

---

[24] Overall black incumbents have won 75 percent of their reelection bids in the last thirty years – as compared to the 85 percent reelection rate for white incumbents between 1970 and 1985 (Wolman et al. 1990). Black incumbents have actually been slightly more successful against white opponents (winning 83 percent of the time) than against black opponents (63 percent).

[25] This suggests that it may be critical for future black challengers to point to the successes of past black incumbents. If, for example, a black challenger can clearly demonstrate to white voters in Boston that black control in Atlanta, Los Angeles, and other cities has led to economic prosperity rather than economic decline, it may be possible to convince white voters that they have little to fear and consequently expand black representation across the country.

may not lead directly to racial equality but it does appear to lead to real change in the white vote and in the nature of the local political contests.

The third lesson is that white behavior is closely tied to the racial makeup of a city in important and complex ways. Generally, as the size of the black population increases, white threat and white resistance also increase – confirming a long line of research into racial context (Giles and Hertz 1994; Key 1949). However, this simple linear relationship gives way to a curvilinear relationship after blacks win the mayoralty. Because the information that whites get from black leadership depends on how much control blacks have over the local political arena, the racial balance of power in a city begins to play a central role. In majority black places where black leadership has more control and a better chance to prove itself, white threat and white resistance decline. In contrast, in cites with a rough balance of power between the black and white communities, black leadership has less of a chance to prove itself and threat remains high. In these racially balanced cities where control of the local community and its resources are most uncertain, white resistance is heightened. If, as this research suggests, actual black control turns out to be less menacing then the threat of black control, racial conflict may reach its peak at racial parity (Blalock 1967; Longshore 1988).

Larger Questions

Perhaps most important, this research raises important questions about the extent of learning that occurs and the generalizability of the information model.

First, what is it exactly that whites learn? Do they simply learn that politics does not matter and incumbents, whether black or white, will not be able to significantly alter the racial status quo? Or do they learn that a particular black incumbent is okay while making no generalizations about the larger black community? Or is learning more extensive? Do whites begin to see the black community as less of a threat and perhaps even as more of a partner? Changes in voting patterns can only hint at the underlying thought processes of white residents.

Fortunately, recent work by Hajnal (2001) has examined white attitudes over time in black and white led cities. This research suggests that black representation at the mayoral level can have a significant and positive effect on white racial attitudes. Under black mayors, feelings of group threat and measures of symbolic racism both decline. However, Hajnal's research also suggests some limitations to the impact of black representation. The same study found no evidence of change in whites' willingness to support a pro-black policy agenda. A cursory glance at cities with long histories of black mayoral representation suggests that racial conflict does not end with the onset of black representation. The 1992 riots in Los Angeles are only one graphic illustration of the enduring nature of racial division.

Second, how generalizeable is the information model? Do the changes that occur under black mayors also happen for blacks in other types of offices?[26] Does this research generalize to other minority groups such as Latino or Asian American candidates? Given that whites have limited experience with members of these groups in positions of power and given a similar set of negative stereotypes, it seems more than likely that information and uncertainty will be important for white voters considering Latino and Asian American candidates. And finally, does this research generalize to a wider range of comparative cases? For example, does the same process govern white reactions to black empowerment in South Africa as it does in New York City? Although racial, religious, and ideological differences often are seen as the critical barrier when one group cedes power to a rival group, it may be that information and uncertainty play a more critical role in political transitions around the world.

---

[26] There is already some interesting anecdotal evidence to suggest that whites react similarly to black incumbents in Congress. When the Supreme Court struck down a series of majority-black congressional districts in the 1990s, most academics and activists felt the decisions would spell doom for black representation in Congress. However, all five black incumbents who ran for reelection in newly created minority black districts won reelection with fairly widespread white support (Bullock and Dunn 1997). Given that before these cases, black candidates had been successful in less than 2 percent of the nation's majority white congressional districts, this string of victories is striking (Handley and Grofman 1994). The pattern over the last century is equally clear. Black challengers rarely win election in minority black districts (only twenty-five blacks have ever served in minority black districts). But, once elected, these black house members are nearly invincible. In minority black districts, incumbent black Congress members have won reelection 97 percent of the time (eighty-two out of eighty-five cases).

APPENDIX

TABLE A.1 *Determinants of Change in White Voting Behavior*

	Change in White Support from Black Challenger to Black Incumbent Election
RACIAL BALANCE OF POWER	
White Majority	−5.1 (7.5)
Racial Balance	−14.3 (.06)*
TRADITIONAL POLITICS	
Change in White Candidate Quality	−1.2 (.82)
Change in Democratic Party Endorsement	15.4 (8.8)
Change in Local Newspaper Endorsement	−.86 (8.7)
Redistributive Spending	−.98 (.39)**
WHITE FLIGHT	
Percent Change in White Population	−.82 (8.7)
Constant	
N	17
adj. R2	.56

OLS regression. Figures in parentheses are standard errors.
*** $p < .01$, ** $p < .05$, * $p < .10$.

TABLE A.2 *Cites Included in the Data Set*

City	Black Candidate	Year first Elected	Margin of Victory	Reelection Year	Margin of Victory
Atlantic City	James Usry	1984	27	1986	10
Baltimore	Kurt Schmoke	1987	58	1991	44
Birmingham	Richard Arrington	1979	2	1983	20
Charlotte	Harvey Gantt	1983	4	1985	22
Chicago	Harold Washington	1983	2	1987	11
Cleveland	Carl Stokes	1967	1	1969	2
Dallas	Ron Kirk	1995	39	1999	54
Durham	Chester Jenkins	1989	6	1991	−12
Flint	James Sharp	1983	3	1987	−6.6
Gary	Richard Hatcher	1967	2	1971	36
Hartford	Thirman Milner	1981	30	1983	32
Houston	Lee Brown	1997	4	1999	41
Kansas City	Emanuel Cleaver	1991	6	1995	10
Los Angeles	Tom Bradley	1973	13	1977	31
Memphis	Willie Herenton	1991	0	1995	48
Minneapolis	Sharon Sayles-Belton	1993	14	1997	10
New Haven	John Daniels	1989	38	1991	12
New Orleans	Ernest Morial	1978	3	1982	7
New York	David Dinkins	1989	1	1993	−1
Newark	Kenneth Gibson	1970	12	1974	10
Oakland	Lionel Wilson	1977	7	1981	60
Philadelphia	Wilson Goode	1983	18	1987	1
Rockford	Charles Box	1989	26	1993	40
Seattle	Norm Rice	1989	3	1993	33
San Francisco	Willie Brown	1995	14	1999	16

TABLE A.3 *Descriptive Statistics*

Variable	Mean	Std. Deviation	Minimum	Maximum
Percent White Vote for Black Challenger	29.7	15.6	58.6	2.6
Percent White Vote for Black Incumbent	34.8	17.4	10.4	66.5
Change in White Vote for Black Candidate	6.1	14.7	−16	39
Newspaper Endorsement 1	.66	.45	0	1
Newspaper Endorsement 2	.92	.18	.5	1
Party Endorsement 1	.73	.41	0	1
Party Endorsement 2	.86	.27	0	1
Percent Black	36.2	15.2	6	58
Change from Development to Redistributive Spending	−.19	6.5	−16	13.9
Incumbent 1	.27	.45	0	1
Quality White Opponent 1	2.5	1.4	0	4
Quality Black Challenger	2.4	1.2	0	4
Quality White Opponent 2	2.2	1.4	0	4
Racial Focus of Black Candidates Campaign 1	.30	.32	0	1
Racial Focus of Black Candidates Campaign 2	.17	.28	0	1
Percent Turnout 1	55.2	15.9	20	82
Percent Turnout 2	48.2	18.8	5	75.5

References

Abney, F. Glenn, and Jr. John D. Hutcheson. 1981. "Race, Representation, and Trust: Changes in Attitudes After the Election of a Black Mayor." *Public Opinion Quarterly* 45:91–101.

Allport, G. W. 1954. *The Nature of Prejudice*. Menlo Park, CA: Addison-Wesley.

Alvarez, Michael R., and John Brehm. 1995. "Are Americans Ambivalent Towards Racial Policies?" Presented at the Midwest Political Science Association Annual Meeting.

Blalock, Hubert M. 1967. *Toward a Theory of Minority-Group Relations*. New York: Wiley.

Blumer, Herbert. 1958. "Race Prejudice as a Sense of Group Position." *Pacific Sociological Review* 1:3–7.

Bobo, Lawrence. 1983. "Whites' Opposition to Busing: Symbolic Racism or Realistic Group Conflict." *Journal of Personality and Social Psychology* 45:1196–210.

Bobo, Lawrence, and Jr. Franklin D. Gilliam. 1990. "Race, Sociopolitical Participation, and Black Empowerment." *American Political Science Review* 84:377–93.

Bosc, Michael. 1987, "Chicago's Mayoral Primary: Racial Lines are Drawn, But Tempers are Cooler." *U. S. News and World Report* Feb: 20–21 (or Feb 23).

Brown, Robert A. 1997. "African-American Urban Representation amid the Urban Transition of the 1970s and 1980s." American Political Science Association Annual Meeting, Washington, DC.

Browning, Rufus P., Dale Rogers Marshall, and David H. Tabb. 1984. *Protest is Not Enough*. Berkeley: University of California Press.

Browning, Rufus P., Dale Rogers Marshall, and David H. Tabb. 1997. "Taken In or Just Taken? Political Incorporation of African Americans in Cities." American Political Science Association Annual Meeting, Washington, DC.

Bullock, Charles S., and Richard E. Dunn. 1997. "The Demise of Racial Districting and the Future of Black Representation." American Political Science Association Annual Meeting, Washington, DC.

Bullock, Charles S. III. 1984. "Racial Crossover Voting and the Election of Black Officials." *Journal of Politics* 46:238–51.

Bureau of the Census. 1994, 1990, 1978. *City and County Data Book*. Washington, DC: Author.

Cameron, Charles, David Epstein, Sharyn Halloran. 1996. "Do Majority-Minority Districts Maximize Substantive Black Representation in Congress?" *American Political Science Review* 90:794–812.

Canon, David. 1999. *Race, Redistricting, and Representation: The Unintended Consequences of Black Majority Districts*. Chicago: University of Chicago Press.

Cantor, George. 1989. "Mayor Coleman Young: A Mayor Who Cried Racism." *Newsday*, p. 56.

Cole, Leonard A. 1976. *Blacks in Power: A Comparative Study of Black and White Elected Officials*. Princeton, NJ: Princeton University Press.

Coleman, Milton. 1983. "Race Clouds Issues for Many Chicago Voters." *Washington Post*, p. A1.

Conover, Pamela J., and Stanley Feldman. 1989. "Candidate Perception in an Ambiguous World: Campaigns, cues and inference processes." *American Journal of Political Science* 33:912–40.

Cox, Gary, and Michael C. Munger. 1989. "Closeness, Expenditures and Turnout in the 1982 House Elections." *American Political Science Review* 83:217–231.

Deane, Glenn D. 1990. "Mobility and Adjustments: Paths to the Resolution of Residential Stress." *Demography* 27:65–79.

Eisinger, Peter K. 1980. *Politics and Displacement: Racial and Ethnic Transition in Three American Cities*. New York: Academic Press.

Eisinger, Peter K. 1982. "Black Employment in Municipal Jobs: The Impact of Black Political Power." *American Political Science Review* 76:380–92.

Fazio, Russel H., Joni R. Jackson, Bridget C. Dunton, and Carol J. Williams. 1995. "Variability in Automatic Activation as an Unobtrusive Measure of Racial Attitudes: A Bona Fide Pipeline?" *Journal of Personality and Social Psychology* 69:1013–27.

Foner, Eric. 1984. *A Short History of Reconstruction*. New York: Harper and Row Publishers.

Franklin, Jimmie Lewis. 1989. *Back to Birmingham: Richard Arrington, Jr., and His Times*. Tuscaloosa: University of Alabama Press.

Gay, Claudine. 2001. "The Effect of Black Congressional Representation on Participation." *American Political Science Review* 95 (3): 603–18.

Gay, Claudine. 1999. "Choosing Sides: Black Electoral success and Racially Polarized Voting." Presented at the Annual Meeting of the American Political Science Association, Atlanta.

Gierzynski, Anthony. 1998. "Money or the Machine: Money and Votes in Chicago Aldermanic Elections." *American Politics Quarterly* 26:160–73.

Giles, Michael W., and Kaenan Hertz. 1994. "Racial Threat and Partisan Identification." *American Political Science Review* 88(2):317–26.

Grofman, Bernard, and Lisa Handley. 1989. "Minority Population Proportion and Black and Hispanic Congressional Success in the 1970s and 1980s." *American Politics Quarterly* 17:436–45.

Hajnal, Zoltan L. 2001. "White Residents, Black Incumbents and a Declining Significance of Race" *American Political Science Review* 95(3):603– 17.

Hamilton, D. L. ed. 1981. *Cognitive Processes in Stereotyping and Intergroup Behavior*. Hillsdale, NJ: Erlbaum.

Hamilton, Charles V. 1977. "De-Racialization: Examination of a Political Strategy." *First World* 1:3–5.

Handley, Lisa and Bernard Grofman. 1994. "The Impact of the Voting Rights Act on Minority Representation: Black Office holding in Southern State Legislatures and Congressional Delegations." In *Quiet Revolution in the South: The Impact of the Voting Rights Act, 1965–1990*, C. Davidson and B. Grofman, eds. Princeton, NJ: Princeton University Press.

Henry, Charles P. 1992. "Black Leadership and the Deracialization of Politics." *Crisis* 100:38–42.

Hurwitz, Jon, and Mark Peffley. 1998. *Prejudice and Politics: Race and Politics in the United States*. New Haven, CT: Yale University Press.

Ingwerson, Marshal. 1981. "L.A.'s Tom Bradley: A Nice Guy Who May Finish First." *Christian Science Monitor*, p. B1.

Jackman, Mary R., and Marie Crane. 1986. "'Some of My Best Friends are Black ...' Interracial Friendship and Whites' Racial Attitudes." *Public Opinion Quarterly* 50:459–86.

Jacobson, Gary C. 1980. *Money in Congressional Elections*. New Haven, CT: Yale University Press.

Jacobson, Gary C., and Samuel Kernell. 1981. *Strategy and Choice in Congressional Elections*. New Haven, CT: Yale University Press.

Joint Center for Political Studies. 1983–1994. *Black Elected Officials: A National Roster*. Washington, DC: Author.

Keiser, Richard A. 1997. *Subordination or Empowerment? African-American Leadership and the Struggle for Urban Political Power*. New York: Oxford University Press.

Key, V. O. 1949 (1984). *Southern Politics in State and Nation*. Knoxville: University of Tennessee Press.

King, Gary. 1997. *A Solution to the Ecological Inference Problem*. Princeton, NJ: Princeton University Press.

King, Gary, and Andrew Gelman. 1991. "Systemic Consequences of Incumbency Advantage in US House Elections." *American Journal of Political Science* 35:110–38.

Krasno, Jonathan S., and Donald Philip Green. 1988. "Preempting Quality Challengers in House Elections." *Journal of Politics* 50: 920–36.

Levine, Charles H. 1974. *Racial Conflict and the American Mayor*. Lexington, MA: Heath.

Lieske, Joel. 1989. "The Political Dynamics of Urban Voting Behavior." *American Journal of Political Science* 33:150–74.

Lieske, Joel, and Jan William Hillard. 1984. "The Racial Factor in Urban Elections." *Western Political Quarterly* 37:545–63.

Loewen, James. 1990. "Racial Bloc Voting and Political Mobilization in South Carolina." *Review of Black Political Economy* 19:23–37.

Loewen, James, and Bernard Grofman. 1989. "Recent Developments in Methods Used in Voting Rights Litigation." *Urban Lawyer* 21(3):589–604.

Long, L. 1988. *Migration and Residential Mobility in the United States*. New York: Russell Sage Foundation.

Longshore, Douglas. 1988. "Racial Control and Intergroup Hostility: A Comparative Analysis." *Research in Race and Ethnic Relations* 5:47–73.

Lublin, David. 1997. *The Paradox of Representation: Racial Gerrymandering and Minority Interests*. Princeton, NJ: Princeton University Press.

Lublin, David Ian, and Katherine Tate. 1995. "Racial Group Competition in Urban Elections." In *Classifying By Race*, Paul E. Princeton, ed. Princeton NJ: Princeton University Press.

Marable, Manning. 1992. *The Crisis of Color and Democracy*. Monroe, ME: Common Courage Press.

Maullin, Richard L. 1971. "Los Angeles Liberalism." *Trans-Action* 8:40–51.

McCrary, Peyton. 1990. "Racially Polarized Voting in the South: Quantitative Evidence from the Courtroom." *Social Science History* 14:507–31.

Mendelberg, Tali. 1994. "The Politics of Racial Ambiguity: Origin and Consequences of Implicitly Racial Appeals." PhD Dissertation. University of Michigan.

Mladenka, Kenneth R. 1989. "Blacks and Hispanics in Urban Politics." *American Political Science Review* 83:165–91.

Perry, Huey L. 1996. *Race, Politics and Governance in the United States*. Gainesville: University Press of Florida.

Peterson, George E. 1994. "Introduction." In *Big City Politics, Governance, and Fiscal Constraints*, G. E. Peterson, ed. Urbana: University of Illinois.

Peterson, Paul E. 1981. *City Limits*. Chicago: University of Chicago Press.

Pettigrew, Thomas F. 1976. "Black Mayoral Campaigns." In *Urban Governance and Minorities*, Herrington J. Bryce, ed. New York: Praeger.

Popkin, Samuel L. 1991. *The Reasoning Voter*. Chicago: University of Chicago Press.

Raines, Howell. 1979. "New York Times Abstracts." *New York Times*, p. A16.

Reed, Adolph. 1988. "The Black Urban Regime: Structural Origins and Constraints." In *Power, Community, and the City*, Michael Peter Smith, ed. New Brunswick, NJ: Transaction Press.

Reeves, Keith. 1997. *Voting Hopes or Fears? White Voters, Black Candidates, and Racial Politics in America*. New York: Oxford University Press.

Rieder, Jonathan. 1985. *Canarsie: The Jews and Italians of Brooklyn against Liberalism*. Cambridge, MA: Harvard University Press.

Rivlin, Gary. 1992. *Fire on the Prairie: Chicago's Harold Washington and the Politics of Race*. New York: Henry Holt and Company.

Rothbart, Myron, and Oliver P. John. 1993. "Intergroup Relations and Stereotype Change: A Social-Cognitive Analysis and Some Longitudinal Findings." In

Prejudice, Politics, and the American Dilemma. Paul M. Sniderman, Philip E. Tetlock, and Edward G. Carmines, eds. Stanford: Stanford University Press.

Russakoff, Dale. 1983. "Birmingham Reelects Black: Once-Split City Unites at Polls." *Washington Post*, p. A1.

Schuman, Howard, Charlotte Steeh, Lawrence Bobo, and Maria Krysan. 1997. *Racial Attitudes in America: Trends and Interpretations*. Cambridge, MA: Harvard University Press.

Scott, Austin. 1977. "Black Mayors in Atlanta, Detroit Expand re-Election Support." *Washington Post*, p. A1.

Sigelman, Carol K., Lee Sigelman, Barbara J. Walkosz, and Michael Nitz. 1995. "Black Candidates, White Voters: Understanding Racial Bias in Political Perceptions." *American Journal of Political Science* 39:243–65.

Singh, Robert. 1998. *The Congressional Black Caucus: Racial Politics in the U.S. Congress*. Thousand Oaks, CA: Sage Publications.

Sleeper, Jim. 1993. "The End of the Rainbow? The Changing Politics of America's Cities." *The New Republic*, p. 20.

Smith, Robert C. 1996. *We Have No Leaders: African Americans in the Post-Civil Rights Era*. Albany: University of New York Press.

Sonenshein, Raphael J. 1993. *Politics in Black and White: Race and Power in Los Angeles*. Princeton, NJ: Princeton University Press.

Swain, Carol M. 1995. *Black Face, Black Interests: The Representation of African Americans in Congress*. Cambridge, MA: Harvard University Press.

Thernstrom, Stephan, and Abigail Thernstrom. 1997. *America In Black and White: One Nation, Indivisible*. New York: Simon and Schuster.

US News and World Report. 1975. "Is a Black Mayor the Solution? Here's How Six Have Fored." April 7:34.

Vanderleeuw, James M. 1991. "The Influence of Racial Transition on Incumbency Advantage in Local Elections." *Urban Affairs Quarterly* 27:36–50.

Watson, S. M. 1984. "The Second Time Around: A Profile of Black Mayoral Election Campaigns." *Phylon* 45:165–75.

Wildstrom, Stephen H. 1998. "After the Victory Party, Frustration in the Black Community." *Business Week* 3140:49.

Williams, Linda F. 1990. "White/Black Perceptions of the Electability of Black Political Candidates." *National Black Political Science Review* 2:45–64.

Wolman, Harold, Edward Page, and Martha Reavley. 1990. "Mayors and Mayoral Careers." *Urban Affairs Quarterly* 25:500–13.

Index

abortion ban, survey on, 169, 170, 171, 175, 179, 181, 183
Adams, Sherman, 33
administrative procedures, 48–71
  agency costs and, 56–60
  consumer movement and, 51, 60, 61–3
  current incentives and, 51–56
  delegation and, 48–9, 50, 67
  dynamic theory and, 49–50
  homogeneity in, 48–9, 50, 57–8, 59
  legislature / governor and, 51–60
  models of, 50–1
  political feasibility and, 51, 53, 56, 58
  radical agency environment, 69–71
  radio licensing and, 51, 63–7
  rulemaking costs and, 53–6
  status quo policy and, 52–6, 69–70
  structural choices and, 48, 49, 60, 61, 65, 68
  See also bureaucratic uncertainty; legislature-agency signaling
affirmative action, 170, 175, 179, 180–1, 183
  antiblack attitudes and, 171, 180

African Americans, 213
  See also black representation, white vote and
agencies
  autonomy of, 78–9
  budgeting process and, 9, 99–100
  costs to, 56–60
  information flow and, 9, 104–5
  See also administrative procedures; bureaucratic uncertainty; legislature-agency signaling
Aggregate Proportional Reduction in Error (APRE), 132, 133–4
Agriculture Department, US, 113
Aldrich, John H., 208
aligned preference environment, 53, 54, 57–8
Alpert, Eugene J., 189
alternative uncertainty, 127
Alvarez, R. Michael, 10n7, 16, 20, 164, 165
  on incumbent insecurity, 193, 200
ambiguity, 7
ambivalence, 10n7, 11, 127, 181
  public opinion and, 164–5, 166, 177, 178, 179, 182